THE *Real* RHYTHM AND BLUES

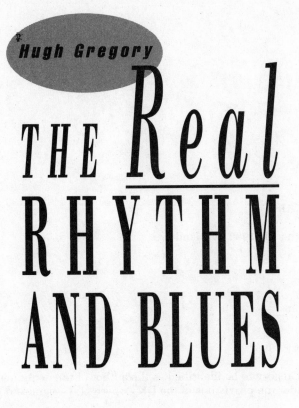

Hugh Gregory

THE Real RHYTHM AND BLUES

BLANDFORD

A BLANDFORD BOOK

First published in the UK 1998 by Blandford
A Cassell Imprint

Cassell plc
Wellington House
125 Strand
London WC2R 0BB

Distributed in the United States by Sterling Publishing Co., Inc.,
387 Park Avenue South, New York, NY 10016–8810

A Cataloguing-in-Publication Data entry for this title is available from the
British Library

ISBN 0-7137-2603-2

Designed by Chris Bell
Printed and bound in Great Britain by MPG Books Ltd, Bodmin, Cornwall

CONTENTS

INTRODUCTION

FOR A WHITE, MIDDLE-CLASS KID born in London in the early 1950s, the arrival of groups such as the Beatles, the Rolling Stones, the Yardbirds, Manfred Mann, and Them, among others, in the 1960s was a jolt to the system. Until then the pop music I had heard – as broadcast by the BBC – had been fairly dire; I mean, Cliff Richard might have been able to curl his lip with that exaggerated sneer, but even a ten-year-old could tell that this was no more than a calculated pose.

As the beat groups took hold of the imagination of the record-buying public, so my interest and fascination in rock 'n' roll intensified. Close study of album liner notes yielded names such as Arthur Alexander, Mose Allison, Chuck Berry, Muddy Waters, Bo Diddley, John Lee Hooker, Willie Dixon, and so on – all these names became far more the focus of attention or, indeed, curiosity.

In the rhythm and blues (R&B) as pioneered in the late 1930s and early 1940s, there lie the seeds of rock 'n' roll and so *The Real Rhythm & Blues* is an attempt to unearth those early stylists and pioneers who laid the foundations for groups such as the Beatles, the Rolling Stones, and the like. Furthermore, it is an attempt to isolate the style of R&B as a genre in itself, which is not to be confused with the electric urban blues or, indeed, soul.

Since Alan Freed allegedly coined the phrase 'rock 'n' roll' in the early 1950s, popular music has undergone more changes than the moods of a schizophrenic. Within these years the perception of what rock 'n' roll actually is has been somewhat muddy and, with that, all of rock 'n' roll's various satellites have been just as indistinct. Nowhere are misnomers more apparent than in the designation of R&B. Some time before this book was commissioned, I was approached by the BBC to set the questions for a television quiz show about black music. Perhaps the most interesting thing to come out of this experience was the extent to which the participants identified R&B as a formative influence in their musical appreciation. However, because these participants were drawn loosely from an 18 to 30 age group, their idea of R&B was at a considerable variance to the general consensus. Marvin Gaye? You've got to be joking! Luther Vandross? Not a chance! Jodeci? Nope. James Brown was the only contender to fit the bill. Even record and PR companies tend to get confused over the fundamental differences between R&B and the blues, or R&B and soul. And that is the purpose of this book: to look at the origins of R&B and where it figures in today's markets.

So what is R&B? And what are the parameters for the context of this book? Starting with its roots in the blues and gospel music, R&B synthesized elements of the blues, gospel, and the big-band jazz of the late 1930s, drawing a fine line between the purism of jazz and the blues and reaching its zenith in the 1950s with performers as different stylistically as Fats Domino and Louis Jordan, or Dinah Washington and the Coasters. At the heart of R&B resided the need to be entertaining: showmanship was always recognized as pivotal to rock 'n' roll; R&B was – and is – no different. Indeed rock 'n' roll and R&B can in this context be deemed synonymous: differences are entirely perceptual and are governed more by a record's or an artist's ability to cross over from an exclusively black-audience market to include a young, white audience. Through that crossover, R&B attracted a wider audience and influence and, ironically, it was young white kids in the 1940s and 1950s who, hearing R&B records, determined that they too would become musicians. Guitarist Steve Cropper once noted that, when he was growing up in the American South during the 1950s and he went to see visiting bands, the white members of the audience were required to watch the show from the gallery because segregation was still a fact of life. In later years he recognized that he could only get close to where the real action was by being a musician on the bandstand: there was no segregation among musicians themselves. That enthusiasm triggered the likes of Cropper and many others to become musicians in the first place. And it is they who, through the years, have managed to keep the flame of R&B burning brightly by inspiring new generations of musicians and performers. Therein lies the crux of this book: that, far from being a moribund form that was superseded by rock 'n' roll, R&B has continued – and continues – to flourish through a host of young performers today. While hip-hop and swingbeat have their origins in the vocal groups of the 1950s, theirs is another story and one which I will not be going into here. Similarly, this is neither the time nor the place to delve too deeply into the soul era of the 1960s or indeed the blues-based, beat-group explosion. No, this book endeavours to deal with R&B in its purest form, so the contemporary performers referred to are those who have based their styles on R&B in its most traditional incarnation.

Obviously with a story that spans the years since the early 1940s, there are few artists left to tell the tale of the very earliest days and so this book remains a synthesis of received opinion, but there have been many musicians who were duly rounded up and were gracious with their time and informative as well. So although *The Real Rhythm and Blues* may well provoke howls of fury or ill-concealed mirth at those who have received name checks and those who haven't, it is not intended to be an encyclopedic litany of every single name that has ever been influenced by or has performed R&B. Rather it is intended to be a signposted celebration of the evolution of one of the most entertaining and enduring musical forms of the twentieth century, which still casts a giant shadow over much of what we hear today.

chapter one

HERE COMES MR JORDAN

W HILE THE BIRTH OF ROCK 'N' ROLL is popularly associated with the likes of Elvis Presley and Bill Haley, it is recognized that probably the first authentic rock 'n' roll records include 'Drinkin' Wine Spo-Dee-o-Dee' by Sticks McGhee in 1949 and 'Rocket 88' by Jackie Brenston with Ike Turner and the Rhythm Kings in 1950. This recognition that rhythm and blues (R&B) was historically the legitimate precursor of rock 'n' roll has been only a relatively recent development. With that in mind, rock 'n' roll can trace its antecedents back to the R&B explosion between 1945 and 1955. To begin to see how R&B started, it is necessary to go back to 1920 when Mamie Smith arrived in Chicago.

A vaudeville singer from Cincinnati, Mamie Smith was encouraged by songwriter Perry Bradford in 1920 to go to Chicago to record some tracks for the OKeh label. Although Smith had been plying her trade on the Harlem music-hall stage, Bradford was aware of the number of other black female songstresses such as Sippie Wallace, Victoria Spivey, and Sara Martin who had made the transition from the music-hall stage to the recording studio. Of the songs Mamie cut, 'Crazy Blues' was the one that had the effect of galvanizing other record companies into signing female blues singers: Ma 'Mother of the Blues' Rainey and Alberta Hunter signed to Paramount, and the 'Empress of the Blues', Bessie Smith, went to Columbia. The other significant factor in the emergence of the female blues singers was the arrangements: their male counterparts had always accompanied themselves singly on the piano or the guitar. The women responded to the demand for blues records by recording with five- or six-piece jazz combos or pianists such as James P. Johnson or Fletcher Henderson; Sara

Martin is best remembered for the tracks she recorded with King Oliver's band. The combination of these elements, however, contrived to give these early blues records a jazzier, more punchy feel than their male counterparts had hitherto achieved.

Therefore while Mamie Smith's 'Crazy Blues' precipitated an explosion of enthusiasm for the blues, the blues-based bands of Lionel Hampton, Lucky Millinder, Cab Calloway, Erskine Hawkins, Tiny Bradshaw, Buddy Johnson and Louis Jordan were catalysts for the R&B explosion.

LOUIS JORDAN

Louis Jordan was first and foremost an entertainer and was described by one critic as 'jazz with a broad grin'. He was born on 8 July 1908, in Brinkley, Arkansas, a one-horse town somewhere between Little Rock and Memphis. After learning to play the saxophone from his father, while majoring in music at the Arkansas Baptist College in Little Rock, Jordan played his first gig with Rudy 'Tuna Boy' Williams at the Green Gables in Hot Springs. With this extensive experience behind him, Jordan joined the Rabbit Foot Minstrels, who had formerly provided the launching pad for both Bessie Smith and Ma Rainey. Remaining with the group for two years, he played clarinet, sang, and danced throughout the South. By 1930 Jordan and the rest of his family had moved north to Philadelphia with Jordan joining trumpeter Charlie Gaines's band. As Jordan was to tell historian Arnold Shaw in 1973, 'I had eyes on the Big Apple [New York City], but it took several years before I could get a union card'.

Eventually Jordan moved to New York and joined first Leroy Smith and then Joe Marshall, who was also Fletcher Henderson's drummer. Playing gigs at the Elk's Rendezvous in Harlem, Jordan came to the attention of Chick Webb and joined his band in 1936. With a residency at the Savoy, Webb's band was never to reach the pinnacle it richly deserved but Webb was quick to spot talent and allowed Jordan to play alto behind Webb's vocalist, Ella Fitzgerald, on his very first recording session. On 15 January 1937, Jordan made his recording debut as a vocalist with Webb's Orchestra on 'Gee, But You're Swell', which was followed by 'Oh Yes Take Another Guess', 'Love Marches On', and 'There's Frost on the Moon' with Ella and Webb's male vocalist, Charles Linton. This hint of the limelight showed Jordan what he really wanted to do and when Webb fired him the following year, Jordan wasted no time in setting up his own band and securing a residency at the Elk's Rendezvous. Known as Louis Jordan's Elk's Rendezvous Band, they cut two sides – 'Barnacle Bill the Sailor', a novelty item penned by country singer Carson Robison, and 'Honey in the Bee Ball' – for Decca on 20 December 1938. While these early performances were undistinguished in themselves, they couldn't disguise Jordan's ebullience and showmanship.

After changing the name of his group to the Tympani Five (that name remained irrespective of the number of musicians in the band), Jordan sought to widen and diversify his appeal. However, Jordan, as the critic Ralph Gleason observed, 'sang black and sang proud' and he never attempted to compromise his blackness to win over white audiences. Inevitably this quest for wider acceptance took him from New York to the rather more salubrious Capitol Lounge in Chicago, working alongside the Mills Brothers and playing for white as well as black audiences; it also put him in touch with Berle Adams, a figure who was to exert a major influence on Jordan's career.

Adams was working for GAC (General Amusement Corporation), but was trying to make his way as an agent. As he recalled in 1992:

> 'The Mills Brothers had been booked into the Capitol Lounge and I phoned New York and asked the office there if they could recommend me a band and they suggested Louis Jordan. Now I worked out that the Mills Brothers would be doing only four shows and so there was a lot of time when there was nothing going on. So I went to the owner of the Capitol Lounge and said did he want another band. Eventually he said, "Yeah, get me another band, but I'll only pay scale". At that time scale was a dollar an hour per man, with a dollar extra for the leader. This meant 35 dollars each, and 36 for Louis. So I called Louis in New York and told him the deal and he said that he couldn't do it for less than 40 dollars, 'cos that's what they were getting in New York. Anyway I talked him round and Louis came out with the Tympani Five and they went down a storm. At the beginning of the second week Louis came to me and said, "Listen I've gotta have more money, 'cos I can't survive on 16 dollars". And I said, "but you're getting 36", and Louis replied, "the band wouldn't come out for less than 40 so I've been making up their money!". I was really shocked about this and so I went to this boss and told him the story and he partly relented, agreeing to pay them their 40 bucks. The band – because they knew how well they were going down – wanted more money and so the boss said, "Fire them. Get another band". When it was put to them like this, they all stayed except the bassist. So Louis had to hire a replacement and the replacement was Dallas Bartley, who became a key member of the group.'

With this break behind him, Jordan started a schedule of touring – one-nighters, mostly – that would continue into the early 1950s and signed with Decca. Working with producer Milt Gabler, Jordan had established his style with a string of tunes such as 'At the Swing Cats Ball', 'You're My Meat', and 'Somebody Done Hoodooed the Hoodoo Man' by 1940. As his popularity grew, so his repertoire began to reflect the different locales on his schedule: at the Fox Head in Cedar Rapids he found 'If It's Love You Want, Baby, That's Me', 'Ration Blues', and 'Inflation Blues'.

In 1942, with a Tympani Five that now featured a guitarist in its line-up, Jordan scored his first hit on the newly established *Billboard* 'race' charts with 'I'm Gonna Move to the Outskirts of Town'. This was followed by 'What's the Use of Getting Sober?' and, in 1943, by 'Five Guys Named Moe' and 'Ration Blues'. The following year Jordan crossed over to the pop charts with 'GI Jive'. Although Jordan had reached the apogee of his sound – the tight rhythm section supporting the infectious, riffing honking of saxophone and trumpet behind his vocals – the lyrical content of his songs was preoccupied with partying and transcended race. With songs such as 'Caldonia (What Makes Your Big Head So Hard?)', 'Choo Choo Ch'Boogie', 'Is You Is, Or Is You Ain't (Ma' Baby)?', 'Boogie Woogie Blue Plate', 'Ain't That Just Like a Woman?', 'That Chick's Too Young to Fry', and 'Let the Good Times Roll', Jordan made the blues jump and jive the way they had never done before.

While Jordan was a strong songwriter, penning five million sellers along the way including 'Caldonia (What Makes Your Big Head So Hard?)' and 'Is You Is, Or Is You Ain't (Ma' Baby?)', he was adept at turning round other people's songs to suit his style: Jessie Mae Robinson – a schoolteacher from Los Angeles – wrote 'Blue Light Boogie'; 'Let the Good Times Roll' was by black comedian Sam Theard; and 'Choo Choo Ch' Boogie' was a country song. However, 'Caldonia (What Makes Your Big Head So Hard?)' and 'Is You Is, Or Is You Ain't (Ma' Baby)?' never earned Jordan the revenue they should have, because in a moment of gallantry or fecklessness he attributed them to his wife Fleecie Moore. When the couple divorced not long after, this attribution backfired on Jordan, providing Fleecie with as nice a little earner as one could imagine (Jordan later commented with commendable altruism, 'I never missed what I didn't have').

Although Jordan was the undisputed leader of the group, his bassist, Dallas Bartley, was an admirable foil. Joining the Tympani Five in 1938, Bartley contributed titles like 'Five Guys Named Moe' and 'Small Town Boy'. Furthermore it was Bartley's influence that encouraged Jordan to lighten up on stage, transforming himself into a comedian as well as a musician. This never detracted from the quality of the music, but it certainly helped him start a career in movies. Appearing in more than half-a-dozen films, including *Follow the Boys* (1944), *Meet Miss Bobby Socks* (1944), *Caldonia* (1945), *Swing Parade of 1946* (1946), *Toot That Trumpet* (1946), *Beware Brother Beware* (1946), *Reet, Petite and Gone* (1947), and *Look Out, Sister* (1948), these helped to broaden his fan-base.

In addition he appeared in more than a dozen one-song 'Soundies'; these ensured that his popularity remained high during the shellac shortage of the war years.

While all these elements were significant in making Jordan the top R&B performer of the era, he was the first popular entertainer to test-market his material. For, as Berle Adams recalls:

> 'Louis would take about eighteen new songs out on the road and as he would be doing something like ninety one-nighters in a single tour, these songs would get heard by a very large number of people. So by the time he recorded them, everybody knew all the new songs.'

To this day Jordan is second only to James Brown in achieving the largest number of Top Ten hits in the R&B charts. In 1951, against the advice of Milt Gabler, Jordan formed a 14-piece orchestra. Even though this earned him kudos by recording with Nelson Riddle and Louis Armstrong, it also softened his hard-biting sound and this in turn led to a down-swing in his popularity. He was never to match the success of the 1940s.

In 1953 Jordan moved from Decca to the West Coast-based Aladdin label. Owned by Leo and Edward Mesner, neither of whom demonstrated much affinity for the record industry, preferring instead to gamble, Aladdin sides such as 'Fat Back and Corn Liquor' and 'Gal You Need a Whippin''' could not arrest Jordan's gradual decline. After Aladdin he moved to the RCA subsidiary Vik in 1955 for 'Baby Let's Do It', among others, but Jordan had already been eclipsed by Elvis Presley and, more embarrassingly, Bill Haley, who – it just so happened – was signed to Decca and was produced by none other than the indefatigable Milt Gabler. Then he moved on to the Mercury label in 1956, which had been founded by his old colleague Berle Adams. For Mercury, with producer Quincy Jones, Jordan re-recorded some of his best-known songs on the albums *Somebody Up There Digs Me* (1957) and *Man We're Wailin'* (1958), but they lacked the lustre of his earlier efforts.

Throughout the 1960s and 1970s, with his health deteriorating and very much a forgotten man, Jordan recorded intermittently and then, more often than not, for old friends. *Hallelujah . . . Louis Jordan Is Back* (1964) was cut for Ray Charles's Tangerine label; *One-Sided Love* (1969) was put out on Paul Gayten's Pzazz label; and finally *I Believe in Music* (1974) for Johnny Otis's Blues Spectrum label. In September 1974 Jordan suffered a heart attack. After recuperating he announced plans to tour Europe, where, through the efforts of musicians such as Chris Barber, he had managed to achieve legendary status. These plans never came to anything as he suffered another heart attack and died at his home in Los Angeles on 4 February 1975.

Since his death, Jordan has come to be regarded as one of the originals of contemporary music – particularly rock 'n' roll. In 1990 the musical *Five Guys Named Moe*, based on the lyrics of Jordan's songs, was launched by impresario Cameron (now Sir Cameron) Mackintosh. It ran in London for six years, toured the world, had a successful run in New York and has largely lived up to its billing of a 'celebration' of Jordan's work. What this has proved is that Jordan's music speaks just as powerfully to audiences of today as it did in the 1940s. Perhaps the final word should go to Jordan, who in the months before his death said, 'when you come out to hear me, I want to make you happy'. And that just about says it all.

CAB CALLOWAY

While Jordan was the man who made the blues jump more authoritatively than anyone else, other band leaders were quick to latch on to the money to be made from a spot of well-turned light entertainment. Of these, Cab Calloway, Lionel Hampton, Lucky Millinder, and Erskine Hawkins were the most adept because not only were they unbothered by accusations of selling out but they also offered opportunities for young musicians trying to make the grade. This ensured that there was a platform for younger and rawer musicians to come through.

A slick and snappy dresser, Cab Calloway was unashamedly a showman and entertainer, who, as one critic noted, exuded 'a joy and festive spirit that moves one to instant gaiety'. He was born on Christmas Day 1907 in Rochester, New York, and raised in Baltimore, Maryland, until the family relocated to Chicago in the 1920s. Starting his career as a drummer and MC, he appeared in *Plantation Days* in 1927, which featured an all-black cast. The following year he became leader of the Alabamians and in 1929 the group moved base to New York. While working in the city he started to front the Missourians, featuring trumpeter Lamar Wright and alto saxophonist Andrew Brown. Hired to appear at the Savoy Ballroom, it was Calloway's flamboyance that held the eye despite the Missourians' excellent backing. Already attired in the trademark 'zoot' suit, with the dangling watch-chain brushing the floor, Calloway changed the group's billing in 1931 to become Cab Calloway and His Orchestra. That year, following the success of 'Minnie the Moocher', Calloway was dubbed the King of Hi-De-Ho on account of the scat-type vocals.

Under the auspices of manager Irving Mills, Calloway enjoyed a residency at Harlem's Cotton Club, alternating with Duke Ellington, that lasted until the club's closure in 1940. Such was Calloway's showmanship that he managed to get away with songs such as 'Kicking the Gong Around' and 'Minnie the Moocher's Wedding Day' in spite of their references to drugs.

White audiences particularly took to the sly lewdness of songs such as Fats Waller's 'Six or Seven Times'. After moving to Vocalion from RCA, Calloway scored his biggest hit with the million-selling 'Jumpin' Jive' in 1939. This, in tandem with Calloway's publication the previous year of *The Hepster's Dictionary* (the official reference book to jive talk), confirmed him as the Dean of Jive – a title bestowed upon him by New York University when he was granted an honorary degree.

While his capacity to entertain remained undimmed, Calloway, like Jordan, combined a high standard of musicianship with the razzmatazz. High-class musicians such as trumpeters Doc Cheatham, Mario Bauza – who later became the leader of Machito's band – and Dizzy Gillespie, alto saxophonist Chu Berry, tenor saxophonists Ben Webster and Illinois Jacquet, and drummer Cozy Cole all passed through the ranks of Calloway's band; indeed Berry's solo on 'Ghost of a Chance' with Calloway's band is regarded by many – including jazz critic Leonard Feather, one of Calloway's biggest detractors – as one of Berry's finest expressions. Despite the comic on-stage routines, many of the younger musicians such as Dizzy Gillespie used to ridicule Calloway. On one occasion this resulted in a famous confrontation between the two (Dizzy allegedly threw a small ball of chewed paper at him during rehearsals), and Calloway attacked Dizzy with a knife. In later years Calloway forgave Dizzy, but it was symptomatic of the ambivalence many of the younger musicians felt about playing second fiddle to Calloway's relentless on-stage shenanigans. The bottom line was the money and Calloway paid his musicians amazingly well; in 1936 a band member could earn anything from 35 to 100 dollars a week.

During this time Calloway started to appear in films, including *The Big Broadcast of 1932* (1932), *The Manhattan Merry-Go-Round* (1937) and, most effectively, *Stormy Weather* (1943). These films, in common with Jordan's later similar outings, only served to underline Calloway's essential qualities as an all-round entertainer. As the Second World War draw to a close, Calloway recognized the shift in popular taste and by 1948 he had dispensed with the big band and started another career in the theatre. He appeared on the New York stage as Sportin' Life in George Gershwin's *Porgy and Bess* in 1952 – a part that was tailor-made for him as he had been Gershwin's role model – and then again, in 1974, in the all-black version of *Hello Dolly!* with Pearl Bailey and Billy Daniels. Other notable parts to come his way were appearances in the Broadway version of *Bubbling Brown Sugar* and a cameo with John Belushi and Dan Akroyd in *The Blues Brothers* (1980), where he reprised 'Minnie the Moocher'.

Even after the dissolution of the big band, Calloway continued touring and wherever he appeared he stole the show; he was still working right up to his death on 19 November 1994. Even when meeting presidents, he managed to get the last laugh: Richard Nixon, on meeting him at the White

House, enthused, 'Mr Ellington, it's so good you're here'. Calloway just beamed and thanked him. For that was Calloway's great contribution: the job was to entertain and it is that spirit that still endures in the best R&B bands today. For the choreographed theatrics of James Brown and Little Richard, and the revues of Ike Turner and Johnny Otis, and British revivalists such as the Big Town Playboys and King Pleasure and the Biscuit Boys all owe a debt to Calloway.

LIONEL HAMPTON

While Cab Calloway brought showmanship to the party, Lionel Hampton brought a rhythmic punch with the blazing horns of Illinois Jacquet on tenor sax and Jack McVea on baritone.

In 1943 the Lionel Hampton Big Band marked the reopening of the Famous Door, a New York jazz club, which had relocated to 52nd Street above a Chinese restaurant and which was bankrolled by Joe Glaser, who was head of the black bands department in the Rockwell-O'Keefe booking agency. While Jacquet and McVea were both the stars and the novelty (in their phrasing, at least), Hampton's exhortations from behind the drums and the vibes showed that here was another musician cast from a similar mould to that of Calloway and Jordan. There was a very fundamental difference, though, for Hampton was motivated by the religiousness of his upbringing and, in the same way as gospel, was concerned with involving his audience with the music.

Born in Louisville, Kentucky, on 12 April 1909, Hampton lived briefly in Birmingham before moving on to Chicago where he lived with his grandparents. He was sent to the Holy Rosary Academy in Kenosha, Wisconsin, where he was taught the rudiments of drumming – apparently by a Dominican nun. After playing drums for the Newsboys' Band run by the *Chicago Defender* (the black newspaper with the largest readership), Hampton moved to the West Coast in 1927. At first he drummed with the Paul Howard Orchestra, then with Eddie Barefield and Les Hite. However, during Hampton's tenure with Hite, Louis Armstrong was fronting the band and Hampton started to play vibes. In 1930, he cut his first vibes solo with Louis on 'Memories of You'. He remained with Hite until 1934 when he organized a pick-up band for a series of dates at Sebastian's Cotton Club in Los Angeles. In 1936, while playing the Paradise Club, Hampton was spotted by Benny Goodman who persuaded him to drop the band and join Goodman for a tour with Gene Krupa and Teddy Wilson.

Remaining with Goodman for four years, Hampton still found time to cut his own records under his own name for RCA. Featuring such luminaries as guitarist Charlie Christian, trumpeter Dizzy Gillespie, and tenor saxophonist Coleman Hawkins, these are some of the finest small-group sides to emerge from the swing era. In 1940 Hampton started to front his own orchestra full-time, which he continued to do for the next fifty years. However, it was during the 1940s that his style complemented that of Jordan and his dynamic leadership echoed that of Calloway. Similarly Hampton's orchestra became a rich breeding ground for developing musicians with Jacquet and McVea being notable products, but also Earl Bostic, Arnett Cobb, and Johnny Griffin coming out of the reed section; other notables included Quincy Jones, vocalists Dinah Washington, Betty Carter and Ernestine Anderson, and Joe Williams's bassist Charlie Mingus and guitarist Wes Montgomery. Hampton's orchestra went on to score a series of hits with titles such as 'Flying Home', which was co-written by Hampton and Goodman, 'Hey! Ba-Ba-Re-Bop' and 'Rag Mop' (later a million-seller for the Ames Brothers). With the powerhouse horns of Jacquet and McVea on 'Flying Home', another piece of the template for future R&B bands slipped into place.

Despite the power of the Hampton Band, many jazz enthusiasts were unenthusiastic about his contribution, with Leonard Feather noting that it had 'become as much a rhythm-and-blues as a jazz attraction, with circus overtones'. Be that as it may, Hampton proved an enduring attraction, and during the 1950s and 1960s he reverted more to type, playing mainstream jazz and recording for Norman Granz's labels, including several with pianist Oscar Peterson. With his advancing years he performed less and less, concentrating more on his publishing interests and property development, which included programmes of urban renewal in Harlem.

ERSKINE HAWKINS

While critics may have railed at Jordan, Calloway, and Hampton for their blatancy in providing entertaintainment at allegedly any cost, Erskine Hawkins was attacked for reflecting popular taste too closely. Hawkins was born in Birmingham, Alabama, on 26 July 1914. When he formed his first band, it was to cover his expenses for the Alabama State Teachers' College. However, in 1936, after his band had been assimilated into the 'Bama State Collegians, they moved to New York and started a residency at the Savoy Ballroom; initially alternating with Chick Webb's band, they remained popular at the Savoy until its closure in 1958. Part of the reason for their popularity at the Savoy can be attributed to the owner Moe Gale, who snapped them up as soon as they hit town and became their manager.

Signed initially to the Vocalion label and then to Bluebird, Hawkins's residency at the Savoy established him as one of the premier outfits of the time. This was mainly due to the high-note trumpet playing of Hawkins and William 'Dud' Bascomb, which had been popularized by Louis Armstrong. Often described as too florid, it struck a loud enough chord with the public to make Hawkins's original version of 'Tuxedo Junction' one of the biggest hits of 1939–40; it was completely outsold by Glenn Miller's later cover version, but it remained Hawkins's theme, despite Bascomb playing the signature solo. Other hits by Hawkins included 'After Hours', which was written by the band's arranger Avery Parrish, 'I've Got a Right to Cry' and Louis Jordan's 'Caldonia (What Makes Your Big Head So Hard?)'.

In the post-war era, as big bands slipped out of favour, Hawkins led a succession of small groups and recorded versions of 'The Tennessee Waltz', 'John Henry Blues', 'Memphis Blues', and 'Teach Me Tonight'. Although posterity will probably not accord Hawkins the credit that is his due, many such as trumpeter Cat Anderson, alto saxophonist Oliver Nelson, and vocalist Della Reese achieved their first big breaks with Hawkins.

BUDDY JOHNSON

Such was Buddy Johnson's his popularity at the Savoy Ballroom that his band was known as Walk 'Em Rhythm, after one of his biggest hits, 'Walk 'Em' (1946). Despite his appeal for dancers, Buddy Johnson's Walk 'Em Rhythm was designed to win over those in his audiences who weren't great dancers:

'I felt sorry for those guys and gals who weren't expert dancers. So I fooled around with this idea of having my band play numbers with a simple back beat . . . I figured that everyone knows how to walk, therefore everyone should be able to dance this rhythm.'

The other reason for his appeal was that he was an impressive arranger and pianist, which meant that he was regarded by his contemporaries as a high-quality musician, and not just a fly-by-night novelty act.

Buddy was born Woodrow Wilson Johnson in 1915 in Darlington, South Carolina, and started to play the piano when he was four. By the time he reached high school, he was an accomplished composer, writing revues. In 1938 he moved to New York to broaden his musical horizons, travelling to Europe with a Cotton Club revue. On his return he was spotted and signed with the Decca label. Johnson then started to assemble a combo, which by 1944 was a 16-piece big band that was a stylish, bluesy outfit capable of satisfying dancers and musicians alike. Much of this was due to the addition of a pair of distinguished vocalists, Ella Johnson and Arthur Prysock.

Johnson was Buddy's sister and she brought to the party the intonations of Billie Holiday and Ella Fitzgerald: Leonard Feather described her as 'one of the great individual stylists of modern blues singing'. More than that, though – as hits such as 'Please Mr Johnson' (1941), 'When My Man Comes Home' and 'That's the Stuff You Gonna Watch' (1944), 'Since I Fell For You' (1946), 'I'm Tired Cryin' Over You' (1947) and the tribute to the baseball player, 'Did You See Jackie Robinson?' (1949) attest – these were all identifiable themes: steeped in the argot of the blues, but couched in contemporary terms.

In 1944 Arthur Prysock joined the band. Prysock was another native of the Carolinas – from Spartanburg in the North – but moved to Hartford, Connecticut, where he worked in the aircraft industry. In the meantime, he sang with a local band, which was where he made the connection with Johnson. Appearing with Johnson on several hits such as 'Jet My Love' (1947) and 'I Wonder Where My Love Has Gone' (1948), Prysock – like Ella Johnson – was a big-band vocalist first and foremost. In later years after embarking on a solo career, the influence of Billy Eckstine was more apparent in his delivery than that of, say, Roy Brown, notwithstanding a major success with a cover of Brown's 'Good Rockin' Tonight' and a disco hit 'When Love Is New' (1977). His métier has remained ballads such as 'I Didn't Sleep a Wink Last Night' (1952) and 'The Very Thought of You' (1960). By the mid-1980s Prysock was on the prowl once again with a striking collection for Milestone entitled *Arthur Prysock* (1985).

The point remains, though, that neither Johnson nor Prysock were R&B vocalists as such; it was the galvanizing, jump-start rhythm of Buddy's band that was the heart-starter. Buddy – like Hampton, Calloway, and Jordan – was not afraid to lead by example as well, for in 1944 he handled the lead vocals on 'Fine Brown Frame', which Nellie Lutcher was to cover in 1948. Johnson's musicianship, coupled with immaculate sidemen such as the exemplary tenor men, Sam 'The Man' Taylor and Purvis Henson, trombonist Slide Hampton, guitarist Mickey Baker, and the faultless drumming of Emmanuel 'Foots' Simms, made the band one of the hottest draws of the R&B era.

Even when his Decca contract expired in 1952 and big bands were very much a thing of the past, Johnson secured a new deal with Mercury, scoring hits with 'Doot Doot Dow' and 'I Don't Want Nobody'. However Johnson's cutest move at developing the affections of the new audience of teenage concert-goers was by providing the instrumental accompaniment for a wide range of performers on Alan Freed's Rock 'n' Roll package tours. This kept Buddy and his band in the limelight long after most of his contemporaries had readjusted to smaller line-ups, reverted to jazz, or just given up the music business completely. In 1964 Buddy called time on his musical career and devoted the rest of his life to the church, becoming a minister before succumbing to cancer in 1977.

TINY BRADSHAW

Tiny Bradshaw never made as many inroads as his pedigree might have suggested for he was literally caught between R&B and jazz. However, like Johnson, Bradshaw's musicianship – in this case as a drummer, pianist, and vocalist – carried the day. Born in 1905 in Youngstown, Ohio, he majored in psychology at Ohio's Wilberforce University. While studying, he started to get involved with the multifarious musical diversions to be found on the campus with Horace Henderson, among others, the brother of band leader Fletcher Henderson. After college he relocated to New York and started to drum for the Savoy Bearcats, before being recruited by impresario Irving Mills as a member of Luis Russell and the Blue Rhythm Band. From this it was but a small leap to forming his own band in 1934. Adopting a vocal style similar to that of Cab Calloway, Bradshaw performed novelty items such as 'The Sheik of Araby', 'The Dark Town Strutter's Ball', 'Shout, Sister, Shout', and 'Jersey Bounce'.

Just as Bradshaw was about to break out into the big league, the Second World War intervened and he was commissioned as a major. For the duration of the war Bradshaw and his orchestra toured the world entertaining the troops. When the war finished, Bradshaw returned to find that big bands were no longer economic and he was forced to reduce the band to a seven- or nine-piece unit. Despite this Bradshaw attracted many top-rate musicians and arrangers such as reed men Bobby Plater and Russell Procope, saxophonists Sonny Stitt and Happy Caldwell, trumpeters Charlie Shavers and Henry Glover, and vocalists such as bluesman Lonnie Johnson and Arthur Prysock.

With the saxophone prominently and fashionably to the fore and the emphasis firmly on R&B, Bradshaw cut a series of sides for the King label that included 'Well, Oh Well' (1950), 'Train Kept A-Rolling' (1951), 'Big Town' (1952) – featuring Roy Brown – and 'Soft' (1952). Despite these successes – a young man from Texas called Buddy Holly was later to cite Tiny Bradshaw as one of his greatest formative influences – Bradshaw was unable to capitalize on the rock 'n' roll era to any great extent. By the mid-1950s the band had folded and Bradshaw had left the music industry through ill health. He died in 1958.

LUCKY MILLINDER AND BULLMOOSE JACKSON

Finally there was the Lucky Millinder Band. In any other epoch Millinder might have found his niche in a record company as an A&R (artists and repertoire) man or even a label boss. For Millinder had no basic musical knowledge – he couldn't read music and he didn't play an instrument – but he did sing sometimes. What he did have was a tremendously good ear for talent and formidable organizational skills. These two qualities enabled him to assemble one of the best bands of the R&B era.

Born Lucius Venable Millinder on 8 August 1900, in Anniston, Alabama, Millinder was raised in Chicago where he became a well-known figure in the late 1920s as master of ceremonies at the Grand Terrace Club (Al Capone was one of the club's clientele). By 1931 he was fronting his own band and the following year he moved to New York. In 1933 he toured Europe and held down a residency in the south of France. On his return to New York he took over the leadership of the Mills Blue Rhythm Band. While this band had been organized by music publisher and manager Irving Mills to operate as cover for Mills's principal clients, Duke Ellington and Cab Calloway, they quickly established themselves in their own right as recording artists for Decca and as backing for Mamie Smith and guitarist and vocalist Sister Rosetta Tharpe. This was hardly surprising as Millinder had already shown a knack for signing up talented sidemen, including trumpeters Henry 'Red' Allen, Charlie Shavers and Harry 'Sweets' Edison, trombonists J. C. Higginbotham and Wilbur De Paris, saxophonist Joe Garland, bassist John Kirby, and many others destined for greater things.

In 1938 Millinder took over the leadership of Johnny Gorham's Band from pianist and arranger Bill Doggett. While this turned out to be a financial nightmare and the band subsequently split up, Millinder formed a new orchestra the following year and, retaining his contract with Decca, hit his stride with titles such as 'When the Lights Go on Again', 'Little John Special', and 'Apollo Jump'. Other titles such as 'Trouble in Mind', the gospel-flavoured 'Rock Me', and 'Shout, Sister, Shout' all featured Sister Rosetta Tharpe, while 'Who Threw the Whiskey in the Well?' (1944) featured Wynonie Harris on vocals. Both Tharpe and Harris illustrated Millinder's knack for hiring fine vocalists as well as fine instrumentalists. Among those to feature in the Millinder line-up in the 1940s were trumpeters Joe Guy, Henry Glover, and Dizzy Gillespie, saxophonist Eddie 'Lockjaw' Davis and pianist Sir Charles Thompson.

After leaving Decca, Millinder joined RCA where he scored more hits with 'D Natural Blues' (1949) and 'I'll Never Be Free' (1950). His sojourn at RCA was short-lived because, at the suggestion of King supremo Syd Nathan, he moved to the King label where Henry Glover – one of Millinder's former trumpeters – had taken up the post of A&R director in 1947. This proved to be a key move in Millinder's attaining the apex of the R&B sound, for not only did he cut hit records such as 'I'm Waiting Just For You' under his own name but he also became effectively leader of the house band at King, backing former sidemen such as Wynonie Harris on 'Bloodshot Eyes' and 'Lovin' Machine' (1951) and Bullmoose Jackson.

If somebody like Millinder had not come along, Bullmoose Jackson could well have languished in semi-obscurity for the best part of his career. But it was the context of Millinder's band that showed Moose the way and it was Millinder who introduced Moose to Syd Nathan and Henry Glover, who between them came up with the notion of Moose starting to record under his own name.

Moose was born Benjamin Clarence Jackson in 1919 in Cleveland, Ohio, and started to sing in church as a child, before going on to study the violin and play the saxophone. After making his debut with trumpeter Freddie Webster's group, both joined Millinder's outfit in 1944. Although Moose cut a session for Capitol, it was with his own group, the Buffalo Bearcats, and the King label that he achieved his biggest hits. Starting with 'I Know Who Threw the Whiskey in the Well' (1945) – an answer record to Millinder's 'Who Threw the Whiskey in the Well?' – Moose combined ballads such as 'I Love You, Yes I Do' (1947) and 'Little Girl Don't You Cry' (1949) with rather more raunchy, overtly R&B flavoured titles such as 'I Want a Bowlegged Woman' and 'Sneaky Pete' (1947) and 'Big Ten Inch Record' (1952). But as Syd Nathan said in later years, 'Bullmoose was a totally wrong name for him, because he crooned so sweetly'. Moose failed to breast the rock 'n' roll tide and went into retirement in Philadelphia to run a bar. Not surprisingly, though, when 'I Love You, Yes I Do' was revived in 1961, it became a hit all over again.

By 1952 the clock was ticking for the big bands and Millinder, with little to offer, ceased operating. Over the years until his death (on 28 September 1966) he would re-form the band periodically for short tours but his time had passed and he found work as a liquor salesman, a fortune-teller, and a DJ on WNEW. While critics often scoffed – and in the light of offerings such as 'We're Gonna Have To Stop That Dirty Little Jap', who can blame them? – Millinder contributed significantly to the rise of R&B through his patronage of artists like Jackson, Tharpe, and Harris. And it is difficult to imagine whether band leaders like Johnny Otis or Ike Turner would have emerged if Duke Ellington and Count Basie had been the only role models.

chapter two

THE STATE OF
THE NATION

WHEN THE SECOND WORLD WAR broke out in Europe in 1939, the charts were still dominated by the 'swing' big bands. Some six years later when the American troops returned from Southeast Asia, the whole fabric of the record industry had changed beyond recognition on account of the formation of the BMI (Broadcast Music International) in opposition to the long-established ASCAP (American Society of Composers, Authors, and Publishers), the shellac shortage of 1942, the cult of the DJ, and the rise of the independent record labels. All these factors were instrumental in determining what the record-buying public would hear and directly contributed to the rise in popularity of R&B and the emergence of rock 'n' roll.

ASCAP VERSUS BMI

ASCAP was formed in 1914 by a group of the most powerful composers, lyricists, and lawyers of the day. The objectives of the society were to ensure that their property rights in their compositions were properly protected and that they received proper remuneration for all public performances of their work. Prior to 1914 it had been standard practice among broadcasters to use copyright materials without permission or payment. Inevitably broadcasters felt hard done by and the issue came to a head when ASCAP took commercial radio stations to court over non-payment of royalties. The resulting judgment in 1923 decreed that all broadcasters were legally bound to pay performance royalties to the copyright holder.

However, ASCAP unofficially operated a cartel and were very picky as to whom they would allow membership; prospective members needed to have scored a minimum of three hits before they were considered for membership. (As Willie Dixon observed, 'How can I get a hit, if no one will publish my songs?'.) Consequently ASCAP's membership comprised the very best commercial writers in the US, such as Cole Porter, Irving Berlin, Jerome Kern, Richard Rodgers, Oscar Hammerstein, and George Gershwin to name but a few. In other words, those who were big in Hollywood or on Broadway were controlling most of the publishing rights and were receiving most of the performance royalties collected by the society. Therefore writers working in country – or 'hillbilly music', as it was then known – jazz, blues, or gospel barely received any remuneration as the society deemed itself above such poor-quality music.

In 1937 ASCAP, asserting its monopoly, proposed a 100 per cent increase in the emoluments paid by the radio stations. This was the last straw for the broadcasters, not that they were about to give in to ASCAP's greedy demands, nor indeed were they about to stop broadcasting the society's music. Instead the broadcasters established their own licensing society, the BMI, in 1939.

Effective as of the expiry of the broadcasters' agreement with ASCAP on 1 January 1941, the BMI immediately took full advantage of ASCAP's rigorous membership stipulations, while adopting the same royalty scale. There was a slight difference, though, as ASCAP tended to pay a higher rate to established writers and composers, while the BMI offered a standard scale to all members. This meant that some ASCAP members swapped their allegiance, but more significantly it meant that those working in jazz, blues, gospel, or country were actively sought out by the BMI. Initially ASCAP members and other music industry bigwigs thought that 'hillbilly music' or R&B would not generate much income. They were proved to be completely wrong.

Throughout the 1940s the lot of the black songwriter improved dramatically. There was still scope for black songwriters to be taken advantage of, as independent label bosses were quick to claim authorship of songs where copyright had not been asserted. Indeed, Willie Dixon in his autobiography, I Am the Blues, states that Leonard Chess 'was just taking the ideas (for tunes) and putting them with other things'. So there were still myriad ways in which the black writer – often through lack of education or business knowledge – could be ripped off, but at least there was a mechanism offering some sort of protection. On a more positive note, the BMI gave black writers a vestige of independence, enabling some such as Louis Jordan, Cab Calloway, and Lucky Millinder to buck the system and record and write what they chose, instead of being perpetually beholden to the record companies.

By 1950 ASCAP's members were so concerned about the ascendancy of BMI-licensed songs that they moved to file a lawsuit against the BMI. The basis of their contention was that because many of the broadcasters held stock in the BMI and that up to 80 per cent of the music played by some radio stations was BMI-licensed, the BMI was guilty of monopolistic practices. In November 1953, 33 ASCAP members filed a $150 million lawsuit against the BMI, the three major broadcasting networks (CBS, NBC, and ABC), and two record companies (Columbia and RCA Victor), charging them with controlling the nation's airwaves and blocking songs from ASCAP members.

Furthermore, ASCAP started to target DJs like Alan Freed, who had become one of the nation's most vociferous champions of R&B, for corrupting the morals of the country's young by playing records such as the Swallows' 'It Ain't the Meat (It's the Motions)', the Dominoes' 'Sixty Minute Man', Peppermint Harris's 'I Got Loaded', the Ravens' 'Rock Me All Night Long', and Ray Charles's 'Roll With My Baby' – all songs that could be loosely interpreted as 'explicit' or, as in the case of 'I Got Loaded', subliminally encouraging the use of drugs and alcohol. Consequently religious groups, teachers, parents, and other concerned bodies joined in the debate and the BMI eventually conceded, instituting a screening committee that would eliminate blatantly pornographic lyrics. Even *Variety* put their spoke in, accusing record companies of allowing their industry to be 'fouled by marketing filth'; *Variety,* however, could not be regarded as dispassionate observers because their publishing *raison d'être* had been to reflect and champion the film and theatrical professions. So, once again, ASCAP was only rallying bi-partisan supporters.

While the lawsuit dragged on, ASCAP announced that it would not credit any performance written by an ASCAP member in collaboration with a BMI writer after 1 January 1955. In 1957, with rumours rife over payola, ASCAP succeeded in bringing a bill before the American Senate preventing individual broadcasters from holding stock in the BMI. The bill was aborted in the committee stages, but it succeeded in maintaining pressure on the BMI and R&B *per se*. The lawsuit eventually petered out in 1964 and broadcasters were not required to divest themselves of their holdings, nor indeed was the BMI barred from offering advances and guarantees to its members in lieu of future royalties, which had been another contentious issue for ASCAP.

The lawsuit, though, had had its casualties, the most notable of which was Alan Freed – whom we shall return to later – but as the war between the rival factions grew, any suggestion of controversy or malpractice was drawn into the fray. And so the seeds were sown for the payola hearings, which brought about the downfall of Freed. Many of the records cited in the payola hearings were R&B or rock 'n' roll and were the products of independent record companies, but the suggestion that individuals were indulging in corrupt practices to get their records played was just another way of getting at the BMI.

In the long term many ASCAP members had feared that R&B/rock 'n' roll was just another passing fad, jeopardizing their livelihoods. Pillars of the establishment like Frank Sinatra were moved to comment that rock 'n' roll was 'the most brutal, ugly, degenerate, vicious form of expression it has been my misfortune to hear'. When Bill Haley's 'Rock Around the Clock' started to sell in quantity, there was never a hint of controversy in the US at least, as it was written by ASCAP members Max Freedman and Jimmy DeKnight; in the UK it was slightly different as gangs of teddy boys tore up cinema seats when it was included on the soundtrack of the film *Blackboard Jungle*. Hopefully this was fury at being made to listen to such a blatant piece of opportunism. By the time the lawsuit had been settled, many ASCAP members themselves were writing for the R&B/rock 'n' roll markets.

WARTIME AND JUKEBOXES

While the song war affected the prosperity of a very few black writers and performers, the shellac shortage affected the very survival of bands, groups, and artists by jeopardizing their ability to get a recording contract in the first place. To place this in context it is necessary to go right back to the 1920s when blues and jazz were marketed on each record company's specialist 'race' label. The term 'race' was coined by OKeh's recording director Ralph Peer. He had decided on this term to market OKeh's 8000 series; then J. Mayo Williams, Paramount's recording director and black, fastened on the term to describe their 12000 series, marketing it as 'The Popular Race Record'. Both Vocalion, a subsidiary of the Brunswick-Balke-Collender Company, and Columbia had specialist series on which to market their records. They were later joined by Victor's Bluebird series and then Decca, founded in 1934 in the US by Jack Kapp, the former guiding spirit behind Vocalion's race records.

Although these labels were lucrative, they could only be made to work if they were significantly cheaper than other lines: Decca retailed Louis Jordan records at 35 cents, but the Andrews Sisters' and Bing Crosby's records were all retailed at 75 cents. After the US was drawn into the Second World War in 1941, the supply of shellac – the raw material used for surfacing records – became restricted and the American Government decreed that record companies had to economize. The special 35 cent labels were the first to be axed. The Government also decreed that the record companies were not allowed to put up the price of the 35 cent labels to 75 cents. In other words, the Government was saying that the record companies had to prune their rosters and stop cutting jazz and R&B records. For many artists this meant that they could not record for the duration of the War, but some had other means at their disposal.

For Jordan, it gave him the opportunity to diversify. Berle Adams recalls:

> 'What we did was we went to the BMI who had just started up and asked them for some money to set up a publishing company. Then we made this twenty minute film called *Caldonia*, starring Louis, and it featured "Caldonia" and "Let the Good Times Roll". And it was massive, it killed everybody and was the number one box office attraction through the South! As it was so successful, we were given some money to make *Beware Brother Beware* (1946). By then the restrictions had eased, but it broke Louis's movie career wide open and he was even more popular than before.'

Although the shellac shortage dealt a body blow to the rise of R&B, other factors acknowledged its growth in popularity: the trade newspaper *Billboard* instituted the 'Harlem Hit Parade' in October 1942, a chart that dealt exclusively with 'race' artists. Up until that time, 'hillbilly' and 'race' were lumped together inconclusively in the 'folk' charts. On 25 June 1949 the term 'race' was dropped in favour of 'rhythm and blues'.

Another significant factor was the emergence of the jukebox. However, jukebox manufacturers were not to escape the exigencies of war, for on 1 May 1942 the War Production Board commandeered the plants of many jukebox manufacturers to help the war effort. This was at a time when the demand for jukeboxes was spiralling out of all proportion. No army base or youth club was complete without a jukebox. By August 1944 record companies were finding it increasingly hard to service jukeboxes, which were accounting for up to 75 per cent of the record output, while the retail market absorbed the balance. Such was the influence of the jukebox that some record labels – Decca, for example – viewed the jukebox as the primary marketing tool, prohibiting radio stations from playing their releases even if they had purchased them. This situation did not last long as the cult of the disc jockey was already beginning to make its presence felt.

THE FIRST DISC JOCKEYS

As the war years saw the jukebox reign supreme, encouraging listeners to splash out on the cresting wave of R&B that was threatening to engulf the record industry, there was initial resistance to the concept of disc jockeys. Record companies expressed fears that playing records over the air would damage sales, with some such as Decca actively prohibiting the practice. By the end of the Second World War, as the number of independent record labels and radio stations proliferated, so opinion gave way and radio and television were set to become the premier promotional tools. Drawing financial resources from the recently established BMI, radio soon became the leading promoter of country music and R&B, with two stations showing the way.

From WLAC Nashville's 50,000-watt transmitter, disc jockeys 'Daddy' Gene Nobles and John Richbourg programmed a combination of jazz and R&B. Both were white men, with Nobles having joined the station in the early 1940s. He initially played the big-band jazz of Count Basie and Lionel Hampton, but when John R arrived after War, both men noticed that they were getting requests for records by Louis Jordan and Bullmoose Jackson, among others, and soon both were programming identical play lists. Of the two, it was Richbourg who exerted the greater influence. With an audience stretching from the east coast of Virginia to west Texas, and as far north as the Canadian border, John Richbourg's weekend shows left an indelible impression on youngsters such as Dan Penn, Steve Cropper, Rick Hall, and Nanci Griffith's band leader James Hooker. In 1995 Hooker recalled:

> 'I remember listening to John R's shows whenever I could get the reception. I used to fix this alligator clip to the antenna and this usually meant that I could hear through even the stormiest conditions. But John R was incredible because you never really heard R&B on the radio then, and it was just such a revelation hearing people like Fats Domino, Ray Charles, Clarence 'Gatemouth' Brown and then all the Stax stuff from out of Memphis.'

Born near Charleston, South Carolina, John Richbourg started his career playing character roles for radio dramas during the 1930s. By 1940 he had returned to Charleston, where he got a job as a DJ on the local radio station, WTMA. After his stint with WTMA and a spell in the navy, he moved to WLAC in Nashville, taking over Ernie Young's 1–3 a.m. slot (Young was to start the Excello label). The success of his radio programmes enabled him to gain access to artists and producers, and in 1955 he started his own Rich label. While never as opportunistic as others, Richbourg guided the careers of performers such as Roscoe Shelton and Lattimore Brown, both of whom were signed to Excello. In 1963 he was hired by Fred Foster to set up the Monument soul subsidiary, Sound Stage Seven. Richbourg took Shelton, Brown, Joe Simon, Sam Baker, and Ella Washington down to the studios in Muscle Shoals, Alabama, or Stax and American in Memphis. In 1970 Richbourg parted company with Foster, who had set up a fresh deal with Columbia. Richbourg set up the Seventy Seven label in 1972, but there was little he could do to stop it from going out of business in 1977. In 1973 he retired from WLAC. With the changes in musical tastes he retired from the music industry, falling ill with cancer soon after. In 1985 a benefit was organized in Nashville, featuring B. B. King, Joe Simon, and the Coasters, among others. Richbourg died in 1986.

While Gene Nobles and John Richbourg were operating from Nashville, two hundred miles to the south-west in Memphis, WDIA started to pro-gramme R&B for white audiences in 1947. In the first year the station lost so much money that they changed the format, using black DJs such as Nat 'The Professor' Williams and Rufus Thomas; it was there that one Riley King would get his first break. After this change, WDIA recouped most of its earlier losses almost overnight.

Across the country, broadcasters started to emulate the success of WDIA and WLAC. In Los Angeles Hunter Hancock, who as early as 1943 had been playing the big-band sounds of Hampton and Millinder, started to host a daily R&B show in 1948. Bill 'Hoss' Allen at WHIN was playing R&B in 1945 and it was his arrival at WLAC in 1949 that made the owners decide to schedule black music exclusively. By the early 1950s most large cities – particularly in the South – had specialist R&B shows: Tom 'Big Daddy' Donahue in Washington, DC; Zenas 'Daddy' Sears in Atlanta; Clarence 'Poppa' Hayman and Ken 'Jack the Cat' Elliott in New Orleans; Danny 'Cat Man' Stiles in Newark, New Jersey; George 'Hound Dog' Lorenz in Buffalo, New York; Phil McKernan in Berkeley, California; and Alan Freed in Cleveland. For many Freed embodied the spirit of R&B.

Born in Johnstown, Pennsylvania, on 15 December 1922, Freed was raised in Salem, Ohio, and played the trombone at high school, joining the Sultans of Swing jazz band for a spell. After leaving the army, he studied engineering, but started to work as an announcer at WKST in New Castle, Pennsylvania. This gave him the opening to work as a relief DJ playing clas-sical music. By 1943 he had moved to WKBN, Youngstown, to work as a sports announcer then, in 1945, he moved on to WAKR, Akron, where he hosted *Request Revue*. In 1951 he moved to WJW, Cleveland, where he con-vinced local record-store owner Leo Mintz to sponsor an R&B show, *Record Rendezvous*. His hoarse delivery, shouting encouragement to the musicians as the records played, went down a storm with young audiences who had never heard anything quite like the unadulterated rawness of groups such as the Orioles and the Harptones and vocalists such as Ruth Brown and Wynonie Harris. After changing the name of his show to *Moondog's Rock 'n' Roll Party*, he promoted a number of concerts, which featured Ruth Brown, the Clovers, and Buddy Johnson's Orchestra, among others. Such was the success of these ventures and his show that he was lured to WINS in New York. Although the year was 1954, the term 'rock 'n' roll' had effec-tively superseded R&B; Freed popularized it as he felt that the latter had too many black connotations for white audiences. He even attempted, unsuccessfully, to copyright the term 'rock 'n' roll'. Later he was disbarred from using the term 'Moondog' as a New York street musician claimed successfully that he had been known as Moondog since the 1930s.

As Freed's influence grew – he appeared in the films *Rock Around the Clock* and *Rock, Rock, Rock* (1956) and *Don't Knock the Rock* (1957) and hosted his own TV show *Rock 'n' Roll Dance Party* – so the controversy surrounding R&B and rock 'n' roll became more intense. Vilified by educationalists and religious leaders for the 'abhorrent' effect these types of music allegedly had upon the young, rock 'n' roll was seen as the devil's music incarnate and Freed was viewed as the devil's disciple. With this type of adverse publicity, Freed was quickly implicated in any scandal: his TV show *Rock 'n' Roll Dance Party* was cancelled when vocalist Frankie Lymon of the Teenagers was shown on camera dancing with a white girl; when a riot broke out at one of his concerts in Boston, Freed was charged with incitement to riot and his legal costs bankrupted him; and in ASCAP's long-running dispute with the BMI, the whole subject of payola was drawn into the controversy, with ASCAP contending that disc jockeys such as Freed were given perks to play records. The payola investigations proved to be Freed's nemesis, as his career was left in tatters after he pleaded guilty to bribery at the Congressional hearings and eventually he was indicted for tax evasion but he died on 20 January 1965 before the case came to trial. The whole point, though, was that as Atlantic producer Jerry Wexler said in his autobiography, *The Rhythm and the Blues*, 'fail to acknowledge the deejays and programme directors and you were out of business' but Freed, being the most vocal champion of R&B and rock 'n' roll, was the scapegoat.

RISE OF THE INDEPENDENTS

Of all the factors in the selling of R&B, the emergence of the independent record labels in the post-war era was the most significant and the least dogged by controversy. Their emergence was, after all, a response only to the failure of the major labels to keep abreast of changes in public taste and post-war economics. More than that, the independent record labels were products of their environments and so they only tended to reflect a microcosm. That these microcosms joined hands, so to speak, and ultimately changed the face of contemporary music was something nobody could have anticipated – let alone planned. However, throughout the US different entrepreneurs started to address the requirements of the community in which they lived. Some were driven by enthusiasm; most saw a void in the market place and were only too happy to try to fill it. Altruism was not a part of the picture: from New York (Ahmet and Nesuhi Ertegun and Herb Abramson at Atlantic and Herman Lubinsky at Savoy) to Los Angeles (Art Rupe at Specialty and the Bihari Brothers at Modern) and from Texas (Don Robey at Duke) to Chicago (Leonard Chess at Chess), labels sprung up with some of the most unlikely characters as proprietors.

The majors were slow to respond to this fresh challenge from a completely different quarter. Ever since the 1930s there had been a smattering of independent record labels: Los Angeles boasted Exclusive and Excelsior, while New York could offer Keynote, Beacon, Savoy, DeLuxe, National, and Varsity. However, it was one record that caused everyone to wake up and see the potential of R&B and that was Cecil Gant's 'I Wonder'.

chapter three

LIFE COULD BE A DREAM: THE VOCAL GROUPS

A S THE SMALL INSTRUMENTAL COMBOS began to pick up steam, and recording studios and pressing plants worked round the clock, more and more kids tried to find the means to gain an entrée into the record business. For many this was an uphill struggle because few had the spending power to buy musical instruments. The church, always an important catalyst in introducing young people to music, provided the principal conduit as many youngsters who had sung in church choirs organized themselves into vocal groups. While barber-shop groups had ben a principal component of the black music tradition, street-corner vocal groups began to spring up across the country. Although many adopted the vocal purity of tone and phrasing associated with gospel, others adopted a more scatological approach, drawing from the vernacular of the ghetto. But it was the success of the Ink Spots and the Mills Brothers that galvanized the growth of vocal groups more than any other factor. This was peer pressure in its most undiluted form. Even early vocal groups such as the Mississippi Sheiks – also known as the Down Home Boys – or the Five Red Caps were unable to match the impact of the Ink Spots and the Mills Brothers, despite their being able to lay a reasonable claim to being the tradition's legitimate progenitors.

ROOTS OF THE VOCAL GROUP

THE INK SPOTS

By the end of the Second World War the Ink Spots – formed in 1934 – had established themselves as purveyors of classy pop music that owed much to gospel stylistically. While their material contained strong elements of blues and jazz initially, their sound was tailored to eradicate any overt racial connotation. As a consequence they succeeded in breaking out of the constricting race markets and started to appeal across the board to white audiences with titles such as 'If I Didn't Care' and 'My Prayer' (1939), 'Whispering Grass' and 'Do I Worry?' (1940). While their appeal for white audiences lay in the sweetness of the harmonies, they indulged in mid-song recitations that were little more than whimsical homilies: there was no attempt made to assert their blackness. Furthermore, appearances in films such as *Great American Broadcast* (1941) and *Pardon My Sarong* (1942) spurred their popularity, while promulgating the concept of the vocal group as a viable unit and worthy of emulation.

Although the Ink Spots had distanced themselves so thoroughly from their gospel roots that occasionally they seemed to be parodying their origins, they still commanded respect. As if to emphasize this claim to being the premier vocal group, they embarked on a package tour with Ella Fitzgerald and the Cootie Williams Orchestra. Lasting for over a year between 1944 and 1945, they even found time for a spot of recording with Ella; the resulting session produced 'I'm Making Believe' and 'Into Each Life Some Rain Must Fall' (1945), with the latter hitting the top of the charts where it remained for a straight 17 weeks. Despite their moving in an altogether more rarefied atmosphere than almost any other vocal group save the Mills Brothers, the Ink Spots' success was the yardstick, which the new wave of young vocal groups sought to emulate. It made little difference that the Ink Spots were as attenuated from traditional black music forms as the new wave vocal groups were from the glitz of showbusiness's elite entertainers. For many, the Ink Spots had made the big time and the ramifications of how they got there were of little significance.

As the 1950s dawned, the Ink Spots began to break up but this only encouraged each successive member who had left to start up his version of the group; this practice would become commonplace in the 1960s and 1970s when different versions of the Platters, the Drifters, or the Coasters could be found at somewhere or another playing anywhere across the globe. To this day the name 'The Ink Spots' is almost generic and could probably have been registered as a trademark, for although the individuals behind the sound have long since passed into legend and obscurity, the monster they created continued to thrive into the 1980s.

THE MILLS BROTHERS

Four years before the Ink Spots emerged, the Mills Brothers (John, born 11 February 1911; Herbert, born 2 April 1912; Harry, born 9 August 1913; and Donald, born 29 April 1915) from Piqua, Ohio, were cutting a swathe with their debut single 'Nobody's Sweetheart' and 'Tiger Rag' for the Brunswick label. While the Mills Brothers were rooted in the tradition of the jubilee quartet gospel style, their career had begun in vaudeville, which was followed by a radio show on Cincinnati's WLW. After the success of 'Nobody's Sweetheart', which became a million-seller, they were lured to the bright lights of Hollywood for a number of film appearances that included *The Big Broadcast of 1932* (1932), *Operator 13* (1933) and, with Dick Powell, *Twenty Million Sweethearts* (1934). Despite this commercial acceptance and their growing appeal for white audiences they remained authentic interpreters of jazz material with hits such as 'Goodbye Blues' and 'Diga Diga Doo' (1932). Indeed the only sop or 'novelty' value to their act was their vocal impressions of instruments such as 'trumpet', 'trombone', 'saxophone', and 'bass', which had come about while working in vaudeville.

In 1936 John, the group's guitarist and the singer of the bass lines, died; his replacement was his father, John Mills Sr. Undaunted, the group continued touring and making radio broadcasts often on Bing Crosby programmes, but they retained their jazzy feel and this was augmented – if anything – by the addition of guitarist Bernard Addison. Sustaining their popularity through the 1940s with appearances in musicals such as *Chatterbox* and *He's My Guy* and hits with 'Paper Doll', which sold an astonishing six million copies, 'You Always Hurt the One You Love', 'Til Then', 'I Wish', 'I Don't Know Enough About You', 'Across the Alley From the Alamo', 'I Love You So Much It Hurts', 'Lazy River', and 'I've Got My Love to Keep Me Warm', they provided inspiration for countless emergent groups.

By the 1950s, they had dispensed with their humorous impressions of instruments and were now dependent on their merits as a vocal group for survival. This they achieved with distinction, particularly in the company of Tommy Dorsey's former arranger, Sy Oliver, who chaperoned them through several revivals of popular standards such as 'Nevertheless (I'm in Love With You)' (1950), 'Be My Life's Companion', and 'The Glow Worm' (1952). In 1956 John Mills Sr retired, but the group continued as a trio, scoring hits with 'Queen of the Senior Prom' (1957) and 'Get a Job' (1958).

Ironically both these hits were blatant attempts by the group to modernize and update their sound in line with groups such as the Drifters and the Coasters. While it was hardly surprising that the Mills Brothers should want to align themselves with the popular success of these R&B vocal groups, they were held in such affection by the public at large that they had become a national institution.

In 1968 they had their final hit with 'Cab Driver'. Still they toured constantly until 1982 when Harry Mills died. Once again a replacement singer was recruited and Herbert and Donald continued to ply their trade, although the pace was less frenetic now. In 1989 Herbert died in Las Vegas, but Donald, now walking with a cane, continued with his son John, performing medleys of the Mills Brothers' best-loved songs.

1945–49

With the incentives offered by the success of the Ink Spots and the Mills Brothers and the immediacy of R&B, independent record labels spotted a niche in the market for vocal groups, particularly on the East Coast where Harlem proved to be an especially fertile hunting ground for A&R men. The first group to catch the ear in the post-war upheaval was the Ravens.

THE RAVENS

Formed in Harlem with a line-up comprising Warren Suttles, Leonard Puzey, Maithe Marshal, and Jimmy Ricks, they made their debut at the Club Baron in 1946. Making no effort to hide their admiration for the Ink Spots, they were signed to the King label, where they knocked out four singles – 'Bye Bye Baby Blues', 'Out of a Dream', 'Honey', and 'My Sugar Is So Refined' – in quick succession. While these sides disappeared without so much as a by-your-leave, the group could certainly 'swing' and Jimmy Ricks's basso profundo infused these early sides with gravitas, causing their style of vocalizing later to be dubbed 'doo-wop'. Not content with King's efforts, they moved to Ben Bart's Hub label, where they promptly reissued 'Bye Bye Baby Blues', 'Honey', and 'My Sugar Is So Refined' ('Out of a Dream' became the B-side of 'My Sugar Is So Refined'). The second time around there was still little enthusiasm shown by the record-buying public, but the group came to the attention of street-wise, fast-talking A&R man Herb Abramson, who at that time was working for Al Green's National label.

Although a jazz enthusiast, Abramson had demonstrated an interested in R&B by recording sides with Joe Turner. Above all, though, he was never slow to spot an opportunity, as his later co-founding of Atlantic attests. Striking a deal with Bart that gave him a co-production credit, Abramson and National obtained the marketing and distribution of future Ravens releases. Over the next three years the Ravens racked up a string of hits that included 'Ol' Man River' and 'Write Me a Letter' (1947), 'September Song', 'It's Too Soon to Know', and 'White Christmas' (1948), 'Deep Purple' and 'Someday' (1949) and 'Don't Have to Ride No More' and 'Count Every Star' (1950). While these hits predicated the economic viability of vocal groups, the Ravens' sound was not much 'blacker' than that of the Mills Brothers and their propensity for covering show tunes displayed an aspiration to emulate the Ink Spots. Having said that, they weren't reticent about performing 'black' material, such as 'Write Me a Letter', which was penned by the youthful, black songwriter Howard Biggs; 'It's Too Soon to Know' was originally cut by the Orioles, and the Ravens' arrangement of 'White Christmas' was copied by the Drifters and turned into one of those hardy festive hits that crop up year after year.

In 1950 National went to the wall – Abramson had gone to Atlantic by this time – and so the Ravens cut 'Marie' for Rendition before signing with Columbia and then OKeh. To some extent this move foreshadowed their demise because major labels like Columbia still had little idea of how to market R&B. Even so, titles such as 'Midnite Blues' (1950) and 'Someone to Watch Over Me' (1951) continued to exert an influence on other emergent doo-wop groups. Another change of labels took place, this time to Mercury, where they scored with 'Wagon Wheels' and the emphatically risqué 'Rock Me All Night Long' (1952), as well as partnering Dinah Washington on 'Out in the Cold' (1952). Remaining at Mercury until 1955, they chose to re-record many of their most influential songs, such as 'September Song' (1953) and 'White Christmas', 'Ol' Man River', and 'Write Me a Letter' (1954). By this time the line-up had undergone many changes of personnel and so these new versions were totally different from the originals in timbre, if not arrangement.

In 1955 the Ravens moved to Jerry Blaine's Jubilee label where they cut another four singles, including another version of 'Bye Bye Baby Blues'. The following year they landed on the Chess subsidiary, Argo, for a few more sides before closing the chapter on their career in show business with another version of 'White Christmas' for the Savoy label in 1957. Although the group's later years paled in contrast with their years at National, the Ravens bridged the gap between the Mills Brothers and the blacker doo-wop groups of the 1950s. Of their immediate contemporaries, the Four Tunes showed the greatest aptitude for crossing over into the white pop markets. Their saving grace was their recruitment of Savannah Churchill as featured vocalist.

SAVANNAH CHURCHILL

Savannah Churchill was born in New Orleans on 21 August 1919. After moving to Brooklyn in 1925, she showed every indication of achieving great distinction as a fashion designer while studying at New York University. Instead she decided to marry her childhood sweetheart and raise a family. After they had had two children, her husband was killed in a car crash and Savannah was left with no alternative but to go out to work. With little work immediately available, she became a dancer at Smalls' Paradise in Harlem and started to study singing. At this point Benny Carter entered the story: after hearing her singing, he was so impressed by her voice that he persuaded her to join his band as the featured vocalist. Joe Davis, who had recently established the Beacon label, was also sufficiently impressed to offer Savannah a short-term contract. Cutting sides such as 'Fat Meat Is Good Meat' and 'He's Commander-in-Chief of My Heart' (1942), it could be suggested that Davis was not as wholehearted in his commitment to Savannah if the material was anything to go by. Three years later Savannah had a new manager, Irving Berman, the owner of the Manor label, and in October 1945 she scored a massive hit with 'Daddy, Daddy'. Not content with this, Berman, recognizing the ascendancy of vocal groups, teamed Savannah with his other protégés, the Four Tunes.

While the Four Tunes on their own achieved some success with titles like 'Marie' (1953) and 'I Understand' (1954), these were drab and characterless in comparison with their output with Savannah. Between 1947 and 1949 their collaborations included 'I Want to Be Loved (But Only By You)', 'I Understand', and 'Time Out For Tears' (1947), 'Little Jane', 'I'll Never Belong to Anyone Else', and 'Would You Hurt Me Now?' (1948), and 'I Want to Cry' (1949). Ironically these collaborations did more for the Four Tunes because Savannah found it increasingly difficult to avoid being pigeon-holed with Dinah Washington. Despite cutting several albums for RCA, Decca, and Columbia, she managed to sidestep any attempts to revive her career. The Four Tunes continued until 1956, having spent the last years of their recording career at the Jubilee label.

THE ORIOLES

Of all the early East Coast vocal groups to break through, the Orioles were probably the most distinguished. Combining the raw emotional commitment of gospel with the gritty realism of street-corner singing, they had a lead singer in Earlington Tilghman (he later changed his name to the less glamorous, but infinitely more manageable, Sonny Til) who possessed the sex appeal of a movie star but the accessibility of the boy down the block. Til, as Sam Cooke in the Soul Stirrers would later demonstrate, was able to whip up a frenzy just by batting his eyelids or combing his hair.

The group were discovered singing on a corner near a Baltimore railway station by a bar owner, who invited them into his bar to entertain the clientele. Serendipity waved her wand and into this bar came a young, aggressive songwriter called Deborah Chessler. Astonished and excited, she swept the group off their feet and into her waiting car, driving them all the way to New York and into an audition with Frank Schiffman, owner of Harlem's Apollo Theatre. Schiffman couldn't believe his good fortune and booked the group, who drove every audience wild with desire.

Originally known as the Vibranaires, the line-up comprised Sonny Til, George Nelson, Alexander Sharp, Johnny Reed, and guitarist Tommy Gaither; the only change came in 1950 when Gaither was killed in a car crash and replaced by Ralph Williams. The other major change was their name because Chessler considered that the Orioles was more appropriate than the Vibranaires – presumably because the Ravens had achieved some success and so names with an ornithological bias were clearly the route to riches. On that point Chessler was correct because throughout the 1950s groups named after species of birds flourished.

Signed by Jerry Blaine, who was in the process of changing his label's name from Natural to Jubilee, the Orioles' debut, 'It's Too Soon to Know' (1948), was strikingly amateurish in its production, but that couldn't disguise its innate earthiness and latent gospel influence. Released initially by Natural, it was re-released when Jubilee got going. For the next eight years, the Orioles established their credentials with a string of hits that struck a fine balance between R&B and pop: 'It's Too Soon to Know' and 'To Be With You' (1948); 'Please Give My Heart a Break', 'Tell Me So', and 'I Challenge Your Kiss' (1949); 'At Night' and 'I Need You So' (1950); 'I'm Just a Fool in Love', 'Baby Please Don't Go', and 'How Blind Can You Be?' (1951); 'Trust in Me', 'Proud of You', and 'See See Rider' (1952); 'Till Then', 'Teardrops on My Pillow', 'Crying in the Chapel', and 'Write and Tell Me Why' (1953); 'Maybe You'll Be There' (1954); and 'I Love You Mostly' (1955).

In the process they created a template for later doo-wop groups such as the Platters and Dion and the Belmonts, but they also started to cross over into the pop charts. With 'Crying in the Chapel', they reached number one on the R&B charts and number 11 on the national charts and, reputedly, sold over a million copies. What this signified was that R&B records *per se* were beginning to sell in greater quantity, although they still constituted a meagre five per cent of total record sales. In 1955 the Orioles disbanded, illustrating once again that the early R&B groups could not overcome the insurmountable barrier that separated R&B from rock 'n' roll in the minds of the record-buying public at least. Til reassembled a new version of the Orioles and signed with the Chicago-based Vee Jay label, but titles such as 'For All We Know' and 'Sugar Girl' were no match for the hip-swivelling gyrations of Elvis and the frenetic piano-pounding of Little Richard.

While the Orioles were of the gospel tradition and literally street-corner singing, they were rooted in the smoother, less testifying blend of spiritual harmony. Similarly, in recording standards or even country songs – the original version of 'Crying in the Chapel' was performed by its writer, country singer Darrell Glenn, and Rex Allen, the star of more than thirty westerns – the Orioles gave no inkling of belonging to the 'rock 'n' roll' era. On the West Coast, however, things were beginning to change, most notably through the Robins.

THE ROBINS/THE COASTERS

Although the Robins were not the most influential of all the vocal groups, through the songwriting and production partnership of Jerry Leiber and Mike Stoller and their spin-off counterpart, the Coasters, they facilitated the possibility that R&B could comment on and reflect, in a humorous way, the concerns of the working man. It does have to be said that as far as the Robins themselves were concerned, being at the cutting edge of social change was of less consideration than turning a fast buck. And it was the lure of the fast buck that scuppered their chances of long-term success.

Formed in 1949 by Johnny Otis in Los Angeles, the A Sharp Trio were appearing at Otis's Barrel House Club at one of the club's many talent shows. At this juncture Otis was starting to cut sides for Herman Lubinsky's Savoy label with A&R man Ralph Bass, featuring the 13-year-old Little Esther. Otis, having heard the A Sharp Trio, added Bobby Nunn to the line-up on the strength of his super-deep bass voice and the group became the Robins. Their first side, 'If It's So Baby' (1949), was a modest hit, prompting Otis and Bass to use the Robins on the Little Esther session. The first – and only surviving – product of this partnership was 'Double Crossin' Blues'. While 'Double Crossin' Blues' had been around for a number of years, Bass and Otis rewrote the song to tell the story of a bear (Bobby Nunn) and a female bear (Little Esther). As Bass was to observe to Arnold Shaw, 'it was just another boy-meets-girl song', but with the protagonists performing 'in character' it gave the Robins, through Nunn's performance, an edge over their rivals on the East Coast such as the Orioles and the Four Tunes. When Lubinsky first heard the recording, he didn't pay any attention to it and it was only through the enthusiasm of a black DJ, B. Cooke, in Newark, New Jersey, that it was released in the first place. When it was issued, it rocketed to number two on the R&B charts and was nominated one of the Best R&B records of 1950.

For Little Esther it broke her career wide open, but the Robins made the mistake of engaging a lawyer to tell Otis that they were the stars of the record and were going to tour on the strength of it. To add insult to injury, they offered Otis the opportunity to work for them as their musical director for 20 dollars a night. Despite their parting of the ways with Otis, they continued working with Bass, cutting titles such as 'Mistrusting Blues' and 'Our Romance Is Gone' (1949) and 'I'm Living O.K.' (1950) for Savoy. In 1950 Bass stopped working for Savoy and moved to New York to work for the King label and the Robins entered an unsettling period, moving between a variety of labels such as Score ('Around About Midnight', 1950), Hollywood ('Race of a Man' and 'School Girl Blues', 1950), and Aladdin ('Don't Like the Way You're Doin'', 1950).

Their luck changed in 1951 when they were signed up by the Biharis, the owners of Modern, to record Leiber and Stoller's 'The Good Book Says'. The Robins were introduced to Leiber and Stoller by the ubiquitous Johnny Otis and 'The Good Book Says' can be viewed as the template for the Robins' output with Leiber and Stoller. Blatantly tongue-in-cheek, it combined a satiric homily with the earthy robustness that was to become Leiber and Stoller's trademark. However this didn't give the group any security because they shuffled on to RCA for a number of worthy – if less than awe-inspiring – outings, the most distinguished of which was another Leiber and Stoller composition, 'Ten Days in Jail' (1953). Once again Leiber and Stoller provided them with another slice of life, with each member of the group taking on a different role within the song.

The following year, in a bid for some creative control, Leiber and Stoller established their own label, Spark, with Lester Sill. One of the first acts they signed was the Robins. Cutting titles such as 'Riot in Cell Block Number 9' (1954) and 'Framed' and 'Smokey Joe's Café' (1955), the Robins were pioneering novelty vignettes of low life that belonged firmly in the traditions of the blues while retaining the images and reference points of contemporary society. Although the group were having considerable success, both commercially and artistically, it was not to last in that particular incarnation because, at a convention in Chicago, Atlantic boss Ahmet Ertegun was so taken by Leiber and Stoller's work that he bought the Spark label, flying the production wizards out to New York. Unhappy with this arrangement, the Robins split up but Nunn and Carl Gardner remained with Leiber and Stoller and recruited Leon Hughes and Billy Guy to become the Coasters – in homage to their coastal origins in Los Angeles.

Because Leiber, Stoller, and Ertegun felt that the Coasters might get lost in the swollen ranks of the Atlantic roster, a new label – Atco – was created for them. Ostensibly a more 'pop'-oriented label, Atco would also become home to Bobby Darin, an Italian-American crooner. Given full artistic control over the output of their protégés, Leiber and Stoller continued where they had left off with 'Down in Mexico' (1956), which reprised the earlier 'Smokey Joe's Café'. This was followed by 'One Kiss Led to Another' coupled with 'Brazil' (1956), and then 'Searchin'' and 'Young Blood'. With the last two, the Coasters scored their first national Top Ten hits, and in so doing illustrated Leiber and Stoller's capacity to fasten on a workaday image from popular culture and reduce it to the equivalent of a cartoon strip. Based around the piano-playing of songwriter Mike Stoller, in 'Searchin'' Carl Gardner alludes to some of detective fiction's most overworked sleuths such as Sherlock Holmes, Boston Blackie, and the Northwest Mounties as he relates the details of his quest and the lengths to which he will go to achieve his objective. As for 'Young Blood', this was the eyeball-popping lust that Cab Calloway connived at and Louis Jordan hinted at, and was such a stereotype that its very usage was ironic.

With these offerings there can have been little doubt that the Coasters had superseded the Robins. However the re-formed line-up of the Robins struggled on fitfully, recording a series of sides for Whippet, which included 'Cherry Lips' (1956) and 'Since I First Met You' and 'A Fool in Love' (1957), and Knight ('Pretty Little Dolly', 1958). These sides only endorsed the consensus that without Leiber and Stoller, the Robins had little to contribute. They were just another vocal group, trading on former glories.

Meanwhile the Coasters had effectively made the transition to the rock 'n' roll era without diluting their credentials as an R&B group; that is to say they had retained their black audience as well as developing a following among whites. Despite their appeal, a question-mark still hung over the line-up, as Hughes departed and was replaced by Young Jessie, and after the group moved to New York, Jessie and Nunn were replaced in due course by former Cadet Cornell Gunter and Will 'Dub' Jones.

The move to the East Coast brought some benefits, most notably through the availability of hard-core R&B session musicians such as horn man King Curtis. Although the group were signed to one of the most prestigious of the independent labels, both Ertegun and Jerry Wexler gave Leiber and Stoller the space they needed to create their aural masterpieces. But if the weight of Atlantic was needed, it was there to be used and that was soon demonstrated with 'Yakety Yak' (1958). Featuring King Curtis's 'Yakety' sax and lyrics that were emblematic of the teenage isolation implicit in rock 'n' roll, 'Yakety Yak' is comparable to Eddie Cochrane's 'Summertime Blues' (1957) and Chuck Berry's 'School Days' (1958): as the quartet barks 'Take out the papers and the trash' – the youthful rejoinder of 'Yakety Yak' is answered by Bobby Nunn's gruff 'Don't talk back'! The spirit of this playlet – as Leiber and Stoller described their songs – was done with an element of humour, but it was also a take on a situation that has been enacted since time immemorial among all families irrespective of race or creed. That 'Yakety Yak' continues to work as a slice of social drama reiterates the continuing importance of Leiber and Stoller as R&B became synonymous with rock 'n' roll.

While now the Coasters were ensconced in the mainstream of rock 'n' roll, Leiber and Stoller made no concessions with the themes of their playlets as 'The Shadow Knows', 'Charlie Brown', and 'Three Cool Cats' (1958) and 'Along Came Jones', 'That Is Rock 'n' Roll', 'Poison Ivy,' and 'I'm a Hog For You' (1959) all attested. Continuing to draw from images and characters of popular culture, the Coasters – with Leiber and Stoller – moved into the 1960s as one of the few surviving exponents of close harmony to survive R&B and flourish in the rock 'n' roll era.

Very gradually, however, their popularity was being eroded, as titles such as 'Shopping For Clothes' and 'Run Red Run' (1960) and 'Wait a Minute' and 'Little Egypt' (1961) successively failed to achieve the same degree of success as their predecessors had done. This was not due to a depreciation in quality. Far from it – both 'Shopping For Clothes', with its poke at consumerism, and 'Little Egypt', with its jibe at the cheap and phoney world of the burlesque cabaret clubs, were as trenchant as anything they had previously recorded. The jokes were just wearing thin. Most white teenagers now preferred the pre-packaged fodder served up on TV shows such as *American Bandstand* and through most of the radio networks. The real reason for the Coasters' decline in popularity was that they sounded 'too black'. The essential conservatism of radio programmers had at last got its way and rock 'n' roll had been effectively neutered with Elvis in the army and a steady diet of Pat Boone, Connie Francis, and Frankie Avalon records filling the airwaves. The Coasters were perceived now as being ever so slightly risqué. But there was another factor. Leiber and Stoller's success with the Coasters had made them the most fêted record producers in New York, and with the Brill Building on Broadway turning out any number of up-and-coming writers such as Doc Pomus and Mort Shuman, Barry Mann and Cynthia Weil, Burt Bacharach and Hal David, and Gerry Goffin and Carole King it was inevitable that Leiber and Stoller should be encouraged to work with other groups such as the Drifters. As a consequence Leiber and Stoller had less time to devote to the Coasters.

By the end of 1961 the line-up had undergone another change with Gunter being replaced by former Cadillac Earl 'Speedo' Carroll. Throughout the 1960s the Coasters continued touring, but their major chart successes were behind them. In 1967 they signed with Columbia subsidiary Date where they were reunited with Leiber and Stoller for 'D. W. Washburn' and 'Down Home Girl' but to little effect. In 1971 they revived 'Love Potion Number 9', which had originally been a hit for the Robins' contemporaries the Clovers. Since the late 1960s the Coasters have been fixtures on the oldies' circuit and a line-up comprising Cornell Gunter, 'Dub' Jones, Billy Guy, and Carl Gardner performed at the Atlantic 40th Anniversary Birthday Concert in 1988. On a rather more macabre note, two members of the group have met violent deaths, with Nathaniel Wilson's dismembered corpse being discovered in 1980 and Gunter being found shot dead in his car in Las Vegas in 1990.

Inducted into the Rock & Roll Hall of Fame, the Coasters have begun to accrue plaudits for their contribution independently of Leiber and Stoller. Even so, taking the Robins and the Coasters as a progression, there are few groups who can trace their lineage back to the infancy of R&B in the 1940s.

1950–51

THE CLOVERS

Although the Coasters' Atlantic recordings did not start until 1956, the Atlantic label was one of the first of the major independent labels to acknowledge the potential of R&B vocal groups. This interest was confirmed in 1951 when the label signed the Cardinals, the Five Keys, and the Clovers. By now Atlantic was regarded as one of the more astute independent labels, properly financed and more significantly not in the least 'fly-by-night' like many of their competitors.

The nucleus of the Clovers comprised high school friends John 'Buddy' Bailey and Harold Winley, augmented by guitarist Bill Harris and vocalists Matthew McQuater and Harold Lucas. Discovered at the Rose Club in Washington, DC, by their future manager, Lou Krefetz, in 1949, the Clovers made their debut with 'Yes Sir, That's My Baby' (1950) for the Rainbow label. Clearly influenced by the Orioles, the group wanted to adopt a smoother style more reminscent of the Ink Spots until they met Ahmet Ertegun. Ertegun was convinced that they should try to sound 'more black' and so he passed on to them a song he had written called 'Don't You Know I Love You'. It stormed to the top of the R&B charts in 1951 and was followed swiftly by another Ertegun composition, 'Fool, Fool, Fool'. Although both these songs were deeply romantic and demonstrated the group's affinity with the Ink Spots, they were solid dance records aimed firmly at a young black audience; both Billy Ward, with his Dominoes, and Hank Ballard, with the Midnighters, listened and learned from them.

For the next five years, the Clovers established a record for commercial consistency that was unmatched by any of their immediate contemporaries with titles such as 'One Mint Julep', 'Ting-A-Ling', and 'I Played the Fool' (1952), 'Good Lovin'', and 'The Feeling Is So Good' (1953), 'Lovey Dovey',

'Your Cash Ain't Nothing But Trash', and 'Blue Velvet' (1954), 'Devil or Angel' (1955), and 'Love, Love, Love' (1956). Despite the group's desire to muscle in on the Ink Spots' territory, the combination of producer and material made it hard for them to be anything other an R&B group, with Bailey's vocals on 'One Mint Julep' sounding, as Charlie Gillett says, 'like a fugitive from a jump blues combo'. Furthermore with songs such as 'Ting-A-Ling' and 'Good Lovin'', the Clovers showed that they were more than capable of handling material with sexual connotations. And they got away with it. A year or so later Hank Ballard would not be so lucky when his 'Work With Me Annie' stirred up a veritable hornet's nest among the morally upstanding.

On a slightly more mundane level, the Clovers underwent the usual personnel changes, with Charles White – a former member of the Dominoes – replacing lead vocalist 'Buddy' Bailey who was drafted into the army in 1952. Then Billy Mitchell replaced White in late 1953 and remained with the group despite Bailey's return in 1954; thereafter Bailey and Mitchell alternated lead vocal duties. These changes did not affect the quality of group's output; the deterioration – when it kicked in – was due to the fact that the group still hankered after a white audience. They still wanted to be the Ink Spots. And so their version of Tony Bennett's 1951 hit, 'Blue Velvet', pointed the direction in which they were headed. However, Buddy Bailey's superbly languorous lead vocals offer a view of romance that is neither kitsch nor steamy. There was nothing inherently wrong with that, but it anticipated a dilution of their sound that would be increasingly apparent through their releases of 1956 and 1957. The only exception to this was 'Down in the Alley' (1957) – an unashamed celebration of the joys of extracurricular activities in urban locales – but it had been recorded some two years earlier. After 'Wishing For Your Love' (1958), the Clovers parted company with Atlantic and scored their final hit with Leiber and Stoller's 'Love Potion Number 9' for United Artists in 1959.

While they never managed to achieve the degree of crossover success that the Ink Spots had, it was a measure of the Clovers' influence that white artists such as Kay Starr, Bobby Vee, and Bobby Vinton covered their material and, naturally, got the bigger hits. The Clovers split up in 1961 and, like many of their counterparts, regrouped and toured on the oldies circuit for many years.

THE DOMINOES

About the same time as the Clovers started their tenure with Atlantic, a vocal coach from Los Angeles was starting to put together a group from his studio at the Carnegie Hall. The coach's name was Billy

Ward and his group was called the Dominoes. Ward had worked in a variety of professions from that of boxer and sports journalist with *Transradio Express* to advertising executive. However, at the root of it all was his fondness for music, which he had studied as a child, winning a talent competition for his composition, 'Dejection'. After service in the Second World War, Ward eventually ended up in New York, where he started to teach singing. As the trend for vocal groups took hold, Ward assembled a gospel group from his finest students. The group comprised lead vocalist Clyde McPhatter, second tenor Charles White, baritone Joe Lamont, and bass Bill Brown, with Ward providing piano accompaniment, but the gospel was quickly phased out to be replaced by a more salacious hybrid.

A harsh disciplinarian, Ward ruled his roost with a rod of iron, imposing fines for any infractions, but he imparted a keen sense of purpose to the group by getting them signed by Ralph Bass to the King subsidiary, Federal. From 1950 until 1953, the Dominoes, with McPhatter's aching vocals, put together a series of hits that included 'Do Something For Me' (1950), 'Sixty Minute Man', 'I Am With You', and 'Heart to Heart', (1951), 'When the Swallows Come Back to Capistrano', 'Have Mercy Baby', and 'The Bells' (1952), and 'These Foolish Things Remind Me of You' and 'Until the Real Thing Comes Along' (1953). Although some of these sides were unabashedly romantic, McPhatter sang as if his very life depended on the outcome: for 'The Bells' he was required to describe a funeral in the ghetto, and McPhatter's distress is palpable as he weeps and shrieks his histrionic way through this curious opus.

Ward was such a disciplinarian that the line-up of the group was generally in a state of turmoil: White moved to the Clovers in 1952 and was replaced by James Van Loan, while Bill Brown's replacement was David McNeill. The biggest upset was caused when McPhatter was eventually fired in May 1953 after some minor dispute. One of his biggest fans, Ahmet Ertegun, came to the rescue. As Jerry Wexler later related to Arnold Shaw, 'The Dominoes were playing Birdland, which was an odd place for them to be playing. Ahmet noticed McPhatter's absence from the group. He exited Birdland like a shot and headed directly uptown'. By the end of the evening McPhatter had a new group, the Drifters, lined up and was signed to Atlantic. For Ward another raw recruit needed to be drilled and that turned out to be Jackie Wilson.

Between 1953 and 1956 Wilson and the Dominoes recorded a combination of blues and standards. Where other vocal groups had cut standards, they had tended to imitate the Ink Spots or the Mills Brothers; Ward was such a fine arranger that he evolved his own style. As a consequence, titles such as 'I'm Going to the Outskirts of Town' and 'If I Never Get to Heaven' (1954) and 'How Long Blues' and a re-worked 'Have Mercy Baby' (1955) fit seamlessly into the grand design of the Dominoes' output. In 1954, they started to record for the parent label, King, cutting sides such as 'Rags to Riches' (1954) and 'Three Coins in the Fountain', 'Little Things Mean a Lot', and 'Over the Rainbow' (1955). The following year they moved to Jubilee for 'Sweethearts on Parade', before moving to Decca, and scoring their first pop hit with 'St Therese of the Roses' (1956). When Wilson left the group for a solo career, Ward himself was the only remaining member from the original line-up but they became increasingly successful as they signed to Liberty, scoring massive hits with 'Stardust' and 'Deep Purple'.

Although the Dominoes' biggest hits were romantic and pop-oriented, the successive vocal talents of McPhatter and Wilson sowed the seeds for the development of 'soul' in the 1960s, while remaining utterly faithful to their origins in the blues and gospel. Despite Ward's reputation for being something of a martinet, he belonged in the tradition of the 1940s band leaders that had defined the formative years of R&B.

THE HOLLYWOOD FLAMES

As the East Coast independents continued to be the baptismal font for most of the key vocal groups, the West Coast threw up two effective interpreters of the tradition in the Hollywood Flames and the Five Keys, as well as Jesse Belvin, who – had he lived longer – would have become undoubtedly one of the most radical stylists of the epoch.

The Hollywood Flames were the brainchild of Robert Byrd, who moved to Los Angeles from his birthplace in Fort Worth, Texas, in 1947. Soon after his arrival he worked with Johnny Otis before forming the Hollywood Four Flames. By 1950 he had secured his first recording contract with the Hollywood label. After cutting a few sides such as 'I'll Always Be a Fool' and 'Baby Please', the group moved to the Unique label for a trio of singles, 'Dividend Blues', 'Tabarin', and 'Please Say I'm Wrong' (1951). The following year, the group recorded 'The Wheel of Fortune' (1952) as the Flames for the Specialty label, but in the same year they made their first appearance as the Hollywood Flames. For the next two or three years, the Hollywood Flames cut titles such as 'One Night With a Fool' and 'Peggy' (1952) for Lucky, 'Let's Talk It Over' (1953) for Swingtime, and 'Fare Thee Well' (1954) for the Money label.

Meanwhile Byrd had adopted an alter ego, Bobby Day. Under this guise, according to Dave Marsh, 'he made some of the wildest doo-wop records' to come out of Los Angeles. From 1955 he cut songs like the original version of 'Little Bitty Pretty One' (1957) for the Class label, under the name of Bobby Day and the Satellites – presumably the Satellites were the Hollywood Flames. In 1958 he released 'Rockin' Robin' coupled with 'Over and Over', which became a monster hit; subsequently both titles were covered, by Michael Jackson and the Dave Clark Five respectively. In January 1959 he perpetuated the ornithological metaphor with 'The Bluebird, the Buzzard, and the Oriole'. However, in 1957 the Hollywood Flames resurfaced and scored their biggest hit with 'Buzz-Buzz-Buzz' for the Ebb label, which was owned by Mrs Lee Rupe, the wife of Art Rupe, the owner of Specialty Records. While 'Buzz-Buzz-Buzz' was the group's biggest hit, it was inferior to the group's earlier output and later material such as 'Give Me Back My Heart' (1957), 'Strollin' on the Beach' and 'Chains of Love' (1958), and 'In the Dark' failed to ignite the public imagination.

In the early 1960s Day re-emerged with former lead vocalist of the Hollywood Flames, Earl Lee Nelson, to form the duo Bob and Earl. Day soon left to resume his solo career and was replaced by Bobby Garrett, also known as Bobby Relf. In 1963 their moment of glory arrived when they cut the dance-floor classic 'Harlem Shuffle' for the Class label. Arranged by Barry White – later to become the Sultan of Slink – it was a minor hit in the US and a club hit in the UK, but they had to wait until 1969 when it was reissued in the UK and became a Top Ten hit; in the 1980s the Rolling Stones covered it and took it up both the US and UK charts. On its first release in the US, the airwaves were littered with songs for unlikely dances, but the 'Harlem Shuffle' has survived through its intrinsic merit as a song rather than a cash-in on some passing fad that was probably out of date before the record had been pressed.

Until Day succumbed to cancer in July 1990, the name 'Bob and Earl' continued to thrive through thick and thin, with either partner choosing a surrogate to reactivate the duo and heading off for lengthy tours in the American Midwest or Europe.

THE FIVE KEYS

The Five Keys – like the Hollywood Flames – enjoyed a brief dalliance with fame. However, the reasons could not have been more different. While Day and the Hollywood Flames made a virtue of signing with any two-bit record label they could find, the Five Keys signed with the prestigious Aladdin label. When Aladdin went to the wall, the Five Keys were signed to the Capitol label, which had been sold to EMI by co-founder and songwriter Johnny Mercer in 1954. Surprisingly, though, for a major label, Capitol were ill-equipped to deal with a pure-bred R&B group like the Five Keys. Capitol had no concept of catering for black audiences – the closest they had ever got was with Nat 'King' Cole and that was after he had crossed over to a predominantly white, middle-class market. So what should have been a safe and lucrative career change turned into the effective demise of the group. They did leave, though, a catalogue that has stood the test of time.

Formed as the Sentimental Four in the late 1940s in Newport News, Virginia, the first line-up comprised two sets of brothers: Rudy and Bernie West and Ripley and Raphael Ingram. They had the same background and style as those of the Orioles – right down to the final detail of singing on street corners – but in 1949 they changed their name to the Five Keys when Raphael Ingram was replaced by Maryland Pierce and Dickie Smith. Embarking on the usual round of talent shows, they were eventually booked to appear at the Apollo. Spotted by Aladdin's Eddie Mesner, they made their debut on 'With a Broken Heart' (1951). The follow-up, 'Glory of Love', coupled with 'Hucklebuck With Jimmy', was a smash hit, embodying literally the two sides of the vocal group style: the soft and gentle ballad and the blacker, up-tempo dance idiom. Later releases for Aladdin attempted to repeat this success by covering standards such as 'Yes, Sir, That's My Baby' and 'Red Sails in the Sunset' (1952), 'These Foolish Things' (1953), and R&B ballads such as Ruth Brown's 'Teardrops From My Eyes' (1953); the last-named side was coupled with another R&B cracker, 'I'm So High'.

On signing with Capitol, they scored with 'Ling Ting Tong' (1955), which, had it not been for Otis Williams and the Charms' cover, would have sold considerably better. Even so it still reached the R&B Top Ten and provided a strong platform for their release of Chuck Willis's 'Close Your Eyes' (1955). With assistance from the Ravens' arranger, Howard Biggs, the Five Keys' version of 'Close Your Eyes' gave wider currency to the term 'doo-wop' through its usage of a background vocal refrain that sounded like 'A doo-wop, A doo-lang' or variations on similar lines. Of course, none of this was a million miles from what the Mills Brothers had been doing with their imitations of instruments. Whereas the Mills Brothers applied it as a 'novelty' or even a gimmick, the Five Keys and the Clovers, among others, used it as a specific trait that was supposed to create a distinctiveness that would separate them stylistically from other vocal groups. The bad news was that, as with any good idea, it became quickly diluted when it was picked up and used by (notably white) imitators. With all the resources that Capitol could muster at their disposal, the Five Keys were able to use much grander arrangements on titles such as 'The Verdict' (1955), 'Out of Sight, Out of Mind' (1956), and the Ink Spots' 'The Gypsy' (1957), which – although this had little to do with the propulsive urgency of R&B in its purest form – anticipated the extent to which vocal groups were able to cross over to pop audiences.

By 1958 the Five Keys had shot their bolt and Capitol – unable to see much mileage in a form that lacked novelty – turned their attention to the wider picture, focusing on the proliferation of white imitators. Signed to King, the group went through a series of personnel changes before disbanding in 1961.

JESSE BELVIN

As we have seen, the vocal group era was the heyday of the manager, producer, or studio boss who guided and shaped the destiny of their protégés. There were very few groups that could boast a leader who wrote or arranged, or was even a member of the group. There were exceptions, though: Billy Ward with the Dominoes, Bobby Day with the Hollywood Flames, Lowman Pauling with the Five Royales, and, to a lesser extent, Sonny Til with the Orioles, but these were the years of the talent scout or promoter or producer, who could stitch together a quick fortune through a mixture of opportunism and good luck. However one man – Jesse Belvin – looked as if he had the potential to turn this all around. For Belvin was not only a fine songwriter and producer, but also possessed a magnificent voice.

Born on 15 December 1933, in Texarkana, Arkansas, Jesse Lorenzo Belvin moved to south Los Angeles when he was five. In 1949 he joined Big Jay McNeely's Band as vocalist in the Three Dots and a Dash until he was drafted into the army. After his discharge he made his debut as a soloist with 'All That Wine Is Gone' (1951) on Imperial. Later the same year he hit his stride with a sequence of sides for the Hollywood label, which included 'Dream Girl' and 'Love Comes Tumbling Down' before he moved on to the Specialty label. Here he scored a Top Ten R&B hit with Marvin Phillips, as Jesse and Marvin, on a reworked version of 'Dream Girl' (1953). Much tighter than the previous version for Hollywood, it highlighted Belvin's instinctive feel for a song, primarily emphasizing his skill as an arranger. Indeed 'Confusin' Blues' (1952), and 'Gone' and 'Where's My Girl?' (1955) combined elements of the vocal group in their arrangements while providing the silky tones of Belvin with the platform of a soloist.

In 1954 he wrote 'Earth Angel' for the Penguins. Selling around four million copies, 'Earth Angel' would have earned Belvin a fortune, but no one could deny him the credit for what was one of the first records from an independent label to burst into *Billboard*'s national charts. Although the Penguins were one-hit wonders, 'Earth Angel' demonstrated links with pop's recent past in the Ink Spots, with lead vocalist Cleveland Duncan singing in a wobbly tenor similar to Belvin's, while remaining firmly locked in the tradition of the R&B ballad that was beginning to achieve currency and popularity as a constituent of the rock 'n' roll era. Despite the success of 'Earth Angel', Belvin was unable to capitalize and was still cutting one-off singles for different labels – 'So Fine' (Federal, 1955), 'I'm Only a Fool' (Money, 1955), and 'Beware' (Cash, 1956) – until 1956 when he signed with Modern. With the Biharis at Modern, Belvin cut a series of sides that, along with the Specialty releases, illustrate his ability to handle a ballad with the mellowness of Nat 'King' Cole and the smooth, sensual urgency of Sam Cooke. These included 'Girl of My Dreams' and 'Goodnight My Love' (1956) and 'Senorita', 'Don't Close the Door', and 'You Send Me' (1957).

Although many have targeted Belvin as a Cooke imitator on the strength of his covers of Cooke's 'You Send Me' and 'Sentimental Reasons', these covers fit seamlessly into the Belvin canon. What they lack in originality is somewhat compensated for in the phrasing and timing, but they did create a pattern that appealed to RCA. When RCA signed Belvin in 1958, the consensus would have it that he was signed to offer competition to Nat 'King' Cole. With hindsight it would seem more logical that what RCA were looking for was an alternative to Sam Cooke, who was signed at that juncture to the independent Keen label. Cooke, an astute businessman, was fully aware of his earning potential, while Belvin had been quietly influential artistically but lacked Cooke's financial acumen and kudos. However, the net result was that Belvin's RCA sides failed to live up to the label's commercial expectations with only 'Funny' and 'Guess Who' approximating the quality of his earlier material with Specialty and Modern. Furthermore, fate stepped in and dealt him a final blow when he was killed in a road accident on 6 February 1960. His driver, Charles Shackleford, fell asleep at the wheel of his Cadillac and ploughed into an oncoming car on Route 67, just outside Fairhope, Arkansas. Belvin and Shackleford were killed immediately, and Belvin's wife, Jo Ann, died two days later. As a further footnote, two weeks before Belvin's death, Cooke was lured to RCA for the then princely sum of $100,000.

THE CARDINALS, THE LARKS, AND THE SWALLOWS

As major labels such as RCA, Decca, and Mercury were gradually establishing competition with the independents by developing A&R departments that could monitor emergent trends, minor vocal groups such as the Swallows, the Cardinals, and the Larks depended upon the limited largesse of their record label for survival. So the Cardinals, who were signed by Atlantic in 1951 and were promoted alongside the Clovers, only had a very limited number of opportunities to achieve the degree of success enjoyed by label-mates the Clovers. Making their debut in 1951 with 'Shouldn't I Know?', the Cardinals maintained an excellent standard with 'Pretty Baby Blues' and 'Wheel of Fortune' (1951), 'She Rocks' (1952), 'Please Baby' and 'The Door Is Still Open' (1954), and 'Come Back My Love' and 'I Won't Make You Cry Anymore' (1955), among others, but they never managed to break into the big time and, after one final push by Atlantic in 1955, the Cardinals and Atlantic ceased to be an item.

A similar fate befell both the Harlem quintet the Larks and the Swallows from Baltimore, but they lacked the benefits of being signed to a label such as Atlantic which – even at this early stage of development – was showing signs of possessing the corporate mentality necessary to building a company that would endure. For the Larks on the Apollo label and the Swallows at King were always going to be the ones to suffer if success wasn't immediate. The Larks managed to issue just six singles for the label before they were shown the door; these included 'Eyesight to the Blind', 'Little Side Car', and 'My Reverie' (1951) and 'In My Lonely Room' (1952). While their style was sweet in flavour and unabashedly romantic, their failure had more to do with market forces than any lack of merit or talent. The same can be said for the Swallows, but there was a slight difference: the Apollo label had had most of its success with gospel or overtly gospel-influenced groups such as the Royal Sons or, as they were later known, the Five Royales.

The Swallows, however, should have had an advantage by being signed to the King label, one of the most experienced purveyors of R&B in the country. It did not work out that way, though. Remaining at King for around three to four years, they only issued about a dozen singles. With lead vocalist Junior Tenby they clearly demonstrated their effectiveness on bluesy ballads such as 'Beside You' and 'Tell Me Why' (1952), while up-tempo items such as the excellent 'It Ain't the Meat' (1951) and 'It Feels So Good' (1954) were noteworthy for their libidinous gusto. Perhaps that was the problem, but in early 1954 the Swallows were told to migrate sooner rather than later.

1952–54

LOWMAN PAULING AND THE FIVE ROYALES

While on the subject of the King label, one of its greatest success stories was that of Lowman Pauling and the Five Royales. Group leader Pauling might not have viewed it in quite the same light because he, like Jesse Belvin and Hank Ballard, showed a knack for getting royally swindled. The similarities did not just end there either because each was a considerable creative force. In Lowman Pauling's case, he could write, arrange, and play the guitar. Unfortunately he made the cardinal error of spending most of his career at Sid Nathan's King label. Consequently Pauling and his group were the last people to reap any significant rewards. In Pauling's case, though, he was just ahead of his time, or as Dave Marsh states in *The Heart of Rock & Soul*, 'From 1945 through 1965, the Royales helped shape vocal group styles and guitar patterns and created landmark songs and recordings'.

The gospel group the Royal Sons was formed by Lowman Pauling in 1942 in Winston-Salem, North Carolina. In around 1948 they cut their first sides, 'Bedside of a Neighbour' and 'Come Over Here', for the Apollo label. By 1952 they had changed their name to the Royals, cutting 'Too Much of a Little Bit'. Later the same year they changed their musical direction and became the Five Royales. Although they ceased working gospel material, they retained the form's vocal characteristics, imposing a style on R&B that paid little or no heed to the predominating influence of the Ink Spots or the Mills Brothers. With Johnny Tanner's rough, intense lead vocals and the hard-edged, single-string guitar solos of Pauling, the group's second R&B side, 'Baby Don't Do It', elbowed its way to the top of the R&B charts in 1953. For much of the remainder of that year, the group was never far away from the top of the R&B charts with such titles as 'Too Much Lovin'', 'Help Me Somebody', 'Crazy, Crazy, Crazy', 'Laundromat Blues', 'I Do', and 'Let Me Come Back Home'.

In 1954 they left Apollo and signed with the King label. In partnership with Ralph Bass, the A&R supremo at King, Pauling wrote some of the most potent R&B compositions of the 1950s. At first, however, they failed to repeat the success of the later Apollo sides. Indeed, Bass was to reflect later that he thought he had lost his touch. The fact was that titles such as 'Behave Yourself' and 'School Girl' (1954), 'You Didn't Learn It at Home', 'I Need Your Lovin' Baby', and 'Women About to Make You Crazy' (1955), 'When You Walk Right Through the Door' and 'Come and Save Me' (1956), and 'Just As I Am' and 'Tears of Joy' (1957) made no concessions to white audiences. Although Leiber and Stoller were riding high with the Robins and then the Coasters, the essential 'blackness' of their records was presented in a very tongue-in-cheek manner, which made them appealing to white audiences. Pauling and Bass offered no such palliatives: the Five Royales performed a form of undiluted R&B that was constantly referring back to its gospel antecedents.

In the latter half of 1957, the Five Royales cut one of their masterpieces – 'Think'. Dave Marsh hits the nail on the head when he asserts that '\'Think' belongs to no particular period; it wouldn't be surprising to wake up tomorrow and find that it . . . had again seized the airwaves'. Tanner's lead vocal anticipates the carefully modulated melisma prevalent in the Southern soul artists of the 1960s, such as James Carr and O. V. Wright, while Pauling's mellow guitar work has the liquid fluidity of Steve Cropper's or Roy Buchanan's playing. Although The Five Royales' version reached *Billboard*'s Top Hundred, Aretha Franklin's version became an early clarion call for feminism in 1968, while James Brown cut three separate versions, all of which made the charts.

It seemed that the group might be on the way to repeating the consistency of their Apollo releases, but 'Messin' Up' failed to make any inroads.

Later in 1958 they cut arguably their best-known song, 'Dedicated to the One I Love'. Complete with a female backing group, 'Dedicated to the One I Love' is built around the incisive guitar work of Pauling and is distinct from the Shirelles' later cover version in that Tanner sings it as a paean to physical separation: producer Luther Dixon turned the Shirelles' version into an ironic reflection on the vagaries of teenage dalliances, replacing the gritty guitar work with smooth vocal harmonies. While this was one of the Five Royales' finest moments, the Shirelles could be described as one of the first all-girl groups to breast the tide of male vocal groups, giving rise to a nationwide search by record companies to discover more all-girl groups. As if to demonstrate the durability of Pauling's material, 'Dedicated to the One I Love' was revived by the Mamas and the Papas in 1967 and then again in 1995 in the UK in a soft reggae-influenced style.

In 1959 the Five Royales cut another Pauling original, 'Tell the Truth'. Once again posterity has decreed that the song should live on through the cover versions by Ray Charles and Eric Clapton. Admittedly, by 1959 any distinctions that might previously have been made between R&B and rock 'n' roll had been lost, and R&B was being consigned to the dustbin of obscurity as less frenzied versions of rock 'n' roll gathered momentum through white imitators. Despite another fine vocal performance from Tanner, it's Pauling's guitar work that calls the tune and shows the way for a host of other young white guitarists such as Robbie Robertson of the Band.

Throughout the 1960s the Five Royales continued to record, but the advent of groups such as the Beatles and the Rolling Stones and Berry Gordy's Motown groups such as the Four Tops, the Supremes, and the Temptations made them sound out of kilter with contemporary taste. Even James Brown – always one of their most fervent admirers – couldn't arrest their decline into obscurity when he stepped in to produce some sides in 1965. After leaving King they recorded briefly for ABC, Smash, and Vee Jay before breaking up in the early 1970s. Pauling died in 1975.

HANK BALLARD AND THE MIDNIGHTERS

Another prolific writer and vocalist who never really achieved his just desserts was Hank Ballard. Ballard, like Pauling, seemed to possess an uncanny knack for getting ripped off as he was the writer of 'The Twist' – the song that launched a thousand dances all with silly names. Ballard was born in Detroit on 18 November 1936 and his musical career started in 1953, while he was working at the Ford car factory. After being heard by Sonny Woods of the Royals he was recruited immediately to become their lead singer. Although the Royals had been popular since their debut in 1951 with Johnny Otis's 'Every Beat of My Heart', which became a hit ten years later for Gladys Knight and the Pips, they lacked that special 'something' that would set them apart from all the other vocal groups. When Woods heard Ballard's high-pitched tenor that was a cross between Clyde McPhatter and Jimmy Rushing, he thought that here might be that 'something' extra that the group needed. He wasn't wrong.

The first session with Ballard taking lead vocal produced 'Get It', which became the group's first R&B Top Ten hit. The reason for this sudden change of fortune was the less stylized timbre of Ballard's voice in contrast with the smoother, sweeter tones of his predecessor, Henry Booth, but also 'Get It' was overtly salacious and suggestive. While the whole point of R&B from its infancy had been to delineate the real side of life – both the good times and the bad – charges from pressure groups that R&B was little more than smut continued to proliferate: the fact that it achieved popularity merely vindicated hardliners. After 'I Feel That-A-Way' and 'Someone Like You', Ballard came up with 'Sock It to Me, Mary' in 1954, but producer Ralph Bass thought it just too risqué. According to Nick Tosches in *The Unsung Heroes of Rock 'n' Roll*, while Bass mused over the song's controversial connotations, Ballard went to work altering the lyrics. This task was made easier when the engineer's wife, Annie – who was pregnant – stopped by the studios and, in a trice, Ballard had turned 'Sock It to Me, Mary' into 'Work With Me, Annie'.

Banned by radio stations the length and breadth of the country, the group was vilified by any pressure group with an axe to grind. Coincidentally, as the group was signed to Federal, a subsidiary of King, and Syd Nathan had just signed the Five Royales from the Apollo label, Nathan deemed it opportune to change the name of the Royals to that of the Midnighters. It certainly had the desired effect of throwing a smokescreen over the whole affair, giving Ballard and the Midnighters an excellent opportunity to reprise the life and times of 'Annie' with 'Annie Had a Baby' and 'Annie's Aunt Fanny' in later months. It also created a vogue for 'answer' records with Etta James's 'Roll With Me Henry' being accorded the same dubious pleasure as Ballard's original offering by having its title changed to 'The Wallflower'. Featuring Richard Berry of the Flairs, 'The Wallflower' provided Etta with the big breakthrough that had hitherto eluded her and, in 1955, she added to the saga with 'Hey Henry'. Ballard responded with 'Henry's Got Flat Feet', but in chart terms all were eclipsed by the bathetic cover version by Georgia Gibbs. Now retitled 'Dance With Me Henry' – just to ensure that any sexual innuendo was completely removed – Gibbs's pale version galvanized many minor groups and vocalists to hop on to the bandwagon with their own thoughts on the life and times of Annie and Henry: the Nu-Tones came up with 'Annie Kicked the Bucket'; the Cadets and the Champions offered 'Annie Met Henry'; three members (Joey D'Ambrosia, Dick Richards and Marshall Lytle) of Bill

Haley's Comets metamorphosed into the Jodimars for 'Annie Eat Your Heart Out'; the El-Dorados suggested 'Annie's Answer'; and one Danny Taylor made the flagrant confession 'I'm the Father of Annie's Baby', which – given the circumstances in which Ballard wrote the song in the first place – must have given the studio engineer one hell of a shock.

As 'Work With Me Annie' climbed the R&B charts through the summer months, Ballard and the Midnighters released 'Sexy Ways', which climbed to number three. By the end of September 1954 the group could boast three records in the R&B Top Ten with 'Annie Had a Baby' holding pole position. However, by the end of 1954, Ballard and the Midnighters had tired of 'Annie', but they continued to put out records with such potentially controversial titles as 'Stingy Little Thing', 'Ring A-Ling A-Ling', and 'Switchie Witchie Titchie'. As these failed to generate much attention, the group reverted to rather more prosaic titles such as 'It's Love, Baby', 'Don't Change Your Pretty Ways', 'Open Up the Back Door', and 'Baby Please'.

In 1959 with the group now officially known as Hank Ballard and the Midnighters, they were moved from the Federal label to the parent, King, for the passionate 'Teardrops on Your Letter', which stylistically anticipated the melismatic inflections that would characterize soul during the 1960s. As it wended its way up the R&B charts, no one paid much attention to the B-side, 'The Twist'. That is until one Ernest Evans – aka. Chubby Checker – got hold of it and turned it into a massive international hit: much of the success of 'The Twist' can be laid at the door of *American Bandstand* presenter Dick Clark, who managed to whip the nation into such a frenzy over the new dance that it is hard to credit that he didn't have a significant vested interest. One person who didn't have much of a vested interest but should have had was Ballard. For, once again, he was in the ignominious position of having written a song but achieving little credit – or indeed cash – for his endeavours. After Checker hit paydirt with it, Ballard's own version was reissued, which climbed to number 28 in 1960.

As a consequence of 'The Twist', Ballard had a string of pop hits such as 'Kansas City', 'Finger Poppin' Time', and 'Let's Go, Let's Go, Let's Go' (1960), as well as a number of 'dance craze' songs such as 'The Hoochie Coochie Coo'. And it was at this point that Ballard seemed to make a vital error of judgement in supposing that eventually he would come up with another dance song that would reap the rewards that had eluded him with 'The Twist'. By 1962 the record-buying public's appetite for new dance crazes had been sated and Ballard's 'Do You Know How To Twist?' only just crept into the Top Hundred. Ironically, if he had persevered in the style of 'Teardrops on Your Letter', he would have found himself aligned with such progenitors of soul as Sam Cooke, Ray Charles, James Brown, and Jackie Wilson, among others.

After parting company with the Midnighters, Ballard started a solo career. At first he recorded for King and then worked regularly with the James Brown Revue while continuing to record as a solo artist. He failed, however, to arrest his continuing decline into obscurity. From 1972 onwards he toured the US constantly, reworking his old hits with creditable fervour. In 1986 he toured the UK and recorded a live album *Hank Ballard Live at the Palais* (1987); it was so well received by the critics that he was dubbed the 'legendary' Hank Ballard. Despite a return with *Naked in the Rain* in 1993, he remains underrated; there are few survivors from R&B's Golden Age and Ballard could so easily have become one of the giants of soul into the bargain.

HARVEY FUQUA AND THE MOONGLOWS

Although Hank Ballard – through his association with James Brown, as well as his own vocal characteristics – was eminently suited to the gradual transmutation of R&B into soul, his inability to transcend the two idioms was indicative of a far deeper malaise that permeated the thinking of many musicians, producers, and label owners in the 1950s. The various markets were so rigidly structured that crossover from one to another was rare. Similarly, for a record to cross over into the 'pop' market from R&B was viewed with suspicion, as in all probability it had been diluted to pander to the tastes of white audiences. There were exceptions: Ray Charles made his mark in jazz and R&B – laying the foundations of soul in the process – but achieved national renown for his country records in the early 1960s, and James Brown's showmanship incorporated elements of gospel and R&B in a revue that referred obliquely to the heyday of the big-band era while providing a subtext for rap and hip-hop in the late 1970s. Of course producers and writers such as Leiber and Stoller were active through both the R&B and rock 'n' roll eras, but even their acuity in predicting the ebb and flow of popular taste was stymied when the Beatles heralded the beat groups' era. In short, it has always been very hard to sustain a career in the record industry in differing milieus.

One of the few to have achieved this is Harvey Fuqua. It could be argued that he had a good start through his Uncle Charlie, who was a member of the Ink Spots. However, forming a group, the Moonglows, that would be lionized by Alan Freed, discovering a young drummer called Marvin Gaye, and marrying Gwen Gordy just as her brother Berry was establishing Motown Records indicates a degree of luck that cannot just be ascribed to good fortune or being in the right place at the right time.

Born on 27 July 1928 in Louisville, Kentucky, Harvey Fuqua started to perform with Bobby Lester, Prentiss Barnes, and Alex Graves as the Crazy Sounds in 1948. By 1952 they had been spotted by a local singer, Al 'Fats'

Thomas, who introduced them to Alan Freed. After auditioning for Freed with a rough version of 'I Just Can't Tell a Lie', the group's name was changed to that of the Moonglows – because, according to Lester, 'we glow in the dark' – and made their debut with 'I Just Can't Tell a Lie', backed with 'I've Been a Dog (Since I've Been Your Man)'. Recorded at radio station WJW, where Freed deejayed, the single was released on Freed's own Champagne label; Freed also helped himself to a songwriting credit as 'Al Lance'. With heavy promotion from Freed, 'I Just Can't Tell a Lie' became a modest local hit, but the group failed to earn enough money despite appearances at Freed's local dances. Soon the group had become a part-time operation with Barnes and Graves returning to the group they had been members of before joining the Crazy Sounds, while Fuqua and Lester still worked at a Cleveland coalyard.

In October 1953, after appearing at one of Freed's biggest R&B shows, the Moonglows were spotted by Art Sheridan and Ewart Abner from the Chicago-based Chance label, who signed them immediately. Cutting five singles for Chance – 'Baby Please' and 'Just a Lonely Christmas' (1953) and 'Secret Love', 'I Was Wrong', and '219 Train' (1954) – hits were still thin on the ground and in 1954 the Chance label closed down. Although Freed was claiming co-writer credits with Fuqua for the group's material, he was still their manager and after the Chance debacle he took them along to the Chess label. At Chess they finally scored with their first release, 'Sincerely' (1954). Employing a vocal delivery style that was described as 'blow harmony', which is similar to crooning, with its closed-mouth, mooing sound, 'Sincerely' sold over two hundred and fifty thousand copies and their style was imitated by other vocal groups such as the Dells and the Spinners. Unfortunately the McGuire Sisters stole their thunder by covering 'Sincerely' in a bland note-for-note carbon copy and sold over a million records in the process.

Having broken their duck, Fuqua diversified by recording 'Shoo-Doo-Be-Doo' (1955), a parody of the Chords' 'Sh-Boom', and 'Hug and a Kiss' (1955) as the Moonlighters for the Chess subsidiary Checker. Meanwhile the Moonglows racked up a succession of hits including 'Most of All' (1955), 'See Saw' (1956), and Percy Mayfield's 'Please Send Me Someone to Love' (1957). By 1958 Fuqua had got a firm hold on the group and had changed their name to Harvey and the Moonglows and scored with 'The Ten Commandments of Love' (1958). That year Fuqua disbanded the group and re-formed with the Marquees, whom he had discovered and which featured a young vocalist called Marvin Gaye. Although Gaye was lead vocalist on just the one side 'Mama Loocie' (1959), Fuqua decided to disband the group and concentrate on production work.

In this new capacity Fuqua rediscovered Etta James and signed her to the Chess subsidiary Argo, before leaving Chess and moving to Detroit. Still with Marvin Gaye under his wing, Fuqua assisted Gwen Gordy with her record label, Anna, before forming his own record labels Harvey and Tri-Phi in 1961. With this trio of labels Fuqua recorded artists such as Marvin Gaye, Johnny (Bristol) and Jacky (Beavers), the Spinners, and Junior Walker. When the labels hit financial problems, they had an eager purchaser in Berry Gordy, who retained Fuqua's services as a writer, producer, and talent scout; in other words, he kept his old job. Producing some of Marvin Gaye's finest duets with Tammi Terrell, as well as nurturing the talents of Junior Walker, the Spinners, and Johnny Bristol, Fuqua was one of Motown's conduits with the traditions of the 'doo-wop' vocal groups as well as the raucous showmanship of rock 'n' roll.

In 1971 Fuqua set up a production company, which was licensed to RCA, where he produced groups such as New Birth and the Nite-Liters. Towards the end of the decade, he produced a number of disco hits by Sylvester for the Fantasy label, including 'You Make Me Feel (Mighty Real)', but in 1982 he teamed up with Marvin Gaye once again, producing *Midnight Love*. Since the development of the oldies' circuit, Fuqua has regularly led a re-formed version of the Moonglows, which resulted in the group rerecording their old material for *The Return of the Moonglows* for Fuqua's own production company in 1972.

THE FLAMINGOS

Despite being less successful than that of the Moonglows, the career of the Flamingos followed a similar course. Formed in 1952 in Chicago, where they all attended the same chuch on the South Side, they specialized in the smooth, romantic ballad that was *de rigueur* in the early 1950s. Despite regular changes in personnel, their style was then adapted to embrace the rock 'n' roll era, before they adjusted their sound once again in the 1960s to embrace the silky and more composed vocal harmonizing of the soul era. And all this was achieved through the simple expedient of changing their record label and producer at regular intervals, so the type of song they sang never changed substantially but the arrangements were contemporaneous. The extent to which this was a carefully contrived plot remains to be seen; it is more likely that synchronicity and luck played the bigger part.

Signed by Art Sheridan and Ewart Abner to the Chance label in 1953, the group at first comprised John Carter, Zeke and Jacob Carey, Paul Wilson, and Sollie McElroy. Initially stealing a march on label-mates the Moonglows, who had joined the label under the influential auspices of Alan Freed, the Flamingos strung together a series of fine R&B titles such as 'That's My Desire' and 'Golden Teardrops', but McElroy left the group and was replaced by Nate Nelson. When Sheridan wound up Chance, the group moved on to the Parrot label where they cut 'I Really Don't Want to Know' and Gene and Eunice's 'Kokomo'.

In 1955 they moved to the Chess subsidary Checker. This was a shrewd move because many had dismissed the group for not sounding sufficiently black. At Checker – once again alongside old sparring partners the Moonglows – they embraced rock 'n' roll and doo-wop with all the fervour of a prodigal son. With titles such as Stan Lewis and Fats Washington's 'I'll Be Home' and 'The Vow', the Flamingos brought a romantic solemnity to the proceedings while all hell broke loose around them. Getting a whiff of stardom, they abandoned Checker for Decca. Historically major labels had never shown much aptitude for vocal groups other than the Ink Spots and Decca were no more suited to the Flamingos than the Flamingos were to Decca. The move did provide them with another stroke of serendipity because when they were dropped, producer George Goldner welcomed them with open arms to his new label, End. Here they cut one of the most widely known and best-loved records of the doo-wop era: Harry Warren and Al Duchin's 'I Only Have Eyes For You' (1959). Although the lavish arrangement belied the notional perception of R&B in its purest form, it anticipated the romantic soft-soul of the late 1960s and 1970s that was to come out of Philadelphia, proving that George Goldner had a firmer grasp on the mercurial trends of popular music than many of his more illustrious counterparts. Other revivals of popular standards such as George Gershwin's 'Love Walked In' (1959) and 'Nobody Loves Me Like You' (1960) followed as the group moved back to Chess for 'Lover Come Back to Me'.

While the line-up of the group continued to chop and change with John Carter leaving to join the Dells only to be replaced by Tommy Hunt, they managed to adapt to the soul market as the 1960s dawned. However, it does have to be said that much of their output during that decade sounded very old-fashioned or just so blatantly opportunistic that titles such as 'The Boogaloo Party' (1969), a classic on the UK's Northern Soul circuit, and 'Buffalo Soldier' (1970), a tribute to the black troopers of the US cavalry, failed to do their track record much justice. That didn't stop them from continuing to ply their trade on the oldies circuit until the early 1980s, when they finally hung up their tuxes.

THE DRIFTERS

For sheer endurance and tenacity, the most successful of all these early vocal groups would have to be the Drifters. Formed in 1953 by Clyde McPhatter, who had been fired as lead singer of the Dominoes by

Billy Ward, the group was the brainchild of McPhatter and Ahmet Ertegun. And here there is a vital difference in the reasons for their formation: they were driven by McPhatter's desire to sing in a very specific type of way, while Ertegun had been searching for a vocalist who could combine the intensity of gospel with the mellowness of contemporary R&B. Few groups could boast of such a unity of purpose in their conception. While it took McPhatter and Ertegun a little bit of time to settle upon the correct line-up, they eventually enlisted Bill Pinckney – formerly of the Jerusalem Stars – and brothers Andrew and Gerhart Thrasher from the family gospel group the Thrasher Wanderers, who had cut 'Moses Smote the Water' for Moe Asch back in 1947.

Their first record 'Money Honey' was written by Atlantic A&R man Jesse Stone, with Ertegun producing. Topping the R&B charts for 11 weeks, it was the first of a series of hits that included 'Such a Night', 'Lucille', 'Bip Bam', and 'Whatcha Gonna Do?'. With McPhatter's silky tenor alternating from the warmly romantic to the flagrantly lascivious, titles such as 'Such a Night' managed to get them banned from many playlists, but with them the Drifters forged the links between R&B and rock 'n' roll. In 1954, as Bill Pinckney sang the memorable bass lead of 'White Christmas', the group demonstrated that they were not exclusively a vehicle for McPhatter. This was probably just as well because in late 1954 McPhatter was drafted into the army and replaced by David Baughan.

As the Drifters suffered from this blow, McPhatter prospered in the army, becoming a forces entertainer. After his discharge in 1955 he started a solo career, notching up a string of hits that were superlative examples of soul in its earliest form; they included 'Seven Days' and 'Treasure of Love' (1956), 'Without Love (There Is Nothing)' and 'Just to Hold My Hand' (1957), 'A Lover's Question' (1958), and 'Since You've Been Gone' (1959). There was, however, the lingering suspicion that as a forces entertainer McPhatter had got the idea that mainstream popularity – in the way of Nat 'King' Cole and later Brook Benton – was more to his liking; it was a mistake that many before him had made and ultimately it spelt the end of his career.

In 1959 he parted company with Atlantic, and signed with MGM and then Mercury, but hits such as 'Ta Ta' (1960) and 'Lover Please' and 'Little Bitty Pretty One' (1962) indicated that, as far as many fans were concerned, McPhatter was to close to his sell-by date. In 1962, in an effort to revive his career, he was taken to Nashville by Shelby Singleton, but his style of singing had been superseded by the more histrionic styles of Otis Redding and Wilson Pickett. Eventually, he died of heart, kidney, and liver disease on 13 June 1972.

However, his legacy – in the words of Bill Millar in his book, *The Drifters* – was that:

'McPhatter took hold of the Ink Spots' simple major chord harmonies, drenched them in call-and-response patterns and sang as if he were back in church. In doing so, he created a revolutionary musical style from which – thankfully – popular music will never recover.'

If McPhatter ultimately fared less well through starting a solo career, the Drifters suffered a gradual loss of identity as Baughan was replaced by Johnny Moore. Although hits such as 'Adorable' (1955) and 'It Was a Tear' (1956) kept them in the public eye, discord raged through the ranks until Andrew Thrasher was fired by their manager, George Treadwell, and replaced by Charlie Hughes. After another spate of changes in personnel, including the departure of Johnny Moore, who was drafted, the whole group was eventually fired by Treadwell. At the behest of Atlantic, claiming ownership of the name, Treadwell hired another group, the Crowns, and rechristened them the Drifters.

In 1959, with Ben E. King taking the lead vocal, they started to record under the guidance of Jerry Leiber and Mike Stoller. Over the next two years they recorded a string of hits that are emblematic of the transitionary years of rock 'n' roll into soul. Although the lyrical preoccupations of songs such as 'There Goes My Baby' (1959) and 'Dance With Me', 'This Magic Moment', 'Save the Last Dance For Me', and 'I Count the Tears' (1960) approximated the pure pop sensibility of New York's Brill Building, King's lead baritone imbued these songs with a gospel-tinged gravitas. This enabled the Drifters to re-establish themselves anew with a sound that was different enough to encourage new admirers while retaining the goodwill of long-time fans.

While the reasons for King's departure have never been made entirely clear, there is a pretty good chance it had something to do with money or billing. For King, who was born Benjamin Earl Nelson on 23 September 1938 in Henderson, North Carolina, had been a career vocalist ever since his childhood when he sang in church choirs before moving to Harlem. Joining the Crowns in 1957, after singing with the Four Bs and auditioning unsuccessfully for the Moonglows, King and the Crowns in their new incarnation as the Drifters enjoyed unparalleled success as the 1950s gave way to the new decade. With the glib soundbites of 'ring out the old, bring in the new' still echoing in the ears, King complained to Treadwell of his lot and offered his resignation, which was promptly accepted.

After signing with Atlantic subsidiary Atco, King started a solo career with Jerry Leiber and Mike Stoller producing. Fortuitously he didn't have to wait long, as 'Spanish Harlem' (1961) – written by Phil Spector and Jerry Leiber – had soon placed him in the vanguard of vocalists able to build a solo career. From the same sessions that produced 'Spanish Harlem', King cut the gospel-slanted 'Stand By Me'. Now established as one of the early classics of the embryonic soul era, 'Stand By Me' has proved its durability by its use in a commercial some twenty-five years after its release, thereby becoming a massive hit all over again. While these were followed by the standard 'Amor' (1961), King and Ertegun's 'Don't Play That Song (You Lied)' (1962), and Jerry Leiber and Mike Stoller's 'I (Who Have Nothing)' (1963), King was overshadowed by the emergence of Berry Gordy's Tamla Motown group of labels and the orthodox Southern soul emanating from Stax in Memphis. He continued to record for Atco until the mid-1970s, including a stint with the much vaunted Soul Clan with Solomon Burke, Joe Tex, and Don Covay. In 1975 he was re-signed to Atlantic for the irre-sistibly funky 'Supernatural Thing' and in 1977 he teamed up with the Average White Band for *Benny and Us*. Although his voice remains impec-cable and he is idolized by a few, nobody seems to have come up with a better way to maximize his potential than by reprising his magic moments.

With King gone, Rudy Lewis from the gospel group the Clara Ward Singers, slipped into pole position in the Drifters. The pre-eminence of Brill Building writers provided the group with a succession of hits that neatly counterpointed the melismatic, gospel-influenced soul of the South. While Lewis's gospel background infused these hits with an earthiness, the romantic sentiments of titles such as Goffin and King's 'Some Kind of Wonderful', Burt Bacharach's 'Please Stay', and Doc Pomus and Mort Shuman's 'Sweets For My Sweet' (1961), Goffin and King's 'When My Little Girl Is Smiling' and 'Up on the Roof' (1962), and Barry Mann and Cynthia Weill's 'On Broadway' and 'I'll Take You Home' (1963) held considerable allure for white audiences, as well as black, and also for the growing Hispanic population.

Part of this success can be ascribed to the influence of the Cuban rhythms that were being felt on Broadway nightly through appearances by Machito, Tito Puente, Eddie Palmieri, Mongo Santamaria, Mario Bauza, and Ray Barretto. The bright, good-natured airiness of these performers crossed racial barriers without difficulty, rendering them acceptable to those from all racial denominations. And so Leiber and Stoller, with their magpie-like instincts right to the fore — and with Jerry Wexler offering encouragement — managed to inculcate titles such as 'This Magic Moment', 'Save the Last Dance For Me', 'Up on the Roof', 'On Broadway', and 'Under the Boardwalk' with something akin to a shimmering heat.

Once again, however, personnel problems threw a spanner in the works. Leiber and Stoller had parted company with the group to devote more time to their Red Bird label and Bert Berns had been drafted in as replacement producer. After two attempts with 'Vaya Con Dios', which had been a massive hit for guitarist Les Paul and Mary Ford, and Berns's 'One Way Love' — later a substantial hit for UK R&B band Cliff Bennett and the

Rebel Rousers – the group were scheduled to cut Artie Resnick and Kenny Young's 'Under the Boardwalk'. On the eve of the session, Wexler was notified that Rudy Lewis had been found dead with a needle in his arm. As Wexler recalls in his autobiography, ' I tried to cancel (the session), but the union said no go; it was a costly string date and players had already been hired. . . . There wasn't even time to change keys for Johnny Moore, now slated to sing lead'.

Moore's ascent to lead vocalist completed the metamorphosis that had started when McPhatter left the group. Embracing a pop sensibility in the same way as the Ink Spots, the Drifters – despite a few lurches back towards their R&B roots under the guidance of Berns with 'I've Got Sand in My Shoes' and 'Saturday Night at the Movies' (1964) – enjoyed a spell of popularity in the UK in the 1970s. Drawing from the notional cream of UK writers such as Roger Cook, Roger Greenaway, Tony Macauley, Les Reed, Barry Mason, and Geoff Stephens, titles such as 'Like Brother and Sister' (1973), 'Kissin' in the Back Row of the Movies' and 'Down on the Beach Tonight' (1974), 'Love Games', 'There Goes My First Love', and 'Can I Take You Home Little Girl?' (1975), and 'Hello Happiness', 'Every Night's a Saturday Night With You', and 'You're More Than a Number in My Little Red Book' (1976) deliberately attempted to evoke the group's golden era. They didn't, but that doesn't stop the body of work they recorded from their inception until the early 1960s from being some of the most consistent and stylistically innovative to come out of the R&B era.

THE PLATTERS

The manner in which the Drifters seemed to dominate the R&B charts from 1953 onwards does need to be set in some sort of context of prevailing trends. While groups had been springing up with regularity ever since the end of the Second World War, this had been as a consequence of the success of the Ink Spots and the Mills Brothers. As the 1950s progressed, new vocal groups sought their inspiration from the success of, for instance, the Clovers or the Orioles. There was, in other words, a completely new set of role models: by 1953 the average age of the Mills Brothers was around forty; with the Ink Spots it was fractionally older. For that reason, new groups were hardly likely to model themselves on groups that were almost old enough to be their fathers: there was a growing perception of R&B being the preserve of the young and this was endorsed by rock 'n' roll. Certainly both the Ink Spots and the Mills Brothers continued to exert an influence, but it was through osmosis and within a wider, less specific term of reference. Consequently the new role models were seen to be the Clovers or the Orioles, although this a drastic oversimplification as it precludes the influence of individual solo artists such as T-Bone Walker or Big Joe Turner – or Johnny Otis, for that matter – but these individuals were influenced by what they chose to play rather than through what was or wasn't in vogue.

As with all generalizations, there were exceptions to this rule and the Platters were a prime example. Discovered at one of the talent shows that Ralph Bass and DJ Hunter Hancock hosted at LA's Club Alabam, vocalist Tony Williams was prevailed upon by Bass not to follow a solo career but to join a group. At about the same time there was a group kicking around Los Angeles called the Platters, which booking agent and songwriter Buck Ram had been planning to sign. However, the lead singer managed to get himself arrested, giving Bass the chance to recommend his protégé, Tony Williams, as replacement lead vocalist. After being signed by Bass to the King subsidiary Federal and cutting 'Give Thanks' and 'Hey Now' (1953), Bass suggested to Buck Ram that he manage and coach them.

Ram was one of the knowledgeable and opportunist entrepreneurs who made up the Los Angeles and New York music scenes. Born in 1908, Ram had worked as a lawyer before turning to songwriting and arrangement with Duke Ellington and Count Basie in the late 1930s. After writing tunes such as 'Afterglow' (1936) for Leo Reisman and 'At Your Beck and Call' (1938) for Jimmy Dorsey, Ram suffered a nervous breakdown and retired from the music industry. Returning to the industry in Los Angeles in the early 1950s was probably not a great idea for one of a nervous disposition, but musically Ram certainly had the credentials to fashion a group that would appeal to white audiences because Williams's pure tenor, with accompanying vocalists David Lynch, Herb Reed, and Alex Hodge, was the direct antithesis of the earthy R&B of the Five Royales or the Dominoes. And without putting too fine a point on it, they seemed to have more in common with the Ink Spots than with the Clovers or indeed any of their immediate contemporaries.

With Ram taking care of the arrangements and determining the type of material they would record, the Platters began to establish themselves as a doo-wop group with an overt pop sensibility. While Ralph Bass continued producing the group, Ram, who also managed the Penguins, chose much of the material. Despite recording ballads such as 'Roses of Picardy' and 'Tell the World' (1954), chart success was still elusive for the Platters, but with the up-tempo material such as 'My Name Ain't Annie' and 'Maggie Doesn't Work Here Anymore' Williams proved himself a finer R&B vocalist than many gave him credit for.

In 1955 they cut 'Only You', which had been co-written by Ram. Although it failed to do much commercially, it was the fulcrum of their later success. The way Ralph Bass tells the story, he wanted to use the group for some studio sessions, but Ram wanted to charge Bass $100 for

Louis Jordan –
described by one
critic as 'jazz with
a broad grin'
(Courtesy of Columbia
Records)

Leader of his own
orchestra, Ray Charles
has always surrounded
himself with the very
best jazz and blues
musicians

Early line-up of
The Ink Spots; a
line-up was still
touring in the 1980s
(Courtesy of MCA Archives)

Early line-up of
The Flamingoes before
they hit the big time
with 'I Only Have
Eyes For You'
(Courtesy of MCA Archives)

Harvey Fuqua with an early line-up of The Moonglows practising their 'blow' harmonies
(Courtesy of MCA Archives)

For years Charles Brown seldom recorded; now he is verging on the prolific
(Courtesy of Rounder Records)

Saxophonist King
Curtis's career was
brought to an abrupt
end when he was
mugged in 1971
(Courtesy of Charly Records)

The skull pictured
here was often to be
seen perched on top of
Screamin' Jay's piano
(Courtesy of Demon Records)

Such was the popularity of Ike & Tina Turner in the 1960s that they even supported the Rolling Stones
(Michael Ochs Archive)

Whenever B.B. King travels, his trusty axe Lucille gets a first class seat as well
(Courtesy of Ace Records)

After years with the Chess label, Muddy Waters
later recorded for Johnny Winter's Blue Sky label
(Courtesy of Columbia Records)

A fresh-faced Johnny 'Guitar'
Watson before he became the
Gangster Of Love
(Courtesy of Ace Records)

their services. King boss Syd Nathan wasn't having any of that as he had groups under contract who would do the same job for him so he signed the release, which effectively terminated the Platters' contract with the label. Coincidentally Ram was on the point of doing a deal for the Penguins with Mercury; the deal was amended so that Mercury had to sign the Platters if they wanted the Penguins. Mercury didn't argue.

Later the same year the Platters re-recorded 'Only You' and it became a massive pop hit. The main reason why it fared so much better the second time around was probably that the Mercury version was marketed better. The fact is that the arrangement was better suited to the qualities of Williams's voice. As Dave Marsh asserts, 'the Federal version makes the song's pledge of eternal love into a burden'. The Mercury version is looser and less constricting, proving that Williams was better equipped to follow Bill Kenny of the Ink Spots than, say, Clyde McPhatter. Having finally struck the template, Ram and the Platters stuck rigidly to the same formula with scant regard for the vagaries of fashion; so accurately did they tap into the Ink Spots' market that when most R&B groups had passed their sell-by date, the Platters were performing on the cabaret circuit in Las Vegas, drawing the same crowd that had stood in line for the Ink Spots.

Between 1955 and 1961 the Platters established themselves as the premier doo-wop group of their generation with hits that included 'The Great Pretender' (1955); '(You've Got) The Magic Touch', 'My Prayer', and 'You'll Never Never Know' (1956); 'On My Word of Honour', 'I'm Sorry', and 'My Dream' (1957); 'Twilight Time' and 'Smoke Gets in Your Eyes' (1958); 'Enchanted' (1959); 'Harbour Lights' and 'To Each His Own' (1960); and 'If I Didn't Care' and 'I'll Never Smile Again' (1961).

Throughout their years of glory the line-up remained remarkably stable with Zola Taylor of the Teen Queens being an early addition while Paul Robi replaced Hodge, who had a disagreement with the police and was compelled to leave. Then in 1961 Williams left the group for a solo career and signed with Frank Sinatra's Reprise label, and was replaced by Sonny Turner. The following year, both Taylor and Robi left to pursue solo careers, to be replaced by two former members of the Flamingos: Sandra Dawn and Nate Nelson. With the departure of Williams, the Platters, sound became more commonplace, but the demand on the cabaret circuit was as strong as ever; Mercury attempted to refuse subsequent Platters' records on the grounds that they didn't feature Williams's voice. Ram and the Platters countered and won on the grounds that other members of the group had sung lead without any complaint from the label. Still going strong in the 1990s, the Platters were inducted into the Rock & Roll Hall of Fame in 1990, which is one honour that has eluded the Ink Spots.

THE DELLS

With the Platters and the Drifters both managing to remain intact despite changes in line-up and the fickle finger of fashion, the Dells have endured without offering many concessions along the way. Formed at Thornton Township High School in Harvey, Illinois, as the El-Rays in 1952, the group initially comprised Vern Allison, Chuck Barksdale, Marvin Junior, John Funches, and Lucius and Michael McGill. Inspired by the records of the Clovers, the Flamingos, and the Five Keys, they used to spend their time hanging around the offices of the Chess label on South Michigan Avenue. Finally their persistence paid off and they met Harvey Fuqua of the Moonglows, who showed them how to sing five-part harmony: 'We sang only two-part harmony,' Michael McGill remembered to Arnold Shaw. 'But they [The Moonglows] had us sing with each of them, tenor with tenor, baritone with baritone' and so on. This advice landed them a deal to record a one-off single for the Checker label. Entitled 'Darling, Dear, I Know' (1953), it was an a cappella and showed that at least they had taken Fuqua's advice to heart. While it failed to sell in any sort of quantity and Chess duly dispensed with their services, Vivian Bracken signed them to his Vee Jay label the following year just as they changed name to the Dells.

After two singles, 'Tell the World' and 'Dreams of Contentment' (1955), they struck with the ballad 'Oh What a Night' (1956). Penned by Funches and Junior, it harked back to the gospel style of call-and-response with Funches intoning 'Oh what a night', while chorus responded with 'To hold you . . .'. Dramatically at odds with prevailing styles among R&B vocal groups, it was an early indication of how R&B would adopt specific traits of gospel as it metamorphosed into soul. Unfortunately their style of delivery could best be described as 'too black' for most palates, and this was not restricted to the Dells because other Vee Jay groups such as the Spaniels were bedevilled by similar problems. With hindsight, as Shaw asserts, 'Vee Jay records were more creative than those produced by other R&B "indies"'. This is a sweeping statement, perhaps, but it is partly vindicated by the lack of success accorded the Dells as their career progressed. Later singles such as 'Why Do You Have to Go?' and 'Pain in My Heart' were rich testaments to the influence of gospel and to this day they possess a timeless soulfulness that traverses the notional boundaries between R&B and soul. Having said all this, the Dells had continuity on their side because there were only two changes in line-up, with Lucius McGill departing in 1955 and former Flamingo Johnny Carter moving to replace John Funches, who was injured in a road accident in 1958. Therefore, the Dells were better equipped than most to evolve musically as the group developed their own agenda as a unit unimpeded by new voices joining the line-up.

In 1962 they rejoined Chess, where they remained until 1973 (apart from another brief spell in the mid-1960s with Vee Jay), and were teamed with producer Bobby Miller and arranger Charles Stepney. In 1968 they were assigned to the Chess subsidiary Cadet, where they hit their chart-making peak with 'There Is', 'Stay in My Corner', and 'Always Together' (1968), 'Does Anybody Know I'm Here?', 'I Can Sing a Rainbow', and 'Oh What a Night' (1969), 'The Love We Had (Stays on My Mind)' (1971), and 'Give Your Baby a Standing Ovation' (1973).

In 1976 the Dells moved to Mercury, where they recorded *No Way Back* (1976) before going to ABC, where New Beginnings was produced by arch-maverick and erstwhile funkster George Clinton. More recently they have recorded for 20th Century under the auspices of producers Carl Davis and ex-Chi-Lite Eugene Record. In 1984 they worked with Marvin Yancy and Chuck Jackson, cutting *One Step Closer*. Despite the changes in style and fashion, they have kept their following and managed to remain a going concern by touring constantly. As recently as 1988 they returned with *The Second Time* for the appropriately titled Veteran label and still, after all these years, they have remained true to their gospel and R&B roots.

THE SPANIELS

While the Dells won hands-down in the longevity stakes, Vee Jay and Vivian Bracken showed their mettle by signing two other key vocal groups, the Spaniels and the El-Dorados; indeed, the Spaniels had the distinction of cutting the first record to be released by Vee Jay. Formed by James Hudson at Gary's Roosevelt High in Indiana, as Pookie Hudson and the Hudsonaires, the Spaniels were distinctive initially in that they chose to re-name themselves after a breed of dog, instead of a species of bird. Making their debut with 'Baby It's You' in 1953 for the Chance label, which was subsequently reissued by Vee Jay, the Spaniels' languid, romantic style was the acme of cool as their 1954 monster 'Goodnight, Sweetheart, Goodnight' attests. Later retitled 'Goodnight, Well It's Time to Go' to avoid confusion with a popular 1930s ballad, it was penned by Hudson and Vivian Bracken's brother, Calvin Carter. Although it was covered by the McGuire Sisters and the country duo Johnnie and Jack, it established the Spaniels as a group capable of embracing the embryonic teenage angst of the rock 'n' roll era without any dilution of their R&B credentials. Later titles such as 'Play It Cool' and 'Doo Wah' suggested that they might be able to establish a measure of continuity, but in 1955 three members of the group Ernest Warren, Willis C. Jackson, and Opal Courtney Jr were drafted for National Service. The replacements were unable – or disinclined – to blend as seamlessly with the lead vocals of Hudson and, after a couple more solid R&B hits such as 'Painted Picture' and 'Do You Really?', they opted for populist renditions of standards such as 'Stormy Weather' and 'People Will Say We're in Love'. These did little to differentiate the group from a thousand others. Despite appearances at various rock 'n' roll revival shows in the late 1960s and 1970s, they gradually subsided from sight.

THE EL-DORADOS

Much the same can be said for the El-Dorados. Originally called the Five Stars, the group came together at Chicago's Englewood High School and won a talent contest. Signed by Bracken to Vee Jay, their name was changed to the El-Dorados in 1954. From the off, the El-Dorados were the antithesis of the Spaniels in that they were sparky and effervescent in their demeanour and brought a glimmer of irony to their debut: the ballad 'Baby I Need You'. The follow-up, 'Annie's Answer', with the group's female vocalist taking lead, offered an alternative view to the sequence of events that befell Hank Ballard's 'Annie'. After another ballad, 'One More Chance', they cut their one and only smash, 'At My Front Door' (1955). Written by John Moore and Ewart Abner – one of Vee Jay's many owners – the El-Dorados showed that they could rise up above the general standard of fare from vocal groups. While today the lyrics could not earn any awards for political correctness, with the crazy little mama doll hammering at the front door trying to get back in again, there was a leering lasciviousness that, with hindsight, makes 'At My Front Door' seem heavily ironic. However, their later material, including the jump-styled arrangement of 'I'll Be Forever Loving You', seemed to indicate that the group lacked a clear direction and identity of its own. This was endorsed when in 1957 'hey cut a version of 'Tears on My Pillow', which was covered by Little Anthony and the Imperials, who converted it into a massive hit a year later. For all that, the El-Dorados remain an undervalued outfit.

THE CHARMS

Similarly undervalued were the Charms, who were massive during their early years between 1954 and 1955, when they generated as many hits as some of their more vaunted counterparts such as the Drifters or the Dominoes. However, they did not break up and fade away like so many of their contemporaries. Instead their lead vocalist, Otis Williams, took the courageous decision to change tack and embrace country music, thereby becoming one of the first documented exponents of what was to become known as country-soul.

Formed by Williams in Cincinnati in 1953, the Charms made their debut in 1953 for the small Miami-based Rockin' label with 'Heaven Only Knows'. While this unabashed piece of schmaltz was undistinguished in itself, it showed that Williams possessed a high-quality, coffee-and-cream voice that had potential. Later that year the Rockin' label was acquired by Syd Nathan and with it the Charms' contract. Assigned to King's De-Luxe label, under the supervision of Henry Glover, the Charms rapidly assumed the status of house vocal group, providing backing vocals for the parent label's strong roster of country artists that included Cowboy Copas and Hawkshaw Hawkins. At first the group stuck to the ballad formula with titles such as 'Please Believe in Me' and 'My Baby Dearest Darling' (1954) but with 'Hearts of Stone' (1954), a cover of the Jewels' hit, Williams showed he could handle up-tempo material as well as ballads; 'Hearts of Stone' was subsequently covered by the Fontane Sisters, then guitarist Bill Justis, and more recently by John Fogerty in his guise as the Blue Ridge Rangers. This was followed by 'Two Hearts', which was covered by Pat Boone, and another cover, this time of the Five Keys' hit 'Ling, Ting, Tong' (1955). Despite these covers, the Charms still managed to establish themselves by dint of Williams's vocal prowess and Glover's arrangements with other hits such as 'Crazy, Crazy Love', 'Rollin' Home', and 'Ivory Tower' (1956) and 'United' (1957). However Williams's penchant for country music showed through with a cover of Patsy Cline's 'I Fall to Pieces' (1960), among others.

When the original Charms broke away from Williams in 1955, a replacement group was pulled together and originally called 'The New Group' but by 1956 they had reverted to the Charms. Although this did not materially affect the group's popularity, Williams was showing interest in a solo career in country music, which neither Nathan nor Glover would countenance. After leaving the Charms, Williams branched out and recorded with steel guitarist Pete Drake for the independent labels Power Pak and Stop, before cutting *Otis Williams and the Midnight Cowboys* (1960). Featuring songs such as Jimmie Rodgers' 'Muleskinner Blues' and Tom T. Hall's 'Do It to Someone You Love', Williams was endorsing a strain that had been prevalent in R&B ever since Ivory Joe Hunter had first taken the stand in west Texas during the 1930s.

While vocal groups continued to proliferate, rock 'n' roll was on the march and dominating the market place through the influence of independent producers such as George Goldner. Groups such as the Isley Brothers and the Impressions would look progessively to their gospel roots for inspiration and they in turn would facilitate the transition from rock 'n' roll to soul. In a sense they would reclaim their music from the hands of white enterpreneurs who had adulterated R&B in the first place and dubbed it rock 'n' roll.

chapter four
THE SEPIA SINATRAS

A S HOSTILITIES IN EUROPE AND SOUTH-EAST ASIA were nearing their conclusion in 1945, many American Soldiers could start to ponder the future. Many young men had been inducted into the armed forces or had actively participated in the war effort by entertaining the troops and a new generation had reached maturity during the war years. With the increased opportunities that the rise of the independent labels offered and the proliferation of regional radio stations, young musicians could actually view a career in music as a possibility. Although the major big bands would continue to flourish until the late 1940s, the small combos like the Tympani Five were economically more viable and, similarly, vocalists – also called 'crooners' – were beginning to step out of the shadows of the orchestras and start careers in their own right.

Nat 'King' Cole was the most successful vocalist at that time. Having initially worked as a pianist, leading his own trio, Cole started to sing in 1943 and scored hits with 'That Ain't Right' (1943) and 'Straighten Up and Fly Right' (1944). With Cole's success, many other vocalists – dubiously dubbed 'sepia Sinatras' – started to come through. But while Cole's mellow and dulcet tones were stylistically akin to those of Sinatra, Bing Crosby, and Al Hibbler, the material the 'sepia Sinatras' chose was 'black' in origin. It was into this vacuum that Private Cecil Gant stepped with 'I Wonder' in the early months of 1945.

CECIL GANT

Gant was born in Nashville, Tennessee, on 4 April 1913. No one seems to know very much of Gant's early years, until his appearance in Los Angeles in 1944 at a war-bond rally. Reputedly he went up to the bandstand in the interval and persuaded the leader to allow him to play. Such was his impact that the organizers sought permission from Gant's commanding officer to allow him to appear that evening at a treasury-bond rally. Gant consequently became a regular feature of all such rallies in the Los Angeles area. In the audience of one of these rallies was Cliff MacDonald, who had been employed by the Los Angeles-based Allied Record Pressing Co. and also had a small studio in his garage. He persuaded Gant to record 'I Wonder', which Gant had co-written with Raymond Leveen, and the record was released on the Gilt Edge label, which had been set up by Richard A. Nelson for the sole purpose of issuing and marketing 'I Wonder'. Nelson promoted Gant as 'Private Cecil Gant', dubbing him 'The GI Sing-Sation'. Gilt Edge also released a special pressing of the record with a beaming Gant, attired in the uniform khaki shirt and tie, and thus issued the first picture disc of the embryonic rock 'n' roll era.

Although the sales of 'I Wonder' were astronomical, *Billboard* were scathing in their review in the issue of 6 January 1945, describing the record's sound quality as if it had been recorded on 'a hidden machine in some smoky back room'. That was hardly the point, though, for when 'I Wonder' entered the Harlem Hit Parade in October it caused a storm and went on to climb all the way to the number one slot; so far-reaching was the song's impact that RCA rushed out a cover version by bluesman Roosevelt Sykes on their specialist 'race' label, Bluebird. That, too, moved quickly to the top of the Harlem Hit Parade.

Despite the success of 'I Wonder', it was restricted to the emergent R&B audiences: Gant played to sell-out audiences at the Paradise Theatre in Detroit and Nashville's Club Zanzibar without making any impression on white audiences. Although a big fan of Bing Crosby, Gant's rolling boogie piano style and vocal style were redolent of bluesman Leroy Carr. Although Gant crooned 'I Wonder', the bluesy inflections of his delivery made him sound 'black'; that was the crucial distinction and ultimately gave the record its appeal. After 'I Wonder', Gant kept in the public eye with other ballads such as 'I'm Tired' (1945), and 'Another Day, Another Dollar' and 'I'm a Good Man, But a Poor Man' (1948). To prove he wasn't just a crooner, he then cut a string of manic rockers that were clearly much more in keeping with his personal proclivities: 'Nashville Jumps' and 'Ninth Street Jive' (1946), 'We're Gonna Rock' (1950), and 'Owl Stew' and 'Rock Little Baby' (1951). Never averse to a drink and the seamier side of life, Gant yelled 'Bring me another drink, and I'll be alright' on 'Nashville

Jumps', while 'Owl Stew' was Gant's own special tribute to a brothel in Nashville.

Although the Gilt Edge label broke Gant as the purveyor of the new style, he also recorded for the Nashville-based Bullet label from 1946 until 1949. On his return to Los Angeles the same year he recorded for the Down Beat and Swingtime labels; other later sessions included two singles, 'You'll Be Sorry' and 'Blues For Cecil' for Imperial, which were cut in New Orleans in 1950, and sides for Decca. The Decca sides were recorded in New York and included 'Someday You'll Be Sorry' (1950), 'Rock Little Baby' (1951) and, curiously, a cover of Leadbelly's 'Goodnight Irene'. However, Gant was unable to repeat the remarkable success of 'I Wonder' and slipped gradually – but inexorably – downhill. Despite attempts to come across with other winning formulae, Gant couldn't arrest the decline and succumbed to pneumonia, dying at Nashville's Hubbard Hospital on 4 February 1951; although pneumonia was the medical diagnosis, it seems more likely that Gant was carried away on a tide of alcohol.

CHARLES BROWN

If Gant was a symptom of the changes in the record industry as the Second World War drew to a close, Los Angeles was the catalyst because the city became the melting pot for the popularization of R&B. Not only had hoards of black migrant workers been drawn to the West Coast in search of work at munitions factories and the Oakland shipyards, but musicians too were drawn by the lure of Hollywood's riches and the fast developing television industry. They also just came along for the ride, in the hope of securing work in the expanding entertainment support that was growing up around the Los Angeles industrial centres.

While Gant epitomized a mood among black Americans in the war years that there just might be better times around the corner, the aftermath proved a different proposition. This was reflected in the bluesy, after-hours style of other 'sepia Sinatras' such as Charles Brown, Ivory Joe Hunter, Lowell Fulson, Amos Milburn, Percy Mayfield, and Roy Milton.

In the final days of the War, Charles Brown scored a massive R&B hit with 'Driftin' Blues' (1945). His musical style was in stark contrast to the frenetic jollity of the jump bands, catching the pervasive mood of melancholy and frustration.

Brown was born in a shack in Texas City on 13 September 1922 and his mother, Mattie, died when he was barely six months old. Raised by her parents, Swannie and Conquest Simpson, Charles was taught the piano by his grandmother, who introduced him to the rolling, swashbuckling style of Fats Waller and to the refined improvisations of Art Tatum, as well as to gospel and classical music; Swanie was the director of the Barbous Chapel Baptist Church Choir and Chorale. By 1936 Brown was playing the piano in church and working the Galveston nightclubs by night and studying at Central High by day. After graduating from high school, he worked as a hospital orderly for the summer vacation before enrolling at Prairie View College in Hempstead, Texas; four years later he graduated with a BSc degree in chemistry and mathematics. After teaching at the George Washington Carver High School in Baytown, where he became head of the science department, he joined the civil service as a chemist. Relocated to Pine Bluff Arsenal, Arkansas, he was researching plastics until an asthmatic condition got the better of him and he was forced to give up his research work. Ineligible for war service because of the asthma, he moved to Los Angeles and won a talent contest at Central Avenue's Lincoln Theatre by playing Earl Hines's boogie-woogie version of 'St Louis Blues' and the 'Warsaw Concerto'. In May 1944 he landed a job in the theatre orchestra; the drummer, incidentally, was one John Veliotes – later known as Johnny Otis. This was short-lived as he moved on to play at Ivie's Chicken Shack; Ivie Anderson had been a vocalist in Duke Ellington's band between 1931 and 1942. This too was short-lived as he was invited to replace Garland Finney in the Three Blazers.

Formed in 1942 by Finney, guitarist Johnny Moore, and bassist Eddie Williams, the Blazers modelled themselves on the Nat 'King' Cole Trio, who were regulars at the 331 Club and had just scored with 'Straighten Up and Fly Right'. According to bassist Williams, Charles was raw at first, but he quickly adopted a smooth professionalism that incorporated the 'call and response' of gospel, by singing a line and then answering himself on the piano.

In late 1944 the group convened at Robert Scherman's small Premier studio on Sunset Boulevard. Introduced to Scherman by Moore's brother Oscar Moore, who was guitarist in Nat 'King' Cole's Trio, they recorded 'Tell Me You'll Wait For Me' and 'Melancholy Madeleine'; Frankie Laine, who was reputedly living in his car at the time, took the vocals on 'Melancholy Madeleine'. While 'Tell Me You'll Wait For Me' sunk without trace – it was later covered by Ray Charles – it gave the Three Blazers the momentum to move over to Leon René's Exclusive label. Their Exclusive debut, 'You Taught Me to Love', coupled with 'Johnny's Boogie', also caused barely a ripple when issued in July 1945. However, later that year, when 'You Taught Me to Love' was coupled with 'Blues at Sunrise', featuring Ivory Joe Hunter on vocals, it became the first hit for both Hunter and the Blazers.

After this brief flirtation with celebrity, the group were booked for the Talk of the Town. Meanwhile Brown, who had already shown his mettle as a writer by co-writing 'Tell Me You'll Wait For Me' with Oscar Moore, had penned 'Driftin' Blues'. By the time the group came to record it, on 14 September 1945, 'Driftin' Blues' was the tune on everyone's lips along Central Avenue. When the record came out on the newly formed Philo label in 1946, it sold almost a million copies and won the 'Best R&B Record of the Year' in the *Cashbox* polls. More than that, though, it made the blues cool – the blues would no longer be associated with down-home hicks from the sticks.

Although 'Driftin' Blues' never took the number one spot, it gave the group the creative edge to record with whom they chose. After the Philo session they returned to Exclusive and continued to record for the Bihari Brothers' Modern label, cutting another version of 'Driftin' Blues' entitled 'Travellin' Blues', and telling Eddie Mesner at Philo that they had been signed to Modern all along. After all, royalties were still a thing of the future.

From 1946 until 1948, the Three Blazers notched up a series of hits that included 'Sunny Road' and 'So Long' (1946), 'Changeable Woman Blues' and the seasonal classic 'Merry Christmas Baby' (1947), and 'Groovy Movie Blues', 'Jilted Blues', 'More Than You Know', and 'Lonesome Blues' (1948). Despite this string of hits, the group never again scaled the heights they had attained with 'Driftin' Blues'. However, since the arrival of Oscar Moore in the group in 1947, there had been some tension brewing: before Oscar joined, everything had been split three ways. With Johnny as the putative leader of the group and Oscar claiming special terms through fraternal ties, there was discussion about the salaries of Brown and Williams. This situation was further exacerbated by a combination of poor financial advice and Johnny's gambling habits, which had reached such a peak that he was obtaining advances against unearned income.

The crunch came while the group were playing New York. Johnny had to return to California in a hurry for treatment of kidney disease; both Oscar and Charles followed him back to the West coast shortly after, leaving Williams in New York. While in New York, Williams was intimidated into signing a new contract that gave him a mere 200 dollars a week. Understandably furious, he left the group and formed his own band. Brown, seeing that he could be the next on the list, left the Blazers. With both Williams and Brown out the picture, the Moore brothers should have been able to capitalize, but they had gravely underestimated the contribution that both Williams and Brown had made to the group's success. Endeavouring to capture the tone of Brown's vocals, the Moore brothers hired Billy Valentine as vocalist. Valentine might have sounded like Brown, but he certainly failed to match his songwriting ability. Valentine didn't last long and was replaced by a succession of female vocalists.

It could be argued that the preceding events turned out to be a blessing in disguise for Brown. He signed with Eddie Mesner, who had now set up the Aladdin label, and formed Charles Brown and His Smarties. Although that particular incarnation only endured long enough to release 'Homesick Blues' and 'Let's Have a Ball', it set the stage for the Charles Brown Trio. Featuring Herman 'Tiny' Mitchell on guitar and Wesley Prince on bass, the trio scored with 'Get Yourself Another Fool' in the early months of 1949.

At this point Brown might still have been trying to shrug off a residual association with the Three Blazers, but in the spring of 1949 he achieved that resoundingly with the gloomily atmospheric 'Trouble Blues'. While 'Driftin' Blues' had been the Three Blazers' calling card, 'Trouble Blues' was inescapably Brown's. Remaining at the top of the R&B charts for the duration of the summer, 'Trouble Blues' made Brown one of the top attractions. Other hits such as 'In the Evening When the Sun Goes Down' and 'Homesick Blues' (1949) and 'My Baby's Gone' (1950) all followed swiftly. In 1951 Brown returned to the top of the charts with Jessie Mae Robinson's 'Black Night', knocking Amos Milburn's 'Bad, Bad Whiskey' from its perch.

However, all was far from well in the Brown ménage as his domestic circumstances tended to reflect the uncertainties of his career and in 1952, when 'Hard Times' was riding the charts – it was to be his final hit – his marriage to singer Mabel Scott was in tatters. Although he continued to record for Aladdin until 1957, there was little to be done to save his flagging career. Rock 'n' roll had hammered the last nail in his coffin and he was consigned to the ignominy of package tours. Sessions with Amos Milburn at Ace in New Orleans in 1959, where they cut 'Educated Fool' and 'I Want to Go Home', and then again at King in Cincinnati in 1960, where he recorded 'Please Come Home For Christmas', were just brief encounters and both men ended up in Kentucky working for some shady characters from the the world of gambling.

Throughout the 1960s and 1970s Brown was the forgotten man of R&B. He still recorded, cutting the odd single for King until 1973, including a revised version of 'Merry Christmas Baby' (1968) and finally a cover of Kris Kristofferson's 'For the Good Times'. But essentially he was the all-purpose freelancer who would record for anyone at any time and through necessity was seen accompanying himself at the organ instead of the piano. Meanwhile a few albums materialized during this period, including *Ballads My Way* (1963) for Bob Shad's Mainstream label and one for ABC-Bluesway. During the 1970s he made albums for Johnny Otis's Blues Spectrum label in 1974 and for the Big Town and Jefferson labels.

In 1986, after years of touring – particularly in Europe – he began to attract attention. It was not just because he had been overlooked for years, but also because he had retained the magic of former years while adding a contemporary slant. That year he cut *One More For the Road* for the Blue Side label (Alligator reissued it in 1989). With Brown seated back in state behind the piano, it opened the door for a string of influential albums – *All*

My Life (1990), *Someone to Love* (1991), *Just a Lucky So and So* (1993), and *Cool Christmas Blues* (1994) – for Bullseye, the blues affiliate of Rounder. With a piano style that echoes Earl 'Fatha' Hines and a band that included tenor horn man Clifford Solomon – an alumnus of Lionel Hampton, Johnny Otis, and Ray Charles – Brown, with producer Ron Levy, showed that not only was he able to reprise his golden years but he was also adding to a musical form that many had regarded as long extinct. Much of this was due to Brown's ability to work with contemporary admirers such as Elvis Costello, who contributed 'I Wonder How She Knows' to *Someone to Love*, and Bonnie Raitt, whose slide guitar work on Brown's version of Brenda Holloway's classic 'Every Little Bit Hurts' is as tender as it is ornery.

In 1995 Brown was invited to guest on *Blues & Rhythm Revue Volume One* by the British R&B band King Pleasure and the Biscuit Boys. While we shall return to that particular group in greater detail later, they provided an accurate context for Brown's nostalgic but potent versions of 'Blues For My Baby' and 'Fool's Paradise'. So, after years of scuffling, Brown is at last accruing the recognition he deserves. The same cannot be said of many of his contemporaries, for most went to their graves unfulfilled and under-appreciated, and none more so than Amos Milburn.

AMOS MILBURN

Amos Milburn was one of the great post-war rockers, who paved the way for Little Richard and James Brown. While both Brown and Little Richard were fuelled – at one point or another – by religious zeal, Milburn relied on the devil's fire-water for inspiration.

Born on 1 April 1927, in Houston, Texas, he graduated from high school in 1942. After lying about his age, he enlisted in the navy, seeing active service in the South Seas, where he served as a steward's mate aboard a landing craft. During his spell in the navy he developed his boogie-woogie style of piano-playing in the officers' messes across the world. When he left the navy on 5 May 1945, Milburn returned to Houston and started to play the club circuit because his father had died and Amos was now the family breadwinner. Organizing a 16-piece band, he played the Keynote club, among others, until he was discovered by a dentist's wife named Loa Anne Cullum, who got him signed to the Aladdin label.

From 1946 until 1957, Milburn cut a string of R&B hits for the label. At first progress was slow with only 'Down the Road Apiece' (1946) making any significant impression. However, in 1948 Milburn peaked at the top of the charts with 'Chicken Shack Boogie' (1948) and then again the following year with Jessie Mae Robinson's 'Roomin' House Boogie' (1949). While Charles Brown may have embodied the bluesy, melancholy side of urban life, Milburn was the life and soul of the party, cutting records that oozed good living, boozing, and women. There was no space in the Milburn repertoire for the faint-hearted; he talked hard and dirty about sex in songs such as 'Walking Blues' (1950), while other songs such as 'Let's Rock Awhile' (1951) and 'Rock, Rock, Rock' (1952) explicitly applied the argot that would become synonymous with rock 'n' roll. Although historian Arnold Shaw attests that Milburn was no great drinker, songs such as 'Bad, Bad Whiskey' (1950), 'Thinking and Drinking' (1952), 'Let Me Go Home, Whiskey', 'Good, Good Whiskey', and 'One Scotch, One Bourbon, One Beer' (1953), 'Vicious, Vicious Vodka' (1954), and 'Juice, Juice' (1956) suggest otherwise. Despite Milburn's records embodying the spirit of rock 'n' roll, his final hit was 'One Scotch, One Bourbon, One Beer' in 1953.

From that point onwards his career went downhill dramatically. This problem was compounded after the collapse of Aladdin; Milburn gamely soldiered on recording briefly for Ace with Charles Brown in 1959, and then King in 1960. He made one final lunge at the big time when he signed with Motown, cutting *Blues Boss* (1962), but his fireball brand of R&B was too raunchy for general consumption and he gigged around the Midwest until he was struck down by a stroke. He continued playing live until 1970 when he had his second stroke and in 1973 he returned for sessions for Johnny Otis's Blues Spectrum label, but these recordings never appeared until 1977. He lived in retirement in Houston – having given up drinking and become a Christian – until his death on 3 January 1980.

ROY BROWN

If it was Milburn whose unabashed use of the terms 'rocking' and 'rolling' gradually acclimatized R&B fans to the concept of rock 'n' roll, it was Roy Brown's 1948 hit 'Good Rockin' Tonight' that was responsible for placing the term 'rock' in a context that – despite the sexual connotations – related more to the non-specific concept of 'just having a good time'.

Such was the popularity of 'Good Rockin' Tonight' that it should have been Roy Brown's meal ticket for the rest of his life. That it failed to be so was more indicative of a music industry that was fundamentally incapable of taking itself seriously as a business and regarded itself as a cottage industry or the terrain for the fly-by-night, fast-buck merchants. On a more practical level, Brown failed to slot into the contemporaneous trend for shouters because there was just a little too much gospel in his delivery. Naturally gospel fans found the base, secular strains in his material distasteful. For all that, despite the many lows in his career, Brown was still performing months before his death in 1981.

Roy Brown was born in New Orleans on 10 September 1925. Roy's mother, Truelove Brown, was part Algonquin (and part black), and led the choir and played the organ at the local church. His father, Yancy, was a builder and so the family moved through the South wherever Yancy was working. Learning to sing gospel at the local church and working in sugar cane fields while still at school, Roy had a settled life until 1939, when his mother died. Three years later, having finished high school and sung in a gospel quartet, the Rookie Four, Brown moved to Los Angeles, where he became a professional boxer winning 16 of his 18 fights.

Despite his evident ability, he packed up boxing and, in 1945, he won a talent contest at the Million Dollar Theatre in Los Angeles. A big fan of crooners like Bing Crosby, at first he sang ballads and covers of show songs like 'Stardust'. He returned to Louisiana and got a job in Shreveport at Billy Riley's Palace Park. Although the blues had not played a significant part in his upbringing, he began to adopt contemporary R&B songs such as Billy Eckstine's 'Jelly, Jelly' and Buddy Johnson's 'When My Man Comes Home' and quickly developed a following because he sounded like a white man.

After Shreveport he moved on to Galveston, Texas, where he wrote 'Good Rockin' Tonight' and worked for a spell with Joe Coleman's group, singing more Ink Spots' and Crosby covers, but he also got the opportunity to cut his first – and only – record for the Gold Star label. Entitled 'Deep Sea Diver', backed by 'Bye Baby Bye', this sunk quickly and further excursions with the label were curtailed by Brown's sudden departure from Galveston.

Returning to New Orleans in 1947 in dire financial straits, he pitched 'Good Rockin' Tonight' for Wynonie Harris to record, but Harris was unimpressed and it was left to the ministrations of Cecil Gant, who was also working in the Crescent City, to pitch the song at Jules Braun, the owner of the New Jersey-based DeLuxe label. Braun immediately took a shine to Brown and placed him under contract, making Braun one of the first to mine the rich vein of New Orleans R&B. Recording in the J&M studios, Brown cut 'Good Rockin' Tonight' with Bob Ogden's band; although Wynonie Harris ironically recorded the song and scored the bigger hit, Brown's original version made the R&B Top Twenty. Brown remained in New Orleans for the remainder of the decade, scoring hits with 'Long About Midnight' and 'Rockin' at Midnight' (1948) and 'Boogie at Midnight' (1949). While Brown's popularity continued to rise, he lived the life of a celebrity to the full, being chauffeured from date to date in a fleet of Cadillacs and acting out his role with all the verve and panache of a Hollywood film star. Despite all this acclaim his vocal style remained as expressive as ever, drawing as it did from both the blues and gospel in equal measure.

By 1950, Brown had relocated to Cincinnati, where the King label was based, because Braun had sold DeLuxe to Syd Nathan, owner of King. Initially this change of environment affected his popularity not one jot for the hits just kept on coming: 'Hard Luck Blues', which was a rewritten version of Charles Brown's 'Driftin' Blues', 'Love Don't Love Nobody', and 'Cadillac Baby' (1950) and 'Big Town' and 'Bar Room Blues' (1951). After cutting 'I've Got the Last Laugh Now' (1951), Brown was shifted on to the parent King label, and for no apparent reason his popularity began to decline. Although the quality of songs such as 'Travellin' Man', 'A Fool in Love', and 'Midnight Lover Man' (1953), 'Trouble at Midnight', 'Ain't It a Shame?', and 'Worried Life Blues' (1954), and 'Letter to My Baby' (1955) were quite the equal of anything he had recorded at his peak, his records just stopped selling because Brown had literally been hoisted by his own petard – rock 'n' roll had arrived.

While many of his contemporaries failed to adjust, Brown merely tightened his belt and was signed to Lew Chudd's Imperial label. Although the label was based in Los Angeles, Brown was assigned to producer Dave Bartholomew. Bartholomew had already made New Orleans R&B a force to be reckoned with through his work with Fats Domino, Shirley and Lee, and Smiley Lewis, as well as producing other Imperial artists such as T-Bone Walker and Big Joe Turner. Linking up with Brown, Bartholomew supervised several sessions at Cosimo Matassa's J&M studios. Because he was backed by the house band, which included horn men Lee Allen, Herb Hardesty, and Clarence Hall, some critics contend that Brown was past his peak and that the Imperial sides showed a man in decline. The evidence is slightly different, though, as Bartholomew was able to combine the bluesy soulfulness of Brown's natural delivery with up-to-date arrangements that were more in keeping with the direction in which black music was moving. The other significant difference was that whereas Brown had previously penned most of his own material, at Imperial Bartholomew, with his regular co-writer Pearl King, wrote nine of the 20 sides Brown cut over the two-year period; Brown contributed just four songs: 'Diddy Y, Diddy O', 'Slow Down Little Eva', 'I'm in Love' and 'Cryin' Over You'. However, Brown's biggest hit, 'Let the Four Winds Blow' (1957), was written by Bartholomew and Fats Domino, rising to number five in the R&B charts and number 29 in the national charts. Despite the commercial success of 'Let the Four Winds Blow' and the artistic excellence of the remainder of his output, Brown was on the way out.

After the completion of his contract with Imperial, no-one was queuing up to sign him and the tax collectors were pursuing him for back taxes – he eventually served time in prison for tax evasion. To raise ready cash he sold the rights to 'Good Rockin' Tonight' and started to work as a door-to-door salesman, selling encyclopaedias and often referring to past glories as an entertainer to land a sale. But the 1960s was a lean time for Brown with just the odd session for independent labels such as Connie, Mobile, and Chess; and these recordings weren't even released. By 1967 he had started to claw his way back, cutting *Hard Times* for ABC's Bluesway subsidiary. Although few copies sold, it raised his stock in Europe and on the flourishing festival circuit. In 1970 Johnny Otis booked him to appear with his Revue at the Monterey Jazz Festival. Appearing alongside other legends of the post-war R&B era such as Ivory Joe Hunter, Roy Milton, Big Joe Turner, Little Esther Phillips, and Pee Wee Crayton, among others, the resulting album is one to which we shall return later in greater detail, but suffice it to say that Brown's version of 'Good Rockin' Tonight' was as full of exuberance as ever and effectively introduced him to a predominantly young, white, collegiate audience. Thereafter Brown was in constant demand across the US and also in Europe – principally at festivals, but also on the club circuit.

Although he continued to record sporadically, the emphasis was firmly on his live performances and it wasn't until 1978 that he went back into the studio to cut another album. *The Cheapest Prize in Town* was issued on Brown's own Faith label and he toured Europe and the UK to promote it – often with Duke Robillard's band Roomful of Blues. By now he was back at the top of his form and his appearance at the New Orleans Jazz and Heritage Festival in early 1981 seemed to confirm this, but on 25 May 1981 he died of a heart attack.

Brown's funeral was presided over by the Reverend Johnny Otis, who had been ordained during the 1970s. It was attended by most of Brown's contemporaries and turned out to be a celebration of Brown's contribution to R&B. While there was little doubt that Brown had many more miles on the clock in terms of his creativity, at least he managed to reap the fruits of his talent and to witness first-hand the respect he was accorded by young white audiences. This was due in no small part to his appearance at the Monterey Jazz Festival. Someone else on the bill that day, who also benefited from this exposure, was Ivory Joe Hunter.

IVORY JOE HUNTER

Although Ivory Joe Hunter was to derive much kudos from his appearance with the Johnny Otis Show at Monterey in 1970, the warmth of his bluesy baritone had already won him admirers in the country fraternity. In his later years he often asserted that his music had always been grounded in country but there can be little doubt that, as his career was approaching its zenith during the late 1940s, he spoke directly to black audiences and not to the conservative, white, blue-collar adherents of country. However, towards the end of his career he appeared at country music's showcase, the Grand Ole Opry, and was also dignified by a commemorative tribute concert at the Ryman Auditorium after his death in 1974.

Born on 10 October 1914, and brought up in Kirbyville, Texas, which lies about 135 miles to the north-east of Houston, Hunter was baptized Ivory Joe. Deeply influenced by gospel and spirituals, it was not uncommon in the Hunter household for the whole family, comprising 11 boys and four girls, to form a choir and sing non-secular music under the tutelage of their mother. After the family moved to Port Arthur, Ivory Joe's education was cut short by the death of both parents, and by the time he was 16 he was working as a professional musician. Influenced by Fats Waller and Duke Ellington, he secured a spot on Beaumont's radio station, KFDM. Billed as 'Rambling Fingers', Ivory Joe led his own band until he settled in Houston in 1936, organizing a residency for himself and his band at the Uptown Tavern.

In 1942 he moved to the West Coast, where he worked initially with Slim Jenkins in Oakland before hitting the Los Angeles and San Francisco club circuits. In 1945, despite the shellac restrictions, Ivory Joe formed his own Ivory label and scored a sizeable jukebox hit with Leroy Carr's ballad, 'Blues at Sunrise'. Featuring the accompaniment of Johnny Moore's Three Blazers, it brought him into contact with Charles Brown, who was a key influence in forming Ivory Joe's vocal style. Despite his warm, balladeering style, his group was typical of the small R&B combo, featuring piano, bass, drums, and tenor sax. The mere suggestion of such a line-up was virtually a passport for a string of dates at some of the most prestigious venues on the club circuit. Although the Ivory label had failed to prosper, he quickly formed another – Pacific – where blues such as 'Grieving Blues' and 'Hard-Hearted Blues' contrasted strongly with the uncharacteristic urgency of jump songs such as 'Boogie in the Basement'. However, the gentle, country-ish orientation in his work was evident in 'Whose Arms Are You Missing?' and 'Why Did You Lie?'.

After a brief sojourn with the Los Angeles-based Four Star label – for whom he cut the ballads 'Did You Mean It?', 'Don't Leave Me', and 'Are You Hep?' – he signed to the Cincinnati-based King label in 1947. In many respects King was the ideal label for Hunter because it included on its roster a significant percentage of country acts and writers such as Hawkshaw Hawkins and Pee Wee King. While the arrangements continued to embody the bluesy gospel bias of R&B, country songs such as 'Jealous Heart' were the antithesis of titles such as 'Guess Who' and 'Landlord Blues'. In 1949 he moved once again, this time to MGM, the home of Hank Williams, where he stayed for the next five years and recorded self-penned material such as 'I Almost Lost My Mind' (1950), which soared to the top of the R&B charts, and 'I Need You So', as well as Eddy Arnold's 'It's a Sin' and a number of Hank Williams covers.

In 1954 Hunter signed with Atlantic, where he continued writing and recording his own compositions, scoring with the million-seller 'Since I Met You Baby' in 1956. While 'Since I Met You Baby' was Hunter's biggest success, it was a distillation of his musical influences – having started life as 'Since I Met You Jesus', which he had written in 1942; then, in 1950, it was reworked to become the country-ish 'I Almost Lost My Mind' before finally appearing as 'Since I Met You Baby' in 1956. Ironically, according to Jerry Wexler, the arrangement for 'Since I Met You Baby' was lifted from Pat Boone's earlier cover of 'I Almost Lost My Mind' – as Wexler says, it was a rare case of the 'imitated imitating the imitator'. Although Hunter went on to cut more sides for Atlantic, such as 'A Tear Fell', 'Empty Arms', and 'You Mean Everything to Me', he was supplanted by the phenomenon of rock 'n' roll. Still his songs found a voice when covered by others – 'No Other One' (Connie Francis and Eddie Fisher), 'Empty Arms' (Teresa Brewer), and 'My Wish Came True' and 'I Need You So' (Elvis Presley).

The late 1950s and 1960s were a lean time for Hunter, as for many of his contemporaries. After being dropped by Atlantic, he recorded a number of singles for a variety of labels, including Dot ('City Lights', 1959), Capitol, Vee Jay, Smash, Stax, Goldwax ('I Can Make You Happy', 1966), Veep ('Did She Ask About Me?', 1967), and Sound Stage Seven ('Ivory Tower', 1968). Although these sides demonstrated Hunter's gospel roots, they also illustrated his affinity with country music. Then, in 1970, he appeared with the Johnny Otis Show at the Monterey Jazz Festival. Performing – naturally – 'Since I Met You Baby', Hunter proved that his vocal style was still umbilically attached to the blues but that, in the manner of Ray Charles, it could be attuned to circumstance.

This versatility was reaffirmed with *The Return of Ivory Joe Hunter* (1971). Featuring Isaac Hayes, Gene 'Bowlegs' Miller, and Sam Phillips's studios in Memphis, *The Return of Ivory Joe Hunter* seems to transcend – and to defy – category, mixing blues, country, gospel, and R&B. Although the album failed to sell, it gave him the impetus to record what turned out to be his final album. Defiantly entitled *I've Always Been Country* (1973), it was cut at Jack Clement's studios in Nashville with a battery of Nashville session men such as Reggie Young (guitar), Charlie McCoy (harmonica), Buddy Spicher (fiddle), Lloyd Green (steel guitar), and Tommy Cogbill (bass). While it included hardy country perennials such as a revised version of Bill Anderson's 'City Lights', Merle Haggard's 'Today I Started Loving You Again', and Bob Wills's 'San Antonio Rose', the voice and the phrasing still dug deep into the roots of the blues and gospel.

When the album was finished Hunter was diagnosed as suffering from lung cancer and as his condition deteriorated, a benefit concert at the Grand Ole Opry was staged. It was indicative of the scope of his influence that both George Jones and Tammy Wynette appeared alongside Isaac

Hayes. Within the month Ivory Joe was dead (8 November 1974), but his epitaph remains his ability to anticipate the marriage of blues and country into a style that was emulated by Ray Charles, Solomon Burke, Arthur Alexander, Joe Simon, and Clarence Carter.

ROY MILTON

While many of the performers discussed up to this point were associated with small groups, they were vocalists first and foremost who prospered initially with a relaxed, bluesy, crooning style but were also able to accompany themselves on the piano. This at least ensured a degree of independence, particularly during the lean times after the emergence and acceptance of rock 'n' roll in the late 1950s and 1960s when many could not economically support a group of any description. Roy Milton was an exception because when R&B lost its appeal, he retired, and it was only the ministrations of Johnny Otis that coaxed him from retirement to appear at the Monterey Jazz Festival in 1970.

Milton was a band leader in the tradition of Louis Jordan. While he achieved his greatest success with a vocal style that was more in keeping with the tough blues shouters from the Midwest, such as Big Joe Turner, at first he adopted the relaxed crooning that was *de rigueur* during the 1940s.

Milton was born on 31 July 1907, in Wynnewood, Oklahoma, and grew up in Tulsa where he got some experience as a vocalist and drummer with the Ernie Fields band during the Depression. In 1935 he moved to Los Angeles, forming the Solid Senders in 1938. While the line-up comprised alto and tenor saxes, trumpet, bass, and piano, it was Milton's drumming and vocals that respectively provided the group's drive and focus. The group managed to sustain a 'double life', playing standards and show tunes for the sophisticated white audiences on the cabaret circuit before metamorphosing into a hard, jump blues band at all-night, after-hours sessions. What Milton lacked in showmanship was compensated for by his ability to blend the Solid Senders into any environment, and with high-calibre musicians such as pianist Camille Howard and saxophonists Buddy Floyd (tenor) and Jackie Kelso (alto) he managed to compete with both Louis Jordan and Lionel Hampton on equal terms.

In 1945 Milton started to record, cutting sides for Gladys, Hamp-Tone – owned by Lionel Hampton – and Jukebox, which was Art Rupe's forerunner of Specialty. In 1946 Rupe set up the Specialty label and Milton's 'R. M. Blues' became one of the first records to sell over a million copies and, according to Charlie Gillett, the first to utilize the beat that would later be described as rock 'n' roll. For the next eight years Milton toured the US, scoring hits with 'The Hucklebuck' (1949), which became one the decade's most popular dances, 'Information Blues' (1950), 'Best Wishes' (1951), and 'So Tired' (1952).

Milton's success had a knock-on effect for his pianist, Camille Howard, who was encouraged by Rupe to record some sides of her own as the Musicians' Union had called a strike starting at midnight on 31 December 1947. Howard – together with Louis Jordan's bassist, Dallas Bartley, and Milton on drums – recorded several sides, including the speedily improvised 'X-Temporaneous Boogie', in an attempt to stockpile masters for the duration of the strike. Although it never charted, 'X-Temporaneous Boogie' became synonymous with Howard and gave her the opportunity to record other titles such as 'Money Blues' and to step from the confines of the Solid Senders for solo engagements.

By 1954, despite his popularity on the club circuit, the hits had dried up and Milton recorded for the Dootone label and then King and Warwick. This was all to little avail and, as the engagements decreased, Milton retired. In 1970 Johnny Otis persuaded Milton to appear at Monterey, where he sang his biggest hit 'R. M. Blues'; this was followed by other appearances with Otis as well as recording the occasional album with him. In 1977 Milton toured Europe and cut *Instant Groove* for the Black & Blue label with guitarists Billy Butler – formerly of Bill Doggett's band – and Roy Gaines, but this was more of a reprise to his earlier career than a serious attempt to revitalize it. Once more he went back into retirement in Los Angeles, where he remained until his death on 18 September 1983. While Milton staked a worthy claim to be one of rock 'n' roll's forefathers, it was diminished by his inability – or unwillingness – to adjust to new trends. This was certainly true of most of his contemporaries, who were vocally able to adapt the relaxed, bluesy crooning that was popular in the 1940s to the boisterous clamour of R&B. However, they lacked the ability to incorporate these stylistic changes and much of the time the partying, good-time feel of up-tempo R&B was construed as a novelty. It was left to label owners and producers to create the agenda in some cases for rather less than altruistic reasons. There were exceptions and these were manifested in the rise of small-group leaders such as Johnny Otis, Ike Turner, Ray Charles, and, later on, James Brown.

chapter five

SHOUTERS AND
SCREAMERS

I F THE 'SEPIA SINATRAS' OFFERED one aspect of R&B, the
shouters presented an altogether different face because they, in tandem with the growling saxophones, were central to the image of
R&B. While both sprung out of the front lines of the big bands, the
traditions from which they came could not have been more different. The shouters had their roots in the urban sprawls of the Midwest:
Kansas City, St Louis, and Indianapolis were all junctions for black
migrants heading north to industrial centres such as Chicago and Detroit,
or west to the land of opportunity in California. These halfway houses
began to appeal on their own account, as pimps and prostitutes, gamblers
and conmen, and bluesmen and jazz musicians gravitated to gather up the
detritus or earn a fast buck. Against this background, each town developed
its own network of bars and juke-joints. These were not places for the
sophisticated. Immediacy was the watchword so it was not unsurprising
that it was from these challenging environments that the boogie-woogie
craze of the 1930s found its feet and went forth to multiply, as notable purveyors of the form such as Albert Ammons, Meade Lux Lewis, Jimmy
Yancey, and Pete Johnson managed to achieve wider acceptance as word of
their abilities spread through the American heartlands. Of them all, Pete
Johnson was to win the most plaudits, being equally at home in a band or
as a vocalist's accompanist, as well as being a fine soloist. Moreover, his
endless inventiveness as a writer enabled him to partner one of the great
shouters of the era, Joe Turner.

JOE TURNER

The portly figure of Joe Turner stands like a corporeal beacon, announcing the birth of R&B with all the gusto and enthusiasm of a town crier announcing the birth of a child to an infertile monarch. For as Nick Tosches asserts in *Unsung Heroes of Rock 'n' Roll*, 'His voice, oceanic and commanding, resonant with that rumbling deep down in the ground which is the voice of the devil chaining his third wife down, is the voice of power'. He was born Joseph Vernon Tucker on 18 May 1911, in Kansas City (KC), Missouri, and started to help to support the family when he was 15 after his father had been killed in a car crash. Within a year or so of his father's death, he had become acquainted with Pete Johnson, the regular pianist at the Backbiter's Club. Although Turner had only sung on street corners up until that time, Johnson saw the potential in Turner's voice and the two of them joined forces. Throughout Prohibition they worked KC's clubs and speakeasies, building up their reputation. Indeed, such was the strength of their appeal that they had no reason to leave until 1936 – Prohibition had ended three years before – when they undertook a whistle-stop tour of the Midwest, taking in Chicago and St Louis before winding up back in KC. On their return they landed a residency at the Sunset Club and it was there that Columbia A&R man John Hammond discovered them.

In 1938 Hammond recruited the two for his first 'From Spirituals to Swing' concert at Carnegie Hall alongside Charlie Christian, Count Basie, Sister Rosetta Tharpe, and Big Bill Broonzy, among others. After the concert, they cut 'Goin' Away Blues' and 'Roll 'Em Pete' (1939) for Vocalion, which was the first of many sides they were to cut for the label. Despite a brief return to KC, Turner and Johnson went back to New York, appearing at some of the swankiest venues around town, including the prestigious Café Society and cutting sides such as 'Cherry Red' and 'Lovin' Mama Blues'; these sides provoked so much attention by black record-buyers that record companies started to sit up and take notice of the huge potential market among black audiences. As their reputations flourished, Turner began undertaking separate recording dates – most notably with the Varsity Seven, featuring Coleman Hawkins and Benny Carter, and with them he cut 'How Long, How Long Blues' (1940). This was followed by sessions with the Café Society's resident Orchestra, led by pianist Joe Sullivan, where he cut 'I Can't Give You Anything But Love' and 'Low Down Dirty Shame' (1940). In 1941 Turner cut several sides with Art Tatum's Band for Decca that included 'Wee Baby Blues'; another session followed which resulted in 'Lucille', 'Rock Me Mama', 'Corrina, Corrina', and 'Lonesome Graveyard'. These sides demonstrated Turner's growth as an accomplished R&B vocalist and sowed the seeds for the sides he would cut with Atlantic some ten years later. However, that is not to belittle in any way what he was to achieve in the interim because, with some of the hottest players on either coast, Turner – sometimes with, and sometimes without Johnson – recorded for National, Swing Time, MGM, Excelsior, Modern, Freedom, Imperial, and Aladdin. And this was not done in the mournful, downtrodden way, often so characteristic of the blues; rather Turner declaimed with all the braggadocio he could muster. Furthermore, his arrival on the scene acted as a catalyst for other shouters such as Wynonie Harris, Eddie 'Cleanhead' Vinson, Big Mama Thornton, Jimmy Rushing, and Jimmy Witherspoon.

In 1951 Turner was offered a contract by Atlantic after he had finished a gig at Harlem's Apollo. His debut for the label, 'Chains of Love', was a monster hit, spending almost six months on the R&B charts. More was to follow as 'Sweet Sixteen' (1952) and 'Honey Hush' and 'TV Mama' (1953) hastened after in hot pursuit. But they were scant preparation for 'Shake, Rattle and Roll' (1954). Written by Atlantic house arranger Jesse Stone, 'Shake, Rattle and Roll' is to rock 'n' roll what D. W. Griffith's *Birth of a Nation* is to the cinema: it announced a fresh series of possibilities that no one had actually thought of before or, at the very least, never thought they could get away with.

Curiously 'Shake, Rattle and Roll' never reached the pinnacle of the R&B charts, despite hanging around for about seven months. For the next five years, Turner knocked out records such as 'Flip, Flop and Fly' and 'Hide and Seek' (1955), 'Corrina, Corrina' and 'Lipstick, Powder, and Paint' (1956), 'Trouble in Mind' (1957), and 'Wee Baby Blues' (1958).

Throughout the 1960s Turner worked with Johnson, appeared at blues festivals and cut albums for Norman Granz's jazz label, Pablo, but above all he gigged regularly on the club circuit, especially down in New Orleans where he was based for much of that decade. After Johnson's death in 1967, Turner showed little inclination to grow old gracefully. Instead he added a walking stick to his formidable armoury, with which he would rap summarily upon bars or floors. Still he continued to tour and record, usually backed by star-studded ensembles. In 1985 he died of kidney failure.

JIMMY RUSHING

While Turner's impact came as a consequence of his work as a soloist, Jimmy Rushing achieved status in his capacity as vocalist in Count Basie's band – a position he held down for 15 years. Therefore, although Rushing was never a purveyor of R&B in the same way as Turner, his declamatory vocal style informed the genre, giving a wider range of musical expression than the blues alone could muster. Born in Oklahoma on 26 August 1902, Rushing learned the violin and piano during his childhood. After working briefly with Jelly Roll Morton, Rushing worked with the Billy King Revue, Walter Page's Blue Devils, and Benny Moten's Band until joining Basie in 1935. With Basie, his slightly nasal high tenor shouting style reached its pitch when pitted against the hard-blowing horns of the front line on songs such as 'Good Morning Blues' (1937), 'Sent For You Yesterday (Here You Are Today)' (1938), 'Evil Blues' (1939), 'Goin' to Chicago' and 'Rusty Dusty Blues' (1941), and 'Jimmy's Blues' (1944). After leaving Basie in 1950, Rushing went on to front a variety of small groups before going solo in 1952. Thereafter he bypassed rock 'n' roll, settling into a comfortable niche as a jazz vocalist *par excellence* until his death from leukaemia in 1972.

JIMMY WITHERSPOON

There is nothing surprising in the fact that Duke Robillard – the former Roomful of Blues and Fabulous Thunderbirds' guitarist – should respond affirmatively to the request to produce Jimmy Witherspoon. For although Robillard has spent most of his musical career indulging his passion for R&B, Jimmy Witherspoon was never just a shouter or a jazz vocalist. Instead he ploughed a very singular furrow, somewhere between jazz and the blues. Where the emphasis fell was due more to the musicians with whom he was recording than to any specific intention on his part to cut a record that conformed to type or category. This malleability was deceptive because Witherspoon bucked the system by surviving. Queues of producers and musicians formed at his front door, eager to pick up any snippet he might cast in their direction.

Witherspoon was born in Arkansas on 8 August 1923 and his career took a familiar path at first when he began singing in his local church choir when he was seven. At 18 he had enlisted in the Merchant Marines – a tour of duty that lasted until 1944. In between times he sang with different impromptu set-ups, including Teddy Weatherford's band. These ad hoc arrangements broadened his style so that he encompassed not only jazz and blues idioms but also gospel. In 1944, when his tour of duty finished, he joined the celebrated Jay McShann Band, taking over Walter Brown's role, starting a relationship that would last until 1948. During those four years, Witherspoon cut sides for Philo – later Aladdin – and Premier and showed that he could swing with the best of them, but he could also sing the blues in its deepest and most sepulchral form. After leaving McShann he started a solo career, cutting a slew of sides for the Supreme and Modern labels; these included ''Tain't Nobody's Business', 'In the Evening When the Sun Goes Down', 'No Rollin' Blues', and 'Big Fine Girl' (1949) and 'The Wind Is Blowin'' (1952).

However, as the 1950s progressed, Witherspoon was increasingly sidelined by rock 'n' roll, until in 1959 his appearance at the Monterey Jazz Festival reversed the process. By now he was working as a jazz and blues vocalist and he pursued a similar route to that of other bluesmen by recording, on the one hand, with younger, white musicians, such as Eric Burdon – formerly of the Animals – on *Guilty* (1971) and Joe Walsh of the James Gang on *Handbags and Gladrags* (1971), and producers such as Dr John and Doc Pomus on *Midnight Lady Called the Blues* (1986) and Mike Vernon on *The Blues, the Whole Blues, and Nothing But the Blues* (1992). On the other hand, he worked with jazz musicians such as organists Richard 'Groove' Holmes and Brother Jack McDuff and saxophonists Coleman Hawkins, Buck Clayton, and Ben Webster. Jimmy Witherspoon remained as vocal as ever, still offering encouragement by example to followers and imitators alike, until his death on 18 September 1997.

WYNONIE HARRIS

The path that Wynonie Harris chose was not all that different from that of Big Joe Turner, for Harris, like Turner, made no excuses about sacrificing all for his art: he became a singer because it was a quicker, more effective route to getting cash and scoring with women. There was no false modesty so, according to Nick Tosches, it was Harris that Elvis Presley studied when he was 'learning' stagecraft back in the early 1950s. Harris was the archetypal 'Sixty Minute Man', but – likely as not – any lady checking her watch might find that that boast had left her wanting. Be that as it may, Harris's R&B was as powerful as it was exuberant.

He was born in Omaha, Nebraska, on 24 August 1915. While his parents encouraged him to be a doctor and he did last the course for two years at Creighton University after graduating from high school, Harris found other things such as dancing more to his liking so he gave up university to be a dancer in some of the less salubrious joints around town. He then married and had started to sing, as well as dance, and often travelled down to Kansas City, where he frequently saw Pete Johnson and Big Joe Turner going through their paces. In 1940 he made his pitch for the big time by moving to Los Angeles where he got a job at the Club Alabam, which led to a small part in the film *Hit Parade of 1944.*

With business slack, Harris returned to Kansas City where he worked the clubs until Lucky Millinder offered him a job as a vocalist in his band. Although he didn't stay with Millinder long, he was there just long enough to cut a couple of sides for Decca. Both 'Hurry, Hurry' and 'Who Threw the Whiskey in the Well?' were good-sized hits, but Harris received only his recording fee for these two hits. It taught him a lesson he never forgot: make sure your own name is on the label. On his return to Los Angeles, he hooked up with the Mesner Brothers and, backed by Johnny Otis's All Stars, he cut 'Around the Clock' and 'Cock-A-Doodle-Doo' (1945). They might not have been hits, but they certainly acted as a powerful magnet for other record labels. Within the month, Harris had landed a deal with Apollo, then a few months later he was recording for Lionel Hampton's Hamp-Tone label, and then it was back to the Mesner Brothers' new label, Aladdin. While many of these sides were derivative, what they lacked in imagination was more than compensated for by the sheer energy of Harris's vocal delivery and the almost instinctive rapport he developed with horn men such as Illinois Jacquet and Jack McVea.

By 1947 Harris was a star and, to prove it, he got himself a deal with the King label. With King, Harris put together a string of hits that included covers of 'Good Rockin' Tonight' and Sticks McGhee's 'Drinkin' Wine Spo-Dee-O-Dee', both of which had been hits before Harris covered them. Indeed, Roy Brown offered 'Good Rockin' Tonight' to Harris before he himself recorded it, but Harris turned it down at first. Other sides included 'Your Money Don't Mean a Thing' and 'Lollipop Mama' (1948), 'All She Wants to Do Is Rock' (1949), 'Rock Mr Blues', and 'Bloodshot Eyes' (1950), 'Night Train' (1952), 'Mama, Your Daughter Done Lied to Me' (1953), and 'Good Mambo Tonight' and 'Shotgun Wedding' (1955). In addition to his solo sides, he was also featured vocalist on titles such as 'Lovin' Machine' (1951) with the Todd Rhodes Orchestra and, in 1953, he cut 'Battle of the Blues' with Joe Turner. Not unreasonably, as the rock 'n' roll era kicked in during the mid-1950s, Harris began to look very old-fashioned and – perhaps – rather quaint in a suitably outlandish way. Although he made the odd comeback, he ran a café in Brooklyn and then Los Angeles before dying in 1969.

SCREAMIN' JAY HAWKINS

For all that, Harris's unremitting salaciousness underlined the essential novelty value implicit in R&B, and some such as Screamin' Jay Hawkins took this novelty value to quite extraordinary heights. He quickly caught on to the potential for instilling a sense of distaste among the older generations, thereby maximizing his appeal for younger audiences. By using shock tactics such as appearing on stage in a coffin, with ghoulish props such as skulls and shrunken heads, he carved a niche for himself that on the one hand echoed the theatrics of Cab Calloway and Louis Jordan and on the other provided a benchmark that later artists such as Alice Cooper and Ozzy Osborne would imitate. However, there the similarity ended because, while Hawkins's capacity for the grotesque was limitless, his material was a finely wrought blend of soulful histrionics and hard-edged R&B.

Born Jalacy Hawkins on 18 July 1929, in Cleveland, Ohio, he learned some of his showmanship in the ring as a boxer. In 1952 he retired from the ring to focus his energies on a career in music, joining Tiny Grimes and his Rocking Highlanders as pianist and vocalist. The following year, having adopted the name Screamin' Jay Hawkins, he started to record for the Timely label, cutting 'Baptize Me in Wine' and 'I Found My Way to Wine'. After recording for the Apollo, Mercury, and Savoy labels, he signed with the OKeh label, cutting 'I Put a Spell on You', which featured guitarist Mickey Baker; never a hit at the time, it has been covered down the years by everyone from Nina Simone to the Crazy World of Arthur Brown. Other releases followed, such as 'Alligator Wine', 'There's Something Wrong With You' and the superbly oblique 'Constipation Blues'.

However, such was Hawkins's success at alienating the authorities that his shows were often cancelled and he became to be regarded solely as a novelty act. From 1958 until 1965 he was relegated to playing obscure one-nighters or endless European package tours. In 1965 the Kinks' producer, Shel Talmy, cut *The Night and Day of Screamin' Jay Hawkins*, which went some way towards rehabilitating him as a major cult artist. This rehabilitation has persisted to the present with Hawkins's appearance in Jim Jarmusch's movie *Mystery Train* and the formation of his own band, the Fuzztones. While his albums have been commercial nightmares, they possess an uncompromising vitality, with *What That Is* (1969), *Screamin' Jay Hawkins* (1970), featuring Earl Palmer (drums) and Plas Johnson (horn), and *Black Music For White People* (1991) being the most accurate representations of what he's about.

Even so, palates for the arcane and the bizarre were tempered by notions of what constituted good taste and R&B and rock 'n' roll were never supposed to be about anything other than transgressing accepted conventions. These were liable to be flouted in the most mundane, muso-ish fashion, one of them being that horn men stood meekly to the side unfurling their licks, as and when required. Now Louis Jordan – a saxophonist by preference – changed that to some extent, but not entirely for, as his fame flourished, he tended to play saxophone less and less. Bullmoose Jackson was another horn man, whose singing generally took precedence over playing saxophone. Eddie 'Cleanhead' Vinson managed to encompass both disciplines with comparable vitality.

EDDIE VINSON

Born in Houston, Texas on 18 December 1917, Vinson learned to play the saxophone while still at school. This ability enabled him to join Milt Larkin's outfit in 1936, where he played alongside Illinois Jacquet and

T-Bone Walker. In 1942 he moved to New York and joined the big band formed by Duke Ellington's former trumpeter, Cootie Williams. For the next three years he toured and cut records with Capitol and OKeh before forming his own band in 1945. Signed by Mercury, he cut a string of fine, suggestive jump blues that included 'Juice Head Baby', 'Kidney Stew Blues', 'Old Mid Boogie', 'Some Women Do', 'Oil Man Blues', 'Cherry Red', and 'Ever-Ready Blues'. Although many of these songs were too blatant in their erotic imagery to obtain much airplay, Vinson's alto, punctuating his predictably wheezy vocals, ensured that his live shows were entertaining, to say the very least.

In 1948 he moved over to King and cut more titles such as 'I'm Gonna Wind Your Clock', 'I'm Weak But Willing' and 'Somebody Done Stole My Cherry Red', but Wynonie Harris and Roy Brown were King's stars and their records were promoted while Vinson's were often sidelined. However, because he had his expertise as a good post-bop saxophonist to fall back on, the 1950s saw him rejoin Cootie Williams and then cut some sides with an offshoot of Basie's orchestra. This was short-lived for he returned to Houston where he remained until he was rediscovered by 'Cannonball' Adderley in 1961. With Adderley's group, Vinson cut *Back Door Blues* (1961) for the Riverside label and this marked his resurgence as a pioneer R&B practitioner whose rooots were grounded firmly in jazz. This tended to give more resonance – perceptually, at least – to his later recordings because they were not dismissed by jazz and blues fans as being the scarifying histrionics of a man trying to cash in on the rock 'n' roll boom. In 1970 he was recruited by his old chum Johnny Otis to appear at the Monterey Jazz Festival, where he was accompanied by such denizens of innumerable sessions as Gene 'Mighty Flea' Connors on trombone. Throughout the 1970s and 1980s, Vinson toured regularly and cut albums, continuing right up to his death in 1988.

BOBBY BLAND

There is one other vocalist who belongs firmly in the tradition of the shouter, despite never really raising his voice once or indulging in any theatrical shenanigans at his live shows. For Bobby 'Blue' Bland is one of those performers whose style was initially formed by singing gospel and evolved through singing blues, but was most at home within the context of a small group or orchestra – usually led by arranger Joe Scott – and none of that has changed in the course of his career. These days, Bland records for the independent Malaco label, who pride themselves on cutting soul, gospel, and R&B for black audiences and he is the remaining link with R&B's golden age in the late 1940s and early 1950s.

He was born Robert Calvin Bland in Rosemark, Tennessee, on 27 January 1930. During the 1940s he moved to Memphis, where he sang in the Miniatures gospel group. Influenced by Roy Brown, Lowell Fulson, and B. B. King, he joined the Beale Streeters in 1949, whose line-up had included at one time or another King, Johnny Ace, and Roscoe Gordon. After a stint as King's driver and valet, he started to record for the Modern label, cutting 'Crying All Night Long' and 'Drifting From Town to Town' (1952). In 1953 he signed with the Duke label, where he recorded singles such as 'Farther Up the Road' (1957), 'I'll Take Care of You' (1959), 'Cry, Cry, Cry' and 'I Pity the Fool' (1961), 'Who Will the Next Fool Be?', 'Turn on Your Lovelight', and 'Call on Me' (1962), 'That's the Way Love Is' (1963), 'Ain't Nothing You Can Do' (1964) and 'I'm Too Far Gone to Turn Around' (1966).

In 1962 he recorded *Two Steps From the Blues*, which, despite its title, is the embodiment of soul: the marriage between the gospel and the secular traditions. After Don Robey sold Duke to ABC, Bland's career went into a decline during the latter half of the 1960s, although he continued to tour regularly with King. In 1972 he recorded *The California Album* with the cream of the West Coast session musicians; this was followed by *The Dreamer* (1974). In much the same way as *Two Steps From the Blues* in the 1960s, *The Dreamer* was the template for a style of soul album in the 1970s where sophistication and warmth were bywords, and not many got the style off pat in quite the same way as Bland. While neither of these records was a huge commercial success, they established him as one of the great vocalists of the period. By 1983 he had signed with Malaco and was cutting albums such as *Members Only* (1985), *After All* (1986), *Blues You Can Use* (1988), and *Midnight Run* and *First Class Blues* (1989); Bland's smooth vocals on these albums combined with the luxurious brass arrangements are reminiscent of a bygone era.

SAXES

It is the brass section – especially a blazing horn riff – that complements the shouts and intemperate hectoring emanating from the lead vocalist. Even on instrumentals these riffs lay bare the bones of R&B. But despite the uncultured vulgarity – or, perhaps the blazing freneticism – of many of the great horn solos, the pedigree lay in the artistry of their exposition. After all, most of the greatest players had benefited from years of toil in the front line of big bands, little bands, or indeed small groups. In short, most were sufficiently acquainted with the technical possibilities their chosen instrument possessed. The same thing cannot be said for the electric guitar. For the horn men the novelty value resided in how they were deployed.

One of the best and earliest examples can be found in Lionel Hampton's 'Flying Home' in 1942. Featuring the towering tenor sax of Illinois Jacquet, the improvised solo on 'Flying Home' blazed away, highlighting the latent erotic properties of such a style of soloing. Jacquet, who was born in Broussard, Louisiana, on 31 October 1922, had been influenced initially by Coleman Hawkins. Growing up in Houston, Jacquet started to play with Milt Larkin's band, alongside Eddie 'Cleanhead' Vinson and Arnett Cobb, before moving to Los Angeles with Floyd Ray's band. After his hit with Hampton, he went on to play with Cab Calloway and Count Basie, before leading his own band or touring with 'Jazz at the Philharmonic'. In later years Jacquet seemed to resort to gimmickry, but at his peak he possesses a fine tone.

It was frequently contended that the repetitive riff only served as an audience-getter, but that in a sense was the whole point of R&B in the first place. It was created as an entertainment: Louis Jordan and the other protagonists didn't sit around thinking about creating high art. They wanted the punters to stream through the doors of the clubs and dance-halls and have fun. It is hardly surprising, therefore, that some of the most enduring tunes of the R&B era were instrumentals or dances: 'The Hucklebuck' by Paul Williams on Savoy in 1949 generated covers by Tommy Dorsey and Frank Sinatra. Instrumentals also anticipated a significant trend of the rock 'n' roll era – namely, records which were based around dance crazes – and possessed that one salient ingredient – a honking horn. Big Jay McNeely did as much as anyone else in turning Jacquet's streamlined honk into a marketable commodity.

McNeely was born Cecil James McNeely on 29 April 1927 in Los Angeles and started recording for Leon René's Exclusive label. McNeely started to get noticed in 1947 with '35-30' for the Savoy label, and this was followed by 'Waxie Maxie' (1948) and 'Deacon's Wig' (1949). Thereafter he was forever typecast and the situation remained unchanged even when his 1959 hit 'There Is Something on Your Mind' featured vocalist Sonny Warner. McNeely is still playing and even cuts the occasional album.

Where McNeely honked, Eugene Earl Bostic bruised, for Bostic – who was born on 25 April 1913 in Tulsa, Oklahoma, and was a graduate of Xavier University in New Orleans – could make his alto sax sound like a baritone. And it caused such a ruckus that he managed to score hits with such unpromising titles as 'Temptation' (1948), 'Sleep' (1950) and 'Moonglow', 'Blue Skies', and 'Flamingo' (1951). While most of his career was spent working out of the King label, he moved to Los Angeles in the mid-1950s, where he eventually died in 1965.

Bill Doggett was another graduate of the King label. Born in 1916 in Philadelphia, Doggett led Jimmy Gorham's band before handing over the reins to Lucky Millinder. His next stop was a stint as arranger and pianist for the Ink Spots before joining Lionel Hampton's band, where he rubbed shoulders with Earl Bostic. In 1949 he took over from organist Wild Bill Davis in Louis Jordan's Tympani Five and then did a spell with Ella Fitzgerald. In 1952, having served his apprenticeship, he took up the baton on his own account and signed with King. For the next ten years or so, he issued a steady stream of instrumentals that included 'Honky Tonk' and 'Slow Walk' (1956), 'Soft' and 'Ram-Bunk-Shush' (1957), 'Hold It' (1958), and 'Rainbow Riot' (1959). Featuring horn man Clifford Scott on tenor, 'Honky Tonk' was Doggett's most memorable moment and it spawned a host of imitations from players such as Boots Randolph, Bill Justis, and Ernie Freeman. Inevitably Doggett's appeal began to wane in the early 1960s, but he was able to fall back on his wealth of experience, expertise, and all-round savvy, which enabled him to find a regular flow of work with jazz musicians such as Jacquet and Rex Stewart.

Many of the great horn men of the period were session guys – some were not even credited – or jazz men doing a spot of moonlighting. These included Buddy Tate, Arnett Cobb, Al Sears, and Sam 'The Man' Taylor. Of these, Taylor is of particular note. Born in Lexington, Kentucky, on 12 July 1916, he first learned to play the clarinet, before changing to tenor sax. After playing with Scatman Crothers and the Sunset Royal Orchestra, he made his mark in Lucky Millinder's band between 1944 and 1945, before moving on to Cab Calloway's band for six years. At the beginning of the 1950s he started working the New York session circuit, where he was particularly favoured by Ahmet Ertegun and, later, Jerry Wexler at Atlantic. Indeed it might be averred with some confidence that it was the innate musicality of Taylor's solos that enabled many of Atlantic's records to transcend contemporary tastes and become classics of their type. For without Taylor, perhaps that other cause célèbre of the New York session circuit, King Curtis, might have found work just that little bit more elusive. King Curtis was born Curtis Ousley in Fort Worth, Texas, on 7 February 1934. When he was 16, he moved to New York and started to play saxophone in Lionel Hampton's Band. By 1953 he had started to record in his own jazz group; however, with Sam 'The Man' Taylor, his robust style of playing quickly secured him work on the burgeoning session circuit. From 1956 until 1971 he backed just about everyone from the Coasters through Jimi Hendrix to Aretha Franklin, and found the time to cut R&B albums with Brother Jack McDuff for labels such as Gem, Groove, Apollo, and Crown.

In 1962 Curtis had his first hit in his own right, 'Soul Twist' (1962), with his group, the Noble Knights, for Bobby Robinson's Enjoy label. In 1967 he had another two hits, 'Memphis Soul Stew' and 'Ode to Billie Joe', with the Kingpins, which featured Tommy Cogbill, Donny Hathaway, Cornell Dupree, and Chuck Rainey. However, these were hardly representative of his solo work, which was as prolific as it was accomplished. On

14 August 1971 he died of stab wounds sustained in a street fight in New York, aged 37. It was a tragic end to a career which, at the time of his death, seemed destined to go through the roof in his new capacity as leader of Aretha Franklin's backing band.

In recent times, that screaming hot syle has gone out of fashion – on sessions at least – to be replaced by an altogether more sophisticated, cultured sound, but some of its main practitioners started working in the front line of Ray Charles's band – Hank Crawford and David 'Fathead' Newman – or in the Crusaders – Wilton Felder. And no one could say that, given the right time and place, these guys couldn't do just as good a job as Big Jay McNeely or King Curtis.

chapter six

SVENGALIS:
JOHNNY AND IKE

WHILE THE ASCENDANCY OF THE SMALL instrumental group in the post-war era was principally due to economic factors, other reasons included the growth of independent labels and the increasing use of tape as the chosen medium for recording. The overriding factor, however, was the spirit of individuality and independence that permeated every level of society. From this attitude there developed an infrastructure of talent scouts, booking agents, and regional amateur talent contests where young hopefuls could show themselves off. Among the most active talent scouts were those for independent record labels such as Specialty, Atlantic, and Imperial, all of whom sent scouts into the Deep South on the look-out for youngsters as well as older blues artists who had never quite managed to establish national recognition. Other labels such as Modern adopted a more informal attitude by taking notice of small-group leaders who, while touring the country, gained a perspective on local talent at grass-roots level. It was from this vantage point that both Johnny Otis and, later, Ike Turner achieved a 'through the keyhole' glimpse of up-and-coming talent.

While the two men could hardly have been more different personally and in their approach to the role of talent scout, each exerted an influence on the way in which record companies went about the business of scouting. Furthermore, both of them established fluid, small groups that – instead of using regular line-ups – drew from pools of musicians, based on who was available from one region to the next. This enabled Otis particularly to present showcases or revues featuring young local instrumentalists or vocalists – a sort of 'all-in' package tour – that reflected local talent. For Otis this method continued throughout his career; in later years both James Brown with the Famous Flames and Ray Charles with his Orchestra and the Raelets would emulate the concept of the all-inclusive package tour.

JOHNNY OTIS – THE EARLY YEARS

Otis was born John Veliotes to Alexander and Irene Veliotes, of Greek extraction, in Vallejo, California, on 28 December 1921. After moving to Berkeley he was raised in the black community where his father ran a grocery store. During his teens he became drummer with Count Otis Matthews' West Oakland House Rockers. Matthews – a bluesman from the Mississippi Delta – had migrated to the West Coast in the years immediately after the Depression and worked as a boogie-woogie pianist before forming the House Rockers. Playing at local events throughout the neighbourhood, Matthews never managed to make the transition to the big time, despite playing a primitive type of R&B in the mid-1930s.

After leaving Matthews, Otis drummed with George Morrison's band in Denver and Lloyd Hunter's in Omaha before returning to the West Coast where he was installed behind the drums with Harlan Leonard's Kansas City Rockets. Based at LA's Club Alabam, Otis was enticed into joining Bardu Ali's band, which had a residency at the prestigious Lincoln Theatre. By 1945 Otis was ready to break out on his own and, after forming his first big band, he struck gold with 'Harlem Nocturne' for Leon René's Excelsior label. With this hit behind him, Otis set off on a coast-to-coast tour with Louis Jordan and the Ink Spots. However, Otis's big band – comprising seven brass, five reeds, four in the rhythm section, and the Trenier Twins – was too big to be economic, and by 1947 it had been trimmed down to two saxophones, trombone, trumpet, piano, guitar, bass, and drums. With this line-up Otis was, in a sense, taking a backward step personally because it was a similar line-up to that of Count Otis Matthews' West Oakland House Rockers, but for Otis it was ideal for the austerity of the post-war years.

In 1948 he opened the Barrel House Club, with Bardu Ali as partner, in the Watts District of Los Angeles. The point of the club was to present a regular showcase for blues musicians in a setting that was designed to entertain. For the two or three years that Otis was involved with the club, it was the place to go for R&B. Featuring established talent such as T-Bone Walker, Lowell Fulson, and Charles Brown, Otis introduced others such as the Robins, Little Esther Phillips, and Mel Walker. Indeed, Otis only left the club when he started gaining recognition for his records. At first he did some sessions with Jules, Saul, and Joe Bihari at Modern before linking up with Herman Lubinsky at Savoy at the suggestion of Ralph Bass. In 1950 Otis scored hits with Little Esther Phillips and Mel Walker on 'Double Crossin' Blues' – featuring the Robins on backing vocals, whom he had dis- covered at one of the Barrel House's talent shows – 'Mistrustin' Blues', 'Deceivin' Blues', and 'Wedding Boogie', and with just Mel, Otis scored fur- ther hits with 'Dreamin' Blues' and 'Rockin' Blues'. The following year Otis scored with 'Mambo Boogie' and 'All Nite Long' and 'Gee Baby' with Mel Walker. While none of these managed to register in the national charts, all made the top three of the R&B charts. As for Walker and Little Esther, Walker quickly disappeared into obscurity but Little Esther proved remark- ably resilient, at least to the swings of fortune.

LITTLE ESTHER

Born Esther Mae Jones on 23 December 1935, in Galveston, Texas, Little Esther was primarily influenced by Dinah Washington. During her childhood she moved to Los Angeles, where she sang in church choirs and at talent shows. In 1948 she was spotted by Otis when she was a mere 13 years old. While her succcess was immediate and meteoric, the constant touring and concomitant publicity made her vulnerable and – like other child stars such as Frankie Lymon – she showed every indication of burn- ing out through drug abuse. In 1954 she stopped touring and for the next eight years seldom worked at all, apart from two separate stints with Savoy in 1956 and 1959.

When she returned to recording it was for the Lenox label. Owned by Lelan Rogers – brother of country singer Kenny Rogers – and based in Houston where Esther now lived, Lenox leased their material out to Atlantic for national distribution. One of the first sides she cut was 'Release Me'. Recorded at Bradley's Barn in Nashville, 'Release Me' had been a country hit for both Ray Price and Kitty Wells. Although it was stereotypi- cally a 'weepie' in the great tradition of country ballads, the gospel grit that Esther brought to her interpretation made it sound as if she was singing about the travails of her own recent experiences.

Despite extensive periods at drug rehabilitation centres, Esther wasn't able to shake off her habit. In the meantime she started to record for Atlantic in 1965. Theoretically this should have been the perfect creative environment for her because she was backed by some of the best session men of the time, such as King Curtis and Richard Tee. As for the material, admittedly juxtaposing Lennon and McCartney's 'And I Love Him' and Percy Sledge's 'When a Man Loves a Woman' with show standards denoted a lack of imagination on the part of her producers, but Esther's background with Otis and her admiration for Dinah Washington should have been sufficient to elicit majestic performances. That these were not forth-coming was evidently to her detriment because she was dropped by the label and consigned to an enforced hiatus in her career, but that enabled her to take stock.

In 1966, after appearing at the Newport Jazz Festival, she booked into Synanon Rehab Center in Santa Monica, California. For the next three years she remained at the centre, trying to kick her habit and 'doing lots of cross-word puzzles'. When she reappeared in 1969, she recorded briefly for the Roulette label, including *Burnin' – Live at Freddie Jett's Pied Piper, LA*, and appeared at the Monterey Jazz Festival. The following year she appeared at Monterey again, this time with the Johnny Otis Show. While her perfor-mance with Otis could perhaps just have been a trip down memory lane, it revitalized her career.

In the aftermath of her Monterey appearances, she was signed to Creed Taylor's Kudu label in 1972. Cutting a string of albums such as *From a Whisper to a Scream* (1972), which has acquired the reputation of being one of the great lost classics, she at last began to realize the potential of which she had always been thought capable. Phillips's version of Gilbert O'Sullivan's maudlin 'Alone Again Naturally' (from her album of the same name) was a moving assertion of resigned independence, illustrating her ability to turn a song on its head. 'What a Difference a Day Makes' gave Phillips her last slice of commercial success with a stunning reworking of Dinah Washington's classic; going Top Twenty in the US, Top Ten in the UK and topping the R&B charts, it showed that her phrasing was as good as ever and if her voice was lacking some of its former power, this was more than compensated for by the sheer emotional drive of her delivery.

While these albums certainly achieved recognition commercially, critical acclaim was muted: jazz-rock and fusion had caused most jazz buffs to run for cover, adopting ever more conservative stances; soul was becoming ever more stylized and streamlined; and the blues was as mar-ginalized as ever, despite its growth in popularity among well-educated collegiate types. Esther nevertheless transcended most attempts at catego-rization through her ability to work alongside jazz musicians such as gui-tarists Joe Beck and Eric Gale, saxophonists Joe Farrell and Hank Crawford, and trumpeter Freddie Hubbard while imposing her own style upon the proceedings and never allowing herself to be outshone by her sidemen. Despite some reservations she at last began to acquire some of the acco-lades – considered by some to be long overdue – when in 1974/5 she picked up awards from *Rolling Stone* and *Ebony* magazines for Best R&B Vocalist and Blues Vocalist respectively, as well as another from the French Académie du Jazz.

However, the emergence of the 'disco' trend threw Phillips's career into decline once again as albums such as *Capricorn Princess* (1976) endeavoured to transform her into some kind of disco diva. Clearly unsuited to such a role, much of the advance she had made in the early 1970s was lost and, although her performances at blues and jazz festivals were well regarded, her albums signally failed to showcase her real abilities. In 1979 Taylor wrapped up Kudu and she was left without a contract. Signing with Mercury, she cut several albums including *All About Esther* (1981) and *Good Black Is Hard to Crack* (1982), but poor material and inappropriate production conspired to make her final albums ill-fitting memorials to her prodigious talent. On 7 August 1984, she died of liver failure in Los Angeles.

LITTLE WILLIE JOHN

While Esther Phillips was one of Otis's greatest discoveries, over the next five years he continued unearthing fresh talent such as Little Willie John, the Royals, Etta James, and Jackie Wilson. Although some of these discoveries were made as a scout for labels such as Don Robey's Peacock label in Houston or Syd Nathan's King label in Cincinnati, the talent shows were an especially fertile source with both Little Willie John and Jackie Wilson coming to Otis's attention in the early 1950s.

Little Willie John was a mere 14 when he was first spotted by Otis at a talent contest in Detroit. Originally known as John Davenport, he had sung with Count Basie's Orchestra and come under the scrutiny of trumpeter Dizzy Gillespie. But when Otis recommended John to Syd Nathan, Nathan was unimpressed at first and John started to record for Prize, cutting 'Mommy, What Happened to the Christmas Tree?' (1954). The following year Otis and Henry Glover got their way and John was signed to King. During his spell with King, Little Willie John cut a string of records that anticipated soul because they owed as much to the blues as to gospel. Despite an impassioned vocal style that was completely out of kilter with the contemporary trends, titles such as 'All Around the World' and 'Need Your Love So Bad' (1955), 'Fever' (1956), 'Talk to Me, Talk to Me' (1958), 'Tell It Like It Is' (1959), 'Let Them Talk', 'Heartbreak (It's Hurtin' Me)', and 'Sleep' (1960) showed the way ahead. In 1960 John's career literally hit the skids when he was arrested and imprisoned for murder after stabbing a railway official. His career was never to recover as he died on 26 May 1968 in Washington's Walla Walla Prison.

While Little Willie John succumbed to the exigencies of success in much the same way as Frankie Lymon or, indeed, Johnny Ace, he self-destructed prematurely: there is little doubt that John would have thrived in the 1960s because he was an instinctive all-rounder who could write and arrange as well as sing.

JACKIE WILSON

        Jackie Wilson was another Otis protégé, who suffered innu-
merable indignities culminating in his death in 1984, nine years after col-
lapsing on stage and hitting his head, which sent him into a coma from
which he never properly recovered. Despite an aura of tragedy that sur-
rounds both John and Wilson, each possessed an adaptable vocal style, but
Wilson spent his career shuffling from one creative environment to the
next. For Wilson the biggest tragedy was that he was unable to establish his
own musical direction and was always dependent on others.

        Born Jack Leroy Wilson on 9 June 1934 in Detroit, Wilson seemed to be
heading for a boxing career while at school. After winning the American
Amateur Golden Gloves Welterweight Title, his mother dissuaded him
from becoming a boxer, suggesting that he concentrate upon singing
instead. Inspired at first by the Ink Spots, the Mills Brothers, and Louis
Jordan, Wilson started entering talent shows, which he duly won. In 1951
Otis heard him one night and contacted Syd Nathan. While Nathan passed
on Wilson – as well as Little Willie John – he signed Billy Ward and the
Dominoes, but Ward was impressed enough with Wilson to take his
address and phone number. For the next couple of years Wilson and some
other guys, who would later join Hank Ballard in the Midnighters, played
in a gospel-style group called the Falcons (not to be confused with the
group Wilson Pickett later joined). In 1953 Wilson was summoned by
Ward, who enlisted him as a backing vocalist in the Dominoes before taking over as lead vocalist when Clyde McPhatter was fired. Wilson remained
with Ward until he left the Dominoes in 1956 to start a solo career.

        Making his debut at the Flame Club, he was courted by the owner, Al
Green, who became his manager. After cutting some demos, Wilson
secured a contract with the Decca subsidiary Brunswick. His first solo
record, 'Reet Petite' (1957), was written by a young writer and producer
called Berry Gordy, who was just beginning to make his way, and Tyrone
Carlo. It was the first of a number of hits for Wilson penned by that songwriting team; these included 'To Be Loved' and 'Lonely Teardrops' (1958),
and 'That's Why (I Love You So)' and 'I'll Be Satisfied' (1959). When Gordy
started to put Motown together, he stopped writing for Wilson and then the
death of Green meant a change of management, too, with Nat Tarnopol,
Green's former assistant, taking over.

        Throughout the early 1960s Tarnopol guided Wilson's career towards
the glitz of Vegas and Hollywood. The results were extraordinary, with
adaptations from classical pieces such as 'Night' from 'My Heart at Thy
Sweet Voice' from *Samson and Delilah* by Saint-Saëns, 'Alone at Last'
(1960) from the *Piano Concerto No. 1 in B flat* by Tchaikovsky and 'My
Empty Arms' (1961) from 'On With the Motley' from *I Pagliacci* by

Leoncavallo, as well as '(You Were Made For) All My Love' (1960), and 'Please Tell Me Why', 'I'm Comin' on Back to You', 'Years From Now', and 'The Greatest Hurt' (1961). Despite some of these extraordinary aberrations, he still managed to leaven the dross with some real stormers such as 'Doggin' Around' (1960) and 'Baby Workout' (1963). His stature as a performer was matched only by his profile as a sex symbol, the latter causing him to be shot in the stomach by a rampant fan, Juanita Jones, while he was trying to disarm her after she had broken into his New York apartment.

From 1963, apart from a duet with LaVern Baker, Wilson continued to record very ordinary material until being teamed in 1966 with writer and producer Carl Davis for 'Whispers' (1966). It showed what could be done when he had halfway decent material. Two more aberrations followed before he recorded '(Your Love Keeps Lifting Me) Higher and Higher' (1967). The following year he recorded *Manufacturers of Soul*, with Count Basie; it included versions of 'For Your Precious Love' and 'Chain Gang'. Despite the purity of his vocals, Wilson was still pitched from one producer to the next with the result that his final success was 'I Get the Sweetest Feeling' (1968). In the years after his death, records such as 'Reet Petite' and 'I Get the Sweetest Feeling' were reissued with spectacular results.

ETTA JAMES

If many of Otis's protégés have failed to endure through either ill-fortune or ill-health, Etta James is the embodiment of the resilience necessary for survival because, in 1995, she was storming up the UK charts with 'I Just Want to Make Love to You', as rambunctious a slab of R&B as one could ever hope to find. Certainly it had got its exposure courtesy of a Pepsi commercial, but it served as an accurate reminder of the essential durability of R&B in its purest form.

James was born Jamesetta Hawkins in Los Angeles on 25 January 1938. Now there are two versions of how Otis discovered her. One has it that she was spotted by Otis while she was singing with a group called Peaches; the other – slightly less plausible and so probably the more likely scenario – has it that Otis was due to perform at the Fillmore in San Francisco. He was asleep in his hotel room when his manager, Bardu Ali, called him to say that there was this young girl who was insisting that she sing for Otis immediately. The upshot of it was that James turned up at the hotel and sang for Otis, who was sufficiently impressed to get out of bed, get dressed, and go off in search of James's mother because Etta was still a minor. Returning to Los Angeles, James took up residence at the Otis abode where she lived as one of the family.

She was signed by the Biharis to Modern, cutting 'Roll With Me Henry' (1955), her answer to Hank Ballard's 'Work With Me Annie'. Although 'Roll With Me Henry' was retitled 'The Wallflower' and Georgia Gibbs covered it as 'Dance With Me Henry', scoring a million-seller with it into the bargain, 'The Wallflower' established Etta James in the front line of R&B vocalists. It was only temporary, for after cutting titles such as 'Good Rockin' Daddy', her contract with Modern was allowed to expire. In 1959 she was signed to the Chess subsidiary Argo. Although James is incredibly scathing about the Chess Brothers, she notched up hits such as 'All I Could Do Was Cry' and 'My Dearest Darling' (1960), 'Trust in Me' and 'Don't Cry Baby' (1961), 'Something's Got a Hold on Me' and 'Stop the Wedding' (1962), and 'Pushover' (1963). These performances show James at the top of her powers, combining the earthy grit of R&B with the raw emotional commitment of soul – as it was now being described.

During the mid-1960s the hits came to an end, and her increasing reliance upon heroin didn't help. In November 1967 she was packed off to the Fame studios in Muscle Shoals where, with producer Rick Hall, she recorded classics such as 'I'd Rather Go Blind' and 'Tell Mama' (1967), and 'Steal Away' and 'Security' (1968).

After the death of Leonard Chess in 1969, and the subsequent sale of the Chess label, her recording contract was allowed to slide and she didn't cut another record until 1973, when she was teamed with producer Gabriel Mekler for the Grammy-nominated album *Etta James*. Recording material by writers such as Randy Newman, much of the former fire seemed to have been quenched. Even a 1978 collaboration, *Deep in the Night*, with Aretha Franklin's former producer Jerry Wexler failed to rekindle her irrepressible urgency. In recent years she has reverted to type, banishing any suggestion of the sophistication she might have picked up along the way by cutting albums such as *Changes* (1978) with producer Allen Toussaint, and *Seven Year Itch* (1989) and *Sticking to My Guns* (1990) with Barry Beckett producing. More appropriately still, she cut a live album, *Blues in the Night* (1986), in Los Angeles with Eddie 'Cleanhead' Vinson, Shuggie Otis, Brother Jack McDuff, and Paul Humphrey. While the glitches still appear from time to time, James is a continuing reminder of what R&B is all about.

JOHNNY OTIS – THE LATER YEARS

Although Otis's energies were split between talent scouting and working as a disc jockey, an accident with a chainsaw had resulted in the partial loss of two fingers and paralysis of the hand. This meant that Otis could no longer drum and so he took up the piano instead. Although the arrival of Elvis Presley had rendered R&B passé in the eyes of many record labels – who immediately devoted their energies to the discovery of young white kids who could sing – for Otis it was business as usual and he just continued doing what he had been doing all along because, as he said to Arnold Shaw, 'rock 'n' roll was a direct outgrowth of R&B'. In 1956 he set up his own label, Dig. Although Dig failed to register nationally, Otis maintained his reputation for delivering authentic slabs of R&B with titles such as 'Midnight Creeper' and 'Driftin' Blues'. It also illustrated his willingness to adapt vaudeville standards such as 'Show Me the Way to Go Home' to his own hard-driving style. The following year he linked up with the Capitol label and scored international hits with 'Ma! He's Making Eyes at Me' (1957), 'Bye Bye Baby'', 'Crazy Country Hop,' and 'Willie and the Hand Jive' (1958), and 'Casting My Spell' (1959). Despite the obvious novelty element to these hits, they conformed to the strong humorous connotation that R&B had engendered in its heyday when Louis Jordan had been setting the charts afire, and Otis still retained the revue-style format with his band, featured vocalist Marie Adams, and vocal backing from the Three Tons of Joy. The fact that Otis's version of 'Ma! He's Making Eyes at Me' became a big hit in the UK seemed to confirm that serendipitously he had managed to align himself with the skiffle boom. This was not lost on Cliff Richard who, in 1960, while trying to reassert his rock 'n' roll credentials, covered 'Willie and the Hand Jive'.

Throughout the 1960s, Otis continued touring, as well as cutting the occasional side for the King label, but gradually his interest in politics began to take up more of his time through campaigning for the Democratic Party. By the time he had finished working with the Democrats, R&B and rock 'n' roll had been superseded in the affections of young blacks by soul – an overt synthesis of gospel and R&B – while the white derivative of rock 'n' roll was now being propagated by rock bands. Still based in the Watts district of Los Angeles, Otis published his autobiography, *Listen to the Lambs*, in which he propounded the reason for the emergence of soul as the principal expression for black artists: 'soul music became so black and gospel-tinged that it couldn't easily be copied' by white artists.

By 1969 Otis returned and recorded *Cold Shot*, featuring his son Shuggie on guitar, for the Kent label. Many critics have claimed that this is just a pale imitation and only of historical interest to students of the genre. But here Otis was reviving a format that he had created almost single-handedly and this revue style of package had been utilized with considerable success by fellow former talent scout and near contemporary Ike Turner, with the Ike and Tina Turner Show at the end of 1960s playing to packed arenas across the US and Europe – often opening for such prestigious white rock bands as the Rolling Stones. Similarly James Brown, the Chambers Brothers, and the Isley Brothers had developed revue-style shows that were attracting young white audiences as a consequence of being booked on to the flourishing festival and college circuits. It was a logical extension, then, that in 1970 Otis was booked to appear at the Monterey Jazz Festival.

While the sociological implications cannot be ignored – with most of the audience aged between 15 and 25 and white – the purpose of his appearance was to create 'a meeting ground where ages, races, and backgrounds coalesce, where grooving together is all that matters'. To achieve that end, Otis assembled a line-up that spanned the generations: alto saxophonist and shouter Eddie 'Cleanhead' Vinson contributed 'Kidney Stew' and 'Cleanhead's Blues'; vocalist and band leader Roy Milton performed 'R. M. Blues' and 'Baby You Don't Know'; the great Kansas City shouter Big Joe Turner chipped in with 'I Got a Gal' and 'Plastic Man'; Ivory Joe Hunter offered a stripped-down reprise of 'Since I Met You Baby'; Roy Brown's sharp reappraisal of 'Good Rockin' Tonight' retained all of the verve and éclat of his original almost 25 years earlier; Little Esther Phillips opened fresh vistas for herself with 'Cry Me a River Blues' and the medley 'Little Esther's Blues', featuring 'Blowtop Blues', 'T-Bone Blues', and 'Jelly Jelly', and as a consequence her career was revived by a fresh contract with Creed Taylor's Kudu label; guitarist Pee Wee Crayton revived Guitar Slim's epochal 'The Things I Used to Do'; and trombonist Gene 'The Mighty Flea' Connors justified the description of 'The Fastest Tongue in the West' with the self-penned 'Preacher's Blues'. Despite the profusion of established performers moving towards their twilight, Otis introduced new talent with Margie Evans and Delmar 'Mighty Mouth' Evans, as well as his son Shuggie Otis, who had started a solo career that year with *Here Comes Shuggie Otis*.

Although it is easy to wax lyrical about a revival that took place as long ago as 1970, the Johnny Otis Show's performance was a vital ingredient in the rehabilitation of R&B as a contemporary form alongside soul, acoustic country blues, and electric urban blues. It set in motion a series of projects – more often than not instigated by white college graduates – that gradually evolved into well established, financially secure independent record labels such as Rounder, Delmark, Alligator, Watermelon, and Malaco.

In 1974 Otis launched his own label, Blues Spectrum. Although it wasn't a great commercial success, its purpose was to revive interest in artists associated with R&B's halcyon years, such as Louis Jordan, Charles Brown, Big Joe Turner, Pee Wee Crayton, and Joe Liggins. While Otis sustained the momentum through the 1970s by touring, he recorded little until he was signed by Bruce Iglauer in 1981 to the Alligator label. The resulting *The New Johnny Otis Show With Shuggie Otis* (1982) was nominated for a Grammy award, but his touring decreased as he concentrated instead on his post of pastor at the Landmark Community Church in Los Angeles. Unable to distance himself for too long from perfoming or recording, he returned with *Spirit of the Black Territory Bands* (1992), on which he paid tribute to the 'jump' bands of the 1940s. Although Otis has never been accorded the respect that is his due, today in the mid-1990s his influence is still felt in UK-based bands such as King Pleasure and the Biscuit Boys and the Jools Holland Rhythm & Blues Orchestra.

IKE TURNER

While Otis got his first breaks on the West Coast, another young man from Clarksdale, Mississippi – Ike Turner – was starting to pay his dues in John Lee Hooker's birthplace. And Muddy Waters'. And Eddie Boyd's. Although Turner was some ten years younger than Otis – almost of another generation – they shared a common goal: to capitalize on the emergent independent record labels. Otis may have been far more altruistic than Turner in his motivation, but both were born to organize and both had the eyes and the ears for spotting raw talent.

Ike Turner was born on 5 November 1931, in Clarksdale, Mississippi. From an early age Ike let it be known that he was the sleekest, coolest dude on the block; by the time he was 18 he was working as a DJ on WROX. Just to make sure nobody made any mistake about his coolness, he formed his first band, the Kings of Rhythm, while he was still at school with Willie Kizart (guitar), Raymond Hill (tenor saxophone), Willie Sims (drums), and Johnny O'Neal (vocals). Although Ike had been taught the piano by Pinetop Perkins, boogie-woogie ace and Sonny Boy Williamson's accompanist, Turner had been monitoring the rapid rise to fame of fellow Clarksdale resident Muddy Waters. Turner felt that if a former cotton-picker could get that far, well, there was no reason why he – a far nattier dresser than Muddy – couldn't outstrip him. There was a problem, though. Johnny O'Neal had just recently left the Kings of Rhythm for the bright lights of Cincinnati and a beckoning contract with the King label. At this point saxophonist Jackie Brenston entered the picture.

JACKIE BRENSTON

Brenston was born on 15 August 1930, in Clarksdale, Mississippi. After rudimentary schooling, Brenston lied about his age to enlist in the army in 1944. In 1947 he returned to Clarksdale and met a local musician, Jesse Flowers, who taught Brenston as much as he knew about the horn and gave him a few more practical tips about drinking. With O'Neal out of the picture, Turner thought that Brenston might just be the man to fill the vacancy so Brenston was recruited and Turner and the Kings of Rhythm travelled up to Memphis to Sam Phillips's Sun Studios at 706 Union Avenue. Basing 'Rocket 88' on Jimmy Liggins's 'Cadillac Boogie', Brenston openly admitted that the two songs were essentially the same and that all he had done was to substitute 'Cadillac' with the new Oldsmobile 'Rocket 88'. Although the song was a blatant rip-off, the arrangement was dramatically different with Willie Kizart's cranked up electric guitar and Ike Turner's rippling triplets on the piano anticipating later rock 'n' rollers like Eddie Cochran and Little Richard: the latter's intro to 'Good Golly Miss Molly' implies something more than mere coincidence at work. That day the group cut three further songs including 'Come Back Where You Belong'. However, when Sam Phillips leased the sides to Leonard Chess for release by the recently formed Chess label, Ike Turner was not best pleased when 'Rocket 88' – credited to Jackie Brenston and His Delta Cats – became the soaraway R&B hit of 1951. The follow-up, 'My Real Gone Rocket', failed to sell and Turner moved from piano to guitar so that he could assert his role as leader of the group from centre stage.

Despite the success of 'Rocket 88', Brenston left Turner and played saxophone in Lowell Fulson's band from 1953 until 1955, before returning to the Kings of Rhythm. But Brenston had gone back to his first love – alcohol – and although Turner was fiercely autocratic, fining band members for drinking, Brenston seemed to know that his five minutes of fame had passed, even though his performance on 'Gonna Take My Chance' for the Federal label espoused something entirely different. Throughout the late 1950s Brenston continued to pay obeisance to alcohol, drinking anything he could get his hands on. Occasionally the alcoholic haze would be punctured by a shaft of light, sufficient to rouse him from his torpor and he would make another stab at stardom. In 1960 such an opportunity arose in the wake of Ike and Tina Turner's hit, 'A Fool in Love', for the Sue label and Brenston was given the chance to cut his own single, 'Trouble Up the Road' and 'You Ain't the One'. It failed to generate much enthusiasm and, finally, in 1962 Brenston made his adieus to Turner and tottered off into the twilight of his career.

The following year he rallied once again for his parting shot, this time with the Earl Hooker band: 'Want You to Rock Me' and 'Down in My Heart' would have been all right if they had been recorded ten years earlier, but as a one-off attempt to break back into the limelight, they sounded like a man living on yesterday's dreams. Brenston returned to Clarksdale and spent the next 16 years living from drink to drink until his death on 15 December 1979, at an Army Veterans' Hospital in Memphis. Despite his inglorious end, it should never be forgotten that as a consequence of 'Rocket 88' rock 'n' roll and the iconography of the automobile were inextricably linked.

Although Turner had been seriously miffed that he could be upstaged by anyone, he was adroit enough to realize that perseverance paid dividends and with just a little luck he couldn't fail. While working as a talent scout for the Bihari Brothers' Modern label, Turner started to work with B. B. King, producing and playing piano on King's 1950 chart-topper 'Three O'Clock Blues', and 'Howlin' Wolf'. Furthermore, the sessions at Sam Phillips's Sun Studios had enabled him to do some scouting for Phillips as well as the Biharis, and because Phillips was leasing material to the Chess label in Chicago, Turner was gradually building up his reputation there as well: 'I travelled round Mississippi with a tape machine in trunk of my car,' Ike told *The Observer* columnist Robert Chalmers in 1995, 'stopping at pool halls and saloons. Junior Parker, Roscoe Gordon, Elmore James – I recorded all those people'. In the meantime he put out his own records, often under pseudonyms such as 'Lover Boy ' or with his wife, Bonnie, as Ike and Bonnie. Early sides such as 'The Way You Used to Treat Me' – a reworking of Guitar Slim's 'The Things I Used to Do' – were credited to Lover Boy but the ferocity of the guitar-playing was unmistakably Ike, doing his damnedest to outshine the original.

TINA TURNER

In 1955 Turner moved north from Memphis and settled in St Louis, signing with the Federal label – a subsidiary of King. Despite the change of location, Ike continued scouting and producing until in 1957 he met Annie Mae Bullock while he and the Kings of Rhythm were performing at a club in East St Louis. The how's and why's of their meeting has become a part of the folklore of rock 'n' roll, attesting on one hand to Ike's intrinsic boorishness and, on the other, how a young woman from Nutbush – or small-town Nowheresville – could be plucked from an audience and turned into a star overnight: 'I was a little girl from Tennessee,' Tina recalled in 1993. 'This man [Ike Turner] had a big house in St Louis, and he had a Cadillac, money, diamonds – all of the stuff that a different class of blacks would look up to'. Such is the stuff of dreams.

Recording first as Little Ann, soon Annie Mae was assimilated into Ike's band. By 1958 she had become pregnant by one of the members of Ike's band. The following year she became pregnant by Ike and, with the characteristic bombast of all putative Svengalis, Ike changed Annie Mae's name to Tina without consulting her. By now the Ike and Tina Turner Show was beginning to establish itself across the US and when they scored their first national hit with 'A Fool in Love' (1960) the die was cast. While Tina, supported by the Ikettes, was the star of the show, Ike – embittered by the number of times he had been ripped off by record companies – made sure that the band was always touring. More records for more labels followed, but it was Tina's voice on songs such as 'It's Gonna Work Out Fine' (1961), and 'Poor Fool' and 'I Idolize You' (1962) and the overt sexuality of her stage show that built the band's reputation. Such was their popularity that even the Ikettes, which included at various times in its line-up P. P. Arnold, Bonnie Bramlett, and Claudia Linnear, had two hit singles in their own right: 'I'm Blue (The Gong-Gong Song)' (1962) and 'Peaches and Cream' (1965).

The band achieved international success at last in 1966, when they were enlisted by producer Phil Spector to record some songs by Brill Building writers Jeff Barry and Ellie Greenwich. The single from the sessions, 'River Deep, Mountain High' (1966), was a big hit all over the world, yet failed to register in the US – much to Spector's intense irritation. However, the band were chosen to support the Rolling Stones on their forthcoming US tour. The decision highlighted the band's growing popularity among young white audiences and enabled Ike to start getting the band booked into Las Vegas and into the Fillmore Auditorium on the West Coast.

In 1969 they signed with the Blue Thumb label, a subsidiary of Minit, and recorded *Outta Season* and *The Hunter*. The following year they covered Lennon and McCartney's 'Come Together' and Sly and the Family Stone's 'I Wanna Take You Higher' (1970), and then John Fogerty's 'Proud Mary' (1971). While all these sides had taken the band – superficially at least – further from Ike's roots in R&B, the format of the stage show remained resolutely in step with the original revues: even Ike's vainglorious asides to the audience recalled the interplay between Cab Calloway and Louis Jordan. And Tina's voice was still able to match any of her contemporaries for its innate soulfulness or sheer power: an early example of this range is best illustrated by her first solo offering – a country album entitled *Tina Turns the Country On* (1974). Powerfully suggestive of influences such as Ivory Joe Hunter, Tina shows a side of her that is not often alluded to as it fails to conform to the universal perception of her.

On the domestic front, the marriage, which had not taken place until 1962, was falling apart. Ike's womanizing was not the real problem for Tina, but the beatings and the drugs were. Finally, in July 1976, after flying from Los Angeles to Fort Worth, Tina was beaten up once again by Ike. That was it, she was out of it. In the years since the duo split, Ike has always maintained that it was his vision that made Tina the star she became. Despite periodic attempts to relaunch his career, Ike has spent most of his time entangled with the law for a variety of offences, including income-tax evasion, drug violations, and even the rigging of electronic devices to avoid paying for use of the telephone. Tina, on the other hand, has gone from strength to strength.

For the next four years she supported herself and her four children by playing the cabaret circuit and cutting *Rough* (1979). In 1980 she met the Australian promoter Roger Davis, who started to book her into rather more salubrious venues than those to which she had become accustomed; consequently he became her manager. In 1981 she played support for the Rolling Stones and was asked by Ian Craig Marsh and Martyn Ware of the UK electro-synth band Heaven 17 to record a cover version of the Temptations' 'Ball of Confusion' for the album *Music of Quality and Distinction* for the British Electric Foundation. Her participation in the project had the desired effect, and she was signed by Capitol. Since *Private Dancer* (1983), Tina has sold over thirty million records and become established internationally as one of the most dynamic solo performers of the rock 'n' roll era. Furthermore, she has ventured beyond the celebrity of rock 'n' roll to develop another career as an actress appearing in the film *Mad Max 3: Beyond the Thunderdome* (1985).

While her life story was recounted in her autobiography, *I, Tina,* which was published in 1985 and turned into a movie as *What's Love Got to Do With It?* in 1993, Tina remains above and beyond her own mythology whereas Ike has become a bit part player in that mythology, although he remains openly dismissive of Tina's ability, proclaiming at every opportunity that it was he who made her. Since his release from prison, Ike has regularly spoken of an imminent comeback: whether his reputation has become so tarnished that no one in his right mind will touch him or he has lost the plot beyond recall – that comeback has not been forthcoming. Whatever Ike does in the future is not all that important because the contribution he made to rock 'n' roll in its infancy remains incalculable: he played dirty, badass music and he endeavoured to live it as well. Many others before and since have tried to subsume themselves in the spirit of rock 'n' roll, and not even Johnny Otis has managed to become so closely identified with it.

chapter seven

GUITAR MEN

WHILE VOCAL STYLES AND LYRICAL CONTENT were funda-mental ingredients of R&B, it would not have become the transcendent style of the rock era had it not been for the inven-tion of the electric guitar. With that single step, the blues was turned around for good. Although the industrial heartlands of Chicago and Detroit were a magnet for migrant workers from the cotton fields, the promise of a putative equality was as enticing. However, it was not to be Chicago to demonstrate the early signs of R&B; that honour went to Los Angeles for, although the shipyards offered copious employment – most certainly after the US entered the Second World War – Los Angeles was the country's entertainment capital with its flourishing film industry, a host of independent record labels, and a club circuit to die for. And so not only from the cotton fields but also from the wide open spaces of Texas and the Louisiana bayous came a tide of migrant musicians keen to try their luck.

LONNIE JOHNSON

At the heart of this lay the examples set by both Charlie Christian and Eddie Durham, who illustrated just what could be done with the electric guitar, but early bluesmen such as Lonnie Johnson demonstrat-ed that the guitar need not be just a time-keeper. Playing the six-string and twelve-string guitar, Johnson's sophisticated musical vocabulary and man-ual dexterity enabled him to play blues and jazz with a greater degree of expression than probably anyone before him had achieved. This supreme proficiency won the attention of jazz men such as Duke Ellington and Louis Armstrong, and resulted in masterful duets with Eddie Lang, who appeared under the pseudonym of Blind Willie Dunn, between 1928 and 1929. Johnson also contributed a delightful solo to the Chocolate Dandies' version of Hoagy Carmichael's 'Stardust'. After touring with Bessie Smith, he slipped out of sight, playing on a Mississippi riverboat with Charlie Heath's Orchestra and then with Putney Dandrich's band in Cleveland. In 1937, now based in Chicago, Johnson started to work with drummer Baby Dodds at The Three Deuces when he got the chance to record some sides for Decca and then Bluebird. While 'He's a Jelly Roll Baker' for Bluebird was clearly in the jump tradition of Louis Jordan, Johnson's resounding success was 'Tomorrow Night' for the King label in 1948. Still deemed one of the definitive R&B records of the 1940s, it illustrated how malleable the blues could be in the right hands. During the 1950s he worked as a hotel janitor before resuming his career in the 1960s and settling in Toronto, whence he toured extensively on the club and festival circuits until shortly before his death in 1970.

EDDIE DURHAM

While Lonnie Johnson made his mark as a soloist, Eddie Durham integrated the electric guitar into the modus operandi of the Jimmie Lunceford band with 'Hittin' the Bottle' in 1935. As Leonard Feather was to note, it was 'probably the first recorded example of any form of guitar amplification'. Durham was born in San Marcos, Texas, on 19 August 1906, and started his career as a trombonist in Lunceford's band until, in 1935, he spotted the potential for an electric guitar by adding a resonator, which enabled him to play at a much greater volume. This in turn had a profound effect on Charlie Christian, who promptly procured himself a Gibson ES-150. Indeed, Durham claims full credit for introducing Christian to the electric guitar in 1937, 'I don't think Christian had ever seen a guitar with an amplifier until he met me'.

With hindsight there is something slightly paradoxical in a stylist of Charlie Christian's evident calibre becoming enthused at the prospect of cranking up the volume. Be that as it may, Durham's contribution was significantly different from Christian's, for Durham was primarily a composer who happened to play the guitar. It was in this capacity that he joined Count Basie's band in 1937, assembling trademark compositions such as 'Topsy', 'Out the Window', and 'Time Out'.

T-BONE WALKER

While Durham might technically have been the originator, it was Christian and one Aaron 'T-Bone' Walker who changed the vocabulary of the guitar. Indeed, through Walker's influence the electric guitar became one of the most emotive and evocative vehicles for musical expression, with his single-note soloing techniques and sophisticated chording illustrating his debt to jazz while remaining firmly grounded in the blues.

Walker was born on 28 May 1910 in Linden, Texas, but moved to Dallas when he was two. After learning the guitar and falling under the spell of family friends Blind Lemon Jefferson and Big Bill Broonzy, he toured the south-west in a medicine show as a tap-dancer and recorded a single, 'Wichita Fall Blues' and 'Trinity River Blues', for Columbia in 1929 as Oak Cliff T-Bone. After touring with Cab Calloway, Ma Rainey, and Ida Cox, and playing with Lawson Brook in Fort Worth, he moved to Los Angeles in 1935; incidentally, Charlie Christian took over Walker's position with Brook. In 1937 Walker joined Les Hite's Orchestra and for the next two years they toured solidly, playing from coast to coast and culminating with some recordings that included 'T-Bone Blues' (1940) for the New York-based Varsity label. Dramatically at odds with Hite's prevailing big-band style, this recording had the jump-style beat that would become synonymous with the embryonic sound of R&B. With that in the bag, Walker left Hite in Chicago and headed back to the West Coast, where he took up the electric guitar and put together his own outfit. More touring followed until, in 1942, Walker settled down to cut 'Mean Old World' and 'I Got a Break, Baby' for the fledgling Capitol label. With these sides, Walker put the blues on the map in Los Angeles for, although black artists had been recording in Los Angeles for many years, their records were aimed at a white crossover audience. Walker broke that particularly divisive mould.

As the war years came to a close and recording restrictions were lifted, other guitarists followed in Walker's footsteps. While his vocal style was easy and conversational, it made no attempt to utilize the cadences and patterns of the standard blues delivery. Furthermore, Walker's incisive and ringing guitar lines offered inspiration to the other youngsters now flocking to the coast. While Walker remained a big draw on the club circuit, his recording career faltered. A spell with the Chicago-based Rhumboogie label, where he cut 'I'm Still in Love With You' and 'Sail on Little Girl', failed to sustain the earlier momentum and, if anything, showed him in slightly regressive mood. In 1946 that all changed when he started to record for the Black and White label.

Owned by Paul Reiner, the label had started to operate at the end of the war and had hit paydirt with 'Open the Door, Richard', a novelty item confected by tenor man Jack McVea and comedians Dusty Fletcher and John

Mason, under the auspices of a youthful A&R man named Ralph Bass. With Bass at his back, Walker set about changing the face of contemporary music. From these sessions issued a steady stream of gems such as 'Don't Leave Me Baby', 'T-Bone Shuffle', and 'Call It Stormy Monday, But Tuesday's Just As Bad'; and even 'Bobby Sox Baby', which could be construed as a notional attempt to cross over, was entrenched in the R&B tradition. Fronting a band that comprised three horns and a rhythm section that swung as effectively as any big band, Walker's flamboyant showmanship – playing his jewel-encrusted guitar behind his head, while doing the splits – provided a role model for others such as Guitar Slim, Johnny 'Guitar' Watson, and Jimi Hendrix.

Throughout the late 1940s and early 1950s Walker maintained a schedule that was jaw-dropping and severely debilitating, which resulted in long-term poor health brought on by a stomach ulcer. Meanwhile, Black and White went to the wall; Reiner had thought that all records sold over five hundred thousand copies, as 'Open the Door, Richard' had done, and just kept on issuing them until he went bankrupt. Despite moving on to Imperial, Walker still managed to keep pace, working with T. J. Fowler's band out of Detroit and Dave Bartholomew's outfit in New Orleans, while retaining his own band in Los Angeles. In 1955 he was hospitalized and when he got out, rock 'n' roll had danced in. Newly signed to Atlantic, however, he eventually cut the immaculate *T-Bone Blues* (1959) with tenor man Plas Johnson and jazz guitarist Barney Kessel.

Throughout the 1960s Walker continued to champion his brand of blues in Europe with visits to the first American Folk Blues Festival in 1962, then again in 1965 and in 1966 with jazz impresario Norman Granz's 'Jazz at the Philharmonic'. In 1968 he made another visit to the festival and tied in recording dates with the French Black & Blue label, cutting *Feeling the Blues*, which was followed by the Grammy-award-winning *Good Feelin'* (1970) with African multi-instrumentalist Manu Dibango.

Curiously, in the UK Walker received fewer plaudits than his Chicago-based counterparts such as Muddy Waters, Sonny Boy Williamson, and Jimmy Reed, who had long been lionized by British groups such as the Rolling Stones, John Mayall's Bluesbreakers, and the Yardbirds. It was left to groups such as the Graham Bond Organisation and Georgie Fame and the Blue Flames to maintain his profile. Even so, despite Walker's frequent dalliances with European operations, his stock in the US remained high, cutting albums such as *Stormy Monday Blues* (1967) and *Funky Town* (1968) for ABC's subsidiary Bluesway. In 1973, with Jerry Leiber and Mike Stoller at the controls, Walker recorded *Very Rare* for Reprise. Today this particular waxing is as rare as hen's teeth, which is a travesty because not only did it contain contributions from jazz men such as trumpeter Dizzy Gillespie, saxophonists Al Cohn, Zoot Sims, and Gerry Mulligan, and flautist Herbie Mann, but also it went some way to defining the essential differences in perception and interpretation between the Los Angeles brand of R&B and its more famous Chicagoan counterpart: Chicago-based musicians tended to align themselves with rock musicians such as the Rolling Stones and the Steve Miller Band. *Very Rare* was another milestone, though, for in 1974 Walker stopped touring as a result of a stroke and the following year he died of bronchial pneumonia.

LOWELL FULSON

The writer of a fistful of R&B classics – 'Everyday I Have the Blues', 'Three O'Clock Blues', and 'Reconsider Baby' – Lowell Fulson breasted the country blues and R&B eras with a basic guitar style that enabled him to accompany himself or to be backed by a full band. While his guitar work was derived from T-Bone Walker's style, his malleability enabled Fulson to sustain a career through the rock 'n' roll era when many of his contemporaries either went into retirement or just sought alternative employment.

Born on 31 March 1921, in Tulsa, Oklahoma, Fulson was raised on gospel. In 1926 his father was killed in an accident and so Fulson and his mother moved to an area between Atoka and Wopanockee, which was inhabited by a mixture of Blacks and Choctaw Indians. By the late 1920s Fulson had started to sing hymns in church and tap-dance at local school functions. As his grandfather played the violin and various uncles played the guitar, Fulson started to learn to play as well although, as he recalled years later to Arnold Shaw, his uncles 'wouldn't let me play their instruments if I got them out of tune, so the first thing I had to learn was to tune it properly'. Having picked up the guitar, Fulson expanded his repertoire to include country and western songs, before moving on to the blues of Blind Lemon Jefferson and Peetie Wheatstraw.

In 1938 Fulson moved to Ada, Oklahoma, and started to play for white audiences in clubs. While the songs he sang were romantic ballads such as 'Sunrise Serenade' and 'Silvery Moon', they showed his adaptability. This was revealed to even greater effect when he moved on to a ten-piece string band that specialized in bluegrass. The following year Fulson married and made some sort of attempt to put music behind him, but after a spell working around the cotton fields and as a short-order cook in a bus terminal in Texas, he continued to play bars, dances and holes-in-the-wall with the legendary Texas Alexander among others.

After the US was drawn into the Second World War in 1941, Fulson was drafted into the army and sent to Camp Shoemaker in Los Angeles. For the next three years until his discharge Fulson worked as a butcher before joining the USS *Wayne* and being shipped out to Guam where he played in the base band. With a line-up of alto and tenor sax, trumpet, trombone, piano, and guitar, the band's repertoire featured popular hits such as Louis Jordan's 'Caldonia', traditional blues, and Fulson's own compositions.

On his return to the US, Fulson returned to catering but quickly tired of it and announced to his wife that he was moving to Los Angeles to pursue his musical career. Arriving in Oakland in 1946, he hooked up with label-owner Bob Geddins whom he had first met while stationed on the West Coast. Working at first with his brother Martin, who was also a guitarist, Fulson cut titles such as 'Cryin' Blues' and 'Miss Katie Lee Blues' (1946) and 'Three O'Clock Blues' (1948). By this time he had come to the attention of Jack Lauderdale, the owner of the Swing Time label, who put him together with pianist and arranger Lloyd Glenn. Together they cut 'Everyday I Have the Blues' (1949), 'Blue Shadows' and 'Lonesome Christmas' (1950), 'I'm a Nite Owl' and 'Guitar Shuffle' (1951), and 'Ride Until the Sun Goes Down', 'Blues Come Rollin' In', and 'Juke Box Shuffle' (1952).

Patterning his vocal style on Jimmy Rushing and his guitar work on T-Bone Walker and Pee Wee Crayton, Fulson was soon in a position to leave his job at the shipyards and start touring locally with a band that comprised Ray Charles, who also recorded for Swing Time, Earl Brown on alto, Tiny Wills on rhythm guitar, Billy Hadnott on bass, and Bob Harvey on drums. Because both 'Everyday I Have the Blues' and 'Blue Shadows' were such big hits, Fulson started to tour the country. Taking in prestigious venues such as the Regal in Chicago, the Howard in Washington, and the Apollo in New York, Fulson augmented his band with two trumpets and baritone and tenor sax and started to play alongside groups such as the Clovers and the Dominoes.

After Charles left the band in 1952, Fulson left Swing Time and recorded briefly in New Orleans for the Aladdin label with the nucleus of musicians who would later join Guitar Slim. However, he moved on to join the Chess brothers' Checker label, where he scored his biggest hit with 'Reconsider Baby' (1955), now a popular classic that has been covered by dozens of others including Elvis Presley. Fulson remained with Chess for the next eight years, cutting a string of hits that included 'Check Yourself' and 'Lonely Hours' (1955) and 'Trouble, Trouble', 'Tollin' Blues', and 'Baby Please Don't Go' (1956). Despite cutting these sides for a Chicago-based label, Fulson retained the swinging big-band vibe characteristic of the West Coast bluesmen and did most of his sessions for the label in LA or Dallas. Indeed the Dallas session that produced 'Reconsider Baby' was overseen by producer Stan Lewis, who would later cut *In a Heavy Bag* (1968) at Muscle Shoals with Fulson and session musicians Jimmy Johnson (guitar), Roger Hawkins (drums), David Hood (bass), and Barry Beckett (keyboards) for the Shreveport-based Jewel label.

After leaving Chess in 1962, Fulson signed with Kent and responded to the invasion of British beat groups by touring Europe frequently and developing a harder style that was as soulful as it was funky. Although blues aficionados found little to admire in hits such as 'Black Nights' (1965) and 'Tramp' (1966), the latter – which he wrote with Jimmy McCracklin – was covered by Otis Redding and Carla Thomas, giving him a degree of financial security.

Fulson is still working to this day and, despite a lull in his activities during the 1970s, he has issued albums with daunting frequency. While many of these have been for minor European labels, *Think Twice Before You Speak* (1984) for JSP and, then, *It's a Good Day* (1988), *Hold On* (1992), with long-time chum Jimmy McCracklin, and *Them Update Blues* (1995) for the Rounder group of labels have shown that Fulson's capacity to turn out high-quality songs such as 'Room With a View' and 'Working Man' is undimmed. Furthermore his guitar work remains economical and his vocals are still refreshingly luxurious. As a footnote it is gratifying to see that he has survived long enough to enjoy some of the accolades that are now being bestowed upon him as he is now a regular recipient of W. C. Handy Awards.

PEE WEE CRAYTON

As with Lowell Fulson, Pee Wee Crayton managed to live long enough to see his fortunes improve radically in the late 1960s and again in the early 1980s just before his death in 1985. Still absurdly undervalued, though, Crayton was a key figure in the chain that started with Charlie Christian and T-Bone Walker and culminated with the formation of a West Coast style of R&B that was totally distinct from its Chicagoan counterpart. Born Connie Curtis Crayton in Liberty Hill, Texas, in 1914, Crayton took up the banjo and ukelele as a child before hearing Christian's records and taking up the guitar. Following a similar route to that of his later mentor, T-Bone Walker, who taught him the electric guitar, Crayton gravitated to the munitions factories in the Bay area of San Francisco. There he fell in with John Collins, who was playing guitar with Nat 'King' Cole, before starting to play the local club circuit, when he was recruited to join Ivory Joe Hunter's band. With Hunter he made his recording debut on Ivory Joe's own Pacific label before moving to 4-Star and cutting his first solo sides. These were unissued until he moved on to the Bihari Brothers' Modern label.

At Modern he began to show his potential, cutting sides in a variety of styles from jump blues to ballads, and from slow blues to jazzy instrumentals. Initially Crayton was backed by just a rhythm section, but that was sufficient to show his mettle on 'Blues After Hours' and Walker's ballad 'I'm

Still in Love With You'. From the same sessions he cut 'Rock Island Blues' and 'Bounce Pee Wee', augmented by a handful of session musicians. By the time the next sessions came around, Walker was using horns to punctuate the rhythm, and his solos on titles such as 'Texas Hop', 'Central Avenue Blues', and 'I Love You So' interpolated the harmonic inventiveness of Walker while adhering to the tried and tested formulae of R&B.

After four years Crayton moved on to the Aladdin label and thence to Imperial after a few none too successful one-off sessions for small-time independents. Working with Dave Bartholomew in New Orleans, the Imperial sessions promised much but ultimately were lost in the turmoil that was rock 'n' roll. In 1956 he moved to Detroit, cutting sessions in Chicago for the Fox and Vee Jay labels before returning to Los Angeles in 1960. Despite sessions with Kent, Edco, and Smash, his career was well and truly in the doldrums and, after cutting Sunset Blues Band for Liberty's subsidiary Sunset in 1965, he retired from the music business to drive a truck and play golf.

By the end of the 1960s, with Europe and the US still in the grip of a rock-fuelled blues boom, Crayton re-emerged briefly to cut *Things I Used to Do* (1970) for Sam Charters' Vanguard label and to appear with the Johnny Otis Show at Monterey where he performed a scintillating reading of 'Things I Used to Do', which showed that he hadn't lost his touch. Ultimately it did little to stimulate interest in his career and more years passed in retirement. In 1980, although there was no blues boom, the market place had expanded sufficiently to allow independent specialist blues and roots labels such as Alligator and Rounder the room to manoeuvre. As a consequence Johnny Otis established his Blues Spectrum label and suggested that Crayton should recut his best known recordings to form a part of a package that would include similar albums by Big Joe Turner and Jimmy Liggins, among others. Known as *Great R&B Oldies Volume Five* (1982) and featuring a group of session musicians, Crayton's guitar work was as incisive as ever, while his vocals had acquired a patina of avuncular warmth. Furthermore it encouraged Norman Granz at Pablo to cut Crayton with Turner on *Everyday I Have the Blues* (1982). Over the next three years Crayton toured regularly – particularly on the festival circuits in North America and Europe – but somehow it was all a little too late, especially as it meant being away from his family and the golf-course.

CLARENCE 'GATEMOUTH' BROWN

Apart from B. B. King – one of the few guitarists to survive R&B's golden era and to reap some of the accrued rewards – few have managed as capably as Clarence 'Gatemouth' Brown. Brown was born on

18 April 1924, in Vinton, Louisiana, but raised from the age of three in Orange, Texas. Learning the fiddle and guitar from his father (Fiddlin' Tom), Brown was influenced by the blues of T-Bone Walker, Tampa Red, and the big bands and later recalled:

> 'I liked Ellington and Basie a lot but Ray Noble also impressed me, because he could really swing. What I heard most of, though, was country and western and so Bob Wills and the Texas Playboys made a lasting impact. You see, my father played the fiddle, mandolin, accordion and lots of other things and he would always be trying out these new tunes around the house – from Gene Autry and Roy Rogers through to Jimmie Rodgers. He had to have variety, you understand, 'cos he would be playing in a bluegrass band one night, and cajun band the next. He would travel right across Texas and into Louisiana. But he would never play zydeco, 'cos that was regarded as lower than the low.'

After touring the South as a drummer in Maxwell Davis's combo, Brown was drafted. When he was discharged, he returned to San Antonio where he developed his guitar style and so impressed Don Robey – the owner of the Bronze Peacock in Houston – that he was taken out to Los Angeles to cut some sides for the Aladdin label in 1947. But as Robey told *Billboard*'s Claude Hall, 'I wanted him to have a record out, because he was playing in my club. Aladdin waited until the last day of the year before releasing Brown's second record. I was so mad'. Robey's response was to take Brown into the studio with Jack McVea and cut sides such as 'Mary's Fine' and 'Time's Expensive'. These were duly issued on Robey's own Peacock label, which he started in 1949, and Brown remained with the label until 1961. During that time he put out a string of titles that were uniquely Texan in flavour because, although his guitar work bore similarities to that of Walker, he incorporated elements of Western swing, cajun, and country.

By the end of his relationship with Peacock, Brown shifted the emphasis more from R&B to country but, by the 1970s, the emphasis had changed once again with Brown making full use of his polymorphism by putting out albums that could appeal to anyone according to their musical persuasions. These included *The Drifter Rides Again* (1973), *Down South in the Bayou Country* (1974), *The Bogalusa Boogie Man* (1975), and *Makin' Music* (1979), with country singer Roy Clark, percussionist Airto Moreira, drummer Jim Keltner, and the Memphis Horns, among others. These days Brown's live shows tend to promote his violin-playing – presumably because there is greater scope for undoubted showmanship – but that doesn't alter the fact that *Alright Again* (1982), *Standing My Ground* (1989), and *The Man* (1994) demonstrated his staccato and punchy guitar style very succinctly.

B. B. KING

While Brown depended on Los Angeles for his early break-through, he relied on the south-west club circuit for his livelihood. Similarly B. B. King, although based in Memphis, was quick to realize that Los Angeles was the place to cut records and as a consequence few have managed to be as resilient and as impervious to the fickleness of passing fads as B. B. King. However, King was suited to the LA style because like most jazz vocalists he sings behind and over the beat: he doesn't project power in the way that the Chicago bluesmen, such as Muddy Waters or Howlin' Wolf, are inclined to do. There is more polish.

Born Riley King on 16 September 1925 at Itta Bena, Mississippi, he worked as a sharecropper and tractor driver from the age of nine. Initially inspired by Blind Lemon Jefferson and Lonnie Johnson, he started to listen to jazz by players such as Charlie Christian and Django Reinhardt. In 1938–9 he was taught the basic chords on the guitar by an uncle. After spells in the army he moved to Memphis in 1946 and stayed with his cousin, bluesman Bukka White. Busking at first and then playing clubs, his guitar style was influenced by T-Bone Walker and Lowell Fulson, and Johnny Moore's Three Blazers. However, his big break came when Sonny Boy Williamson, whom he knew through Williamson's guitarist, Robert Lockwood, gave him an opportunity to play on one of his programmes for radio station KWEM. As a result he began to work regularly on the club circuit and, by 1949, had his own show on another radio station, WDIA, where Rufus 'Do the Funky Chicken' Thomas was employed as a DJ.

It was at this time that King became known as the 'Beale Street Blues Boy', a nickname eventually reduced to 'Blues Boy' – hence the initials B. B. With his popularity on the up, he formed a band that included Lockwood and John Alexander (who would achieve popularity in his own right as Johnny Ace, before playing Russian roulette one moonlit New Year's Eve, and losing). The same year King cut his first sides for the Bullet label, which included 'Miss Martha King', 'Got the Blues', 'Take a Swing With Me', and 'How Do You Feel When Your Baby Packs Up To Go?'. In 1950 the Bullet sides were heard by the Bihari Brothers who signed King to the Modern subsidiary RPM.

In 1951, he scored a number one R&B hit with 'Three O'Clock Blues', the first of a series of R&B hits. Others included 'You Didn't Want Me' and 'Story From My Heart' (1952), 'Woke Up This Morning', 'Please Love Me', and 'Neighborhood Affair' (1953), 'You Upset Me Baby' (1954), 'Sneaking Around' and 'What Can I Do (Just Sing the Blues)' (1955), 'Crying Won't Help You', 'Sweet Little Angel', and 'On My Word of Honour' (1956), and 'I Want to Get Married' (1957). In 1957 he moved over to the Biharis' Kent label, as the company shifted its emphasis from singles to albums.

Throughout the 1950s King toured continually, backed by a 13-piece band, building a live act that would remain essentially unchanged for the rest of his career. In 1962 he was given an advance of $25,000 to join ABC: this, coupled with Modern's inability to sell his records beyond the 'race' market, was the reason for his move, but also ABC had shown a certain affinity with black musicians, having scored major success with Ray Charles. His first records for ABC were overproduced but in 1965 they released *Live at the Regal* – the first time that the raw excitement of one of his concerts had been successsfully captured on record. Its success was part of a process that would culminate in his decision in 1969 to aim at white rock-oriented audiences instead of continuing to play the chitlin' circuit.

His attraction for white audiences was based on the large number of US and UK blues musicians such as John Mayall, Eric Clapton, Mike Bloomfield, Paul Butterfield, Bob Hite of Canned Heat, and Alexis Korner, among others, who had consistently championed his work by recording their own versions of his material, consequently his biggest hits – 'Rock Me Baby' (1964) and 'The Thrill Is Gone' (1970) – had become famous through the many cover versions. Furthermore, as an indication of the concessions King was prepared to make to get an audience, *Completely Well* (1970) included string arrangements, most notably on 'The Thrill Is Gone'. Later the same year he teamed up with white musicians such as Leon Russell and Joe Walsh for *Indianola Mississippi Seeds* (1970), which included 'Ask Me No Questions'. After another live album, *Live in Cook County Jail* (1971), he got together with what amounted to a who's who of British R&B for *B. B. King in London* (1971).

With hindsight it could be said that, having decided against embracing rock 'n' roll – unlike Chuck Berry and Little Richard – King acknowledged his potential among the white rock audiences and so made sure that he did not miss out again. Be that as it may, King's style has remained essentially unchanged. Certainly as the 1970s gave way to the 1980s, King contented himself by updating the sound – the style never changed – and so albums such as *To Know You Is To Love You* (1973), whose title track was composed by Stevie Wonder, or his collaborations with the Crusaders, such as *Midnight Believer* (1978), can be viewed as extensions of what King perceived trends in black music to be.

Now based in Las Vegas, King has accrued the prosperity denied many of his antecedents and contemporaries, but his albums continue to demonstrate his proximity to his roots while keeping a close eye on what is happening all around him. In 1992 he cut *Blues Summit* , a collection of duets with various kindred spirits, such as Ruth Brown, Buddy Guy, John Lee Hooker, Lowell Fulson, Robert Cray, Etta James, Irma Thomas, Albert Collins, and Koko Taylor. He was also on hand to duet with country legend George Jones on the Clarence Carter hit, 'Patches', for the *Rhythm Country*

& Blues compilation in 1994. Similarly, when U2 proclaimed their allegiance, King didn't need to think twice before agreeing to go on the group's world tour in 1989–90 so showmanship has never been far from the King mandate, but then it is in that spirit that R&B first came about.

GUITAR SLIM

While King's showmanship was always inclined to be unobtrusive, he knew how to entertain – or perhaps manipulate – an audience. Both Guitar Slim and Johnny 'Guitar' Watson took the T-Bone Walker tack by employing every trick imaginable to wind up an audience. In so doing they gave a young James Marshall Hendrix a few ideas about attention-seeking. Guitar Slim was born Eddie Jones on 10 December 1926, in Greenwood, Mississippi, and spent his early years working on the New Orleans club circuit. Initially influenced by 'Gatemouth' Brown, Slim employed an emotional, gospel-influenced vocal style with a heavily distorted guitar sound. In 1953 he was signed to the Los Angeles-based Specialty label and the following year he hit paydirt with the immaculate 'Things That I Used To Do'. Featuring an arrangement by pianist Ray Charles, it is one of those chunks of gritty R&B that came out of the blue and went to the top of the R&B charts where it remained for six weeks. Thereafter Guitar Slim slipped out of sight nationally but continued to ply his trade on the southern club circuit on the strength of 'Things That I Used To Do'. Furthermore, on stage he would play his guitar behind his head and with his teeth and was the first to use an extended lead on his guitar, making it possible for him to wander all around the stage as he played. Although he scored a minor success with 'Something to Remember You By' (1956), he died in 1959 after contracting pneumonia while touring the East Coast.

JOHNNY 'GUITAR' WATSON

It is just conceivable that, had Guitar Slim not met his maker prematurely, his career might well have developed along similar lines to that of Johnny 'Guitar' Watson, who also had a flair for stagecraft coupled with an extraordinary ability for penning appealing tunes with wryly witty lyrics. However, Watson was such an iconoclast that for much of his career he failed to achieve the fame that was his due because no one was able to take him at face value. Born on 3 February 1935, in Houston, Texas, Watson – inspired by T-Bone and Clarence 'Gatemouth' Brown – moved to Los Angeles in 1950, where he joined the Chuck Higgins Band as pianist two years later. With Higgins, Watson made his vocal debut on 'Motor Head Blues' for the Combo label. Chart action for this waxing might have been negligible but Ralph Bass detected potential in the young Watson and signed him to the Federal label. Almost immediately Young John Watson, as he was now called, drew attention to his guitar work with 'Highway 60' (1953) and 'You Can't Take It With You' (1954), but it was the instrumental 'Space Guitar' with its liberal use of feedback and reverb that caused jaws to hit the floor. Not surprisingly, perhaps, this all proved a little too much for his record label and Watson was allowed to move on to the Bihari Brothers' RPM label.

Now answering to the name of Johnny 'Guitar' Watson, which had been bestowed upon him by Joe Bihari, Watson proceeded to knock out a succession of singles such as 'Hot Little Mama' (1954), 'Too Tired', 'Those Lonely, Lonely Nights', and 'Oh Baby' (1955), and 'Three Hours Past Midnight' (1956). Of these 'Those Lonely, Lonely Nights' was the most successful, reaching the R&B Top Ten. However, it was his extravagant stage act that was generating interest and so his solo career took a back seat as he was hired to tour with Little Richard and Don and Dewey, among others. In common with Guitar Slim, Watson, too, had a 150-foot lead for his guitar, which gave him the leeway to cavort around the stage, playing the guitar with his teeth and such like.

By 1961, with rock 'n' roll and R&B gradually losing their appeal, Watson revived his recording career when he was signed to the King label. This time his benefactor was the equally idiosyncratic Johnny Otis. Although this proved to be a short-lived arrangement, Watson scored with 'Cuttin' In'. While 'Cuttin' In' might have sounded anachronistic coming from anyone else, Watson's jaunty style transcended trivial considerations such as fashion, and closer study reveals startling similarities with his later disco-funk outings such as 'I Need It'. This was later followed by 'The Gangster of Love'. Nominally described as a novelty item, the fluid, incisive guitar work belied that pejorative. Although it sold well enough on the West Coast, it didn't reap its full rewards until it was covered by Steve Miller some six years later.

As the British beat group invasion gathered momentum, Watson cut the curious *I Cried For You* (1963), a suave and swanky affair that included such hoary old chestnuts as 'Witchcraft'. Then he was signed to the Columbia subsidiary OKeh by producer Larry Williams, of 'Short Fat Fannie Fame' fame. The two of them started to tour and record together, most notably adding lyrics to Joe Zawinul's 'Mercy Mercy Mercy'. Although they couldn't compete with Sam and Dave as a duo, their combined experience enabled them to provide a very entertaining live act, which was captured on record as *The Larry Williams Show* (1965) and *Two For the Price of One* (1967).

After cutting a tribute to pianist Fats Waller with *In a Fats Bag* (1968), Watson started to get funky with albums such as *Listen* (1973) and *I Don't Want To Be Alone, Stranger* (1976). When disco arrived, Watson was on hand with such gems as 'I Need It' (1976) and 'A Real Mother For Ya' (1977). Although those two songs proved to be his final hits, Watson continued playing the Los Angeles club and R&B festival circuits right up to his death in 1996.

While Los Angeles had its appeal for those bluesmen from the south-west, Chicago was the most obvious destination for southern bluesmen and they flocked there in droves. Like Los Angeles with its munitions factories and shipyards, Chicago and Detroit were the twin peaks of the industrial heartland of the Midwest, offering employment on car assembly lines, should all else fail. However, because Chicago had never boasted an entertainment business on the scale of Los Angeles, independent record labels did not tend to spring up over night in quite the same way as they were inclined to do on the West Coast, or indeed the East Coast, come to that. What Chicago did have was a flourishing club circuit that was geared to entertaining the vast number of blue-collar workers and it was clubs such as the Macomba on Chicago's South Side that acted as a catalyst for the development of what has come to be regarded as 'urban blues'.

The Macomba was owned by two Polish émigrés, brothers Leonard and Phil Chess. Based on Thirty-ninth Street and Cottage Grove, the Macomba attracted the biggest names in jazz and R&B: Lionel Hampton, Louis Jordan, Ella Fitzgerald, Billy Eckstine, and Louis Armstrong. By 1946 the Chess brothers had started to diversify by opening a record label. Called Aristocrat, it was none too successful initially but it offered a glimmer of hope to the many performers who nightly crowded the stage of the Macomba and other smaller venues. Operating from a store front, the Chess brothers later asserted that many of their artists literally turned up, almost begging to be heard. What is certain is that in the early years of Aristocrat, the Chess brothers started to record some of the artists who would later earn them a fortune, including Muddy Waters, Willie Mabon, and Sonny Boy Williamson. As Muddy Waters would later say to Arnold Shaw, 'We're doing the stuff like we did way years ago down in Mississippi'. However, it wasn't quite the same, because now the bands were amplified and, despite the presence of horn sections, it was the electric guitars that were the centrepieces of these blues bands. And it was Muddy Waters who spearheaded the charge.

MUDDY WATERS

Muddy Waters occupies centre stage as one of the most important architects of rock 'n' roll. His brisk, business-like style gave the Chicago blues an identity in the post-war period that would serve as a template for an entire generation of bluesmen and rock musicians. He was born McKinley Morganfield on 4 April 1915, in Rolling Fork, Mississippi, but was raised in Clarksdale by his grandmother after his mother died. Quickly he acquired the nickname 'Muddy Waters' on account of his tendency to frolic in a nearby stream. At first he took up the harmonica, but that was sidelined when he formed his first band in 1932 with Charley Patton's former fiddler, Henry Sims, and guitarist Scott Bowhandle. With Bowhandle teaching him the rudiments of the instrument, the rest he picked up by himself or by listening to Robert Johnson records or watching Eddie 'Son' House.

In 1940 Muddy left Clarksdale and headed north for St Louis, but returned to Clarksdale shortly after and was recorded in 1941 by archivist and historian Alan Lomax for the Library of Congress. By 1943 Muddy took the initiative and moved to Chicago, staying with his sister and obtaining work in a paper factory. Despite his rural upbringing, Muddy was soon playing house parties, but the acoustic blues he had been playing up until this point were plainly inappropriate for the noisy rough and tumble of the club circuit. In 1944 his cousin Joe Brant, recognizing Muddy's dilemma, bought him an electric guitar, which not only augmented his range, but also made his playing more expressive. Within the year, Muddy was getting encouragement from Big Bill Broonzy and doing the occasional gig accompanying Sonny Boy Williamson. This led to a couple of recording sessions for Muddy where he cut 'Mean Red Spider', among other things.

Very gradually, through working the circuit, Muddy began to gather around him a regular group of young hopefuls in a similar situation to his own. These included Jimmy Rogers, who at this juncture was playing harmonica, and Claude 'Blue Smitty' Smith; Smith failed to last as he was inclined to disappear halfway through a gig after picking up a young lady. This was a shame because Smith, an ardent follower of Charlie Christian, was by far the most accomplished guitarist Muddy had come across thus far. With Smith out of the picture, a lively character called Leroy 'Baby Face' Foster was recruited and was discovered to be a better drummer than guitarist.

In late 1947 Sunnyland Slim, another musician from the Delta, had talked himself into a session with the fledgling Aristocrat label and he wanted Muddy to accompany him. That was the start. In 1950 the now familiar chequered logo took over as Aristocrat became Chess and, for the next 15 years, Muddy and his band provided the bedrock to Chess's prosperity and reputation.

While Muddy's deft chording and restrained lyrical solos inspired reverence, his compositional talents were awesome and included: 'I Got My Mojo Working', 'I'm Ready', 'I Can't Be Satisfied', 'Rolling Stone', 'Rollin' and Tumblin'', 'Hoochie Coochie Man', 'Just Make Love to Me' and 'Just to

Be With You'. His band came to resemble a who's who of the Chicago blues scene with Little Walter and James Cotton on harmonica, pianist Otis Spann, and guitarists Jimmy Rogers, Hubert Sumlin, Pat Hare, Robert Lockwood, Earl Hooker, Buddy Guy, and Luther Johnson, and the *éminence grise* of the Chess label, bassist and producer Willie Dixon, all passing through the ranks at one time or another. Despite Muddy's immense local popularity and influence, a glance through *Billboard's* R&B charts shows a slightly different story with only a comparatively small number of records making an impression. These included '(I Feel Like) Going Home' (1948), 'Louisiana Blues', 'Long Distance Call', 'Honey Bee', and 'Still a Fool' (1951), 'She Moves Me' (1952), 'Mad Love' (1953), 'Hoochie Coochie Man', 'I Just Want to Make Love to You', and 'I'm Ready' (1954), 'Mannish Boy' and 'Sugar Sweet' (1955), 'Trouble No More', 'Forty Days and Forty Nights', and 'Don't Go No Further' (1956), and 'Close to You' (1958).

During the early 1960s, Muddy sought to revive his faltering career as R&B and the blues were losing ground in urban environments to labels such as Berry Gordy's Detroit-based Tamla Motown. For Muddy and others of his ilk, salvation was at hand in the form of blues enthusiasts and devotees in the UK such as Manfred Mann, the Rolling Stones, Van Morrison of Them, Alexis Korner, John Mayall, and Graham Bond, all of whom had championed Muddy's work, citing him as one of their inspirations. This swell of enthusiasm in the UK corresponded with a similar outpouring in the US, where young white collegiates such as Johnny Winter, Paul Butterfield, Mike Bloomfield, John Hammond Jr, and Canned Heat started forming blues-based bands or performing in coffee bars. And so Muddy, like B. B. King, started to draw from a well of enthusiasm and appreciation that was emanating not from young black kids or factory workers, but from educated white middle-class kids. Indeed, in the years preceding his death in 1983 Muddy recorded a number of albums including *I'm Ready* (1977) and *Hard Again* (1978) for Winter's Blue Sky label.

HOWLIN' WOLF

Despite Muddy's pre-eminence at Chess and in Chicago, he was not the only influence. As more bluesmen turned up in Chicago and plugged in, the basic twelve- or ten-bar format of the blues was experimented with and started to lose its rigidity. Arguably one of the most original bluesman was Howlin' Wolf. Wolf didn't make the move to Chicago until he was 37 years old and his characteristic growl came from his early enthusiasm for country singer Jimmie Rodgers, whose yodelling Wolf endeavoured to imitate; he couldn't, so he settled for growling, and then howling instead. Wolf was born Chester Arthur Burnett on 10 June

1910 in West Point, near Ruleville, Mississippi. For much of his early life he worked as a farm labourer, but in the meantime he played on farms and around the environs of the Delta, having acquired a guitar when he was 18. While his guitar-playing was influenced by Robert Johnson – whom he apparently played with – and Charley Patton, he was also influenced by a duo called the Mississippi Sheiks, which featured Memphis Slim and his brother. After the US entered the Second World War, Wolf was drafted immediately and remained for the duration. After his discharge he went back to labouring on a farm before moving across the Mississippi to West Memphis in Arkansas, where he got his first electric guitar and started laying plans for a career as a musician.

In 1948 he formed an electric R&B band with Little Junior Parker and James Cotton and started to broadcast over KWEM in West Memphis. One of these broadcasts was heard by talent scout Ike Turner who recommended him to the Bihari Brothers in Los Angeles. While Modern issued several of Wolf's recordings, including 'Moanin' at Midnight', on the RPM subsidiary label, Turner was overseeing sessions at Sam Phillips's studios in Memphis; these sides were licensed to the Chess brothers. For Wolf the next step was obvious – he moved up to Chicago.

After settling in Chicago in 1954, Wolf started to pack clubs such as Sylvio's or the Big Squeeze and his band, featuring guitarists Hubert Sumlin and Jody Williams, was supplemented by pianist Otis Spann, drummer Earl Phillips and bassist Willie Dixon. While Wolf performed a lot of his own compositions, including 'Smokestack Lightnin'', 'Evil', 'Sittin' on Top of the World', 'Killin' Floor', and 'No Place to Go', he was quick to use Dixon songs such as 'Red Rooster', 'Back Door Man', and 'Wang Dang Doodle'. Although these sides retained some of the brooding intensity characteristic of most Delta bluesmen, the roistering house style of Chess and Wolf's simple chording technique imbued them with a tough majesty. It is not surprising that when the blues explosion of the 1960s reached the UK, Wolf and songs such as 'Smokestack Lightnin'' or 'Killin' Floor' became as familiar as Muddy's best-known tunes. Five years before he died in 1976, he recorded *The London Howlin' Wolf Sessions* (1971) with Eric Clapton, Bill Wyman, and Keith Richards, but Wolf's powerful influence on the style of Chicago R&B is as discernible today as it was right back in the early 1950s.

OTIS RUSH

Although the Chess brothers had created a pantheon of legends, they needed assistance to do it and bassist, writer, and producer Willie Dixon was Leonard's right arm, but Leonard didn't always take his advice. One bluesman who only cut eight sides for the label and slipped through the net because of his ostensible closeness to Muddy was Otis Rush. Rush was born on 29 April 1934 in Philadelphia, Mississippi, and moved to Chicago in 1949, where he attended Dunbar High School on the South Side. After finishing school, Rush worked as a labourer and in steel mills before landing work at the Campbell's Soup cannery. In 1955 he turned to music full-time, appearing frequently at the 708 Club, and then approached Chess. He was turned down but Dixon, who had by now left Chess, arranged sessions for him at the small Cobra label in 1956. Among the sides Rush cut were 'Double Trouble', 'I Can't Quit You Baby', 'Groaning the Blues', 'All Your Love', and 'Keep on Loving You Baby', which were characterized by his moaning and groaning vocals to the accompaniment of ferocious flurries of stinging solos. Indeed, such was the excellence of these early sides that later records were hard pressed to compete. In 1960 he was briefly contracted to Chess, cutting 'So Many Roads, So Many Trains', but Chess were beginning to lose interest in R&B and the blues and trying to feather their nest elsewhere. After Chess he was contracted to Don Robey's Duke label but Robey, arguably one of the least philanthropic record-company moguls, ensured that Rush didn't record again until 1965 when he took part in Sam Charters' overview of the Chicago blues scene for the Vanguard label.

Thereafter Rush recorded occasionally, often with white bluesmen such as Mike Bloomfield and Nick Gravenites, but albums like *Mourning in the Morning* (1969) lacked the visceral attack of his earlier sides. Throughout the 1970s he toured regularly, appearing in Europe with guitarist Jimmy Dawkins. A number of live albums appeared as a result of visits to France, Sweden, and Japan, and to a San Francisco blues festival. Critically rated by John Mayall, Eric Clapton, and Mick Taylor, Rush remains undervalued to this day.

BUDDY GUY

The other principal beneficiary of Dixon's practised ear was Buddy Guy. Born George Guy on 30 July 1936 in Lettsworth, Louisiana, he learned to play on a pretty basic home-made guitar and then copied records he heard on the radio. By the mid-1950s Guy had started playing with local bluesmen such as Slim Harpo and Lightnin' Slim, but his relocation to Chicago in 1957 gave his career the required fillip. Initially playing with the Rufus Foreman Band, he met Otis Rush at a 'Battle of the Blues' contest. Guy won the contest and Rush took him along to Dixon at the Cobra label, where Guy cut sides such as 'Sit and Cry' and 'Try to Quit You Baby'. After Cobra collapsed, Guy joined the Chess label, where he became a member of the label's house band, accompanying Muddy Waters and Howlin' Wolf. At the suggestion of Waters and Dixon, he started to cut sides in his own right, including the raw and scintillating 'First Time I Met the Blues' and the memorable 'Stone Crazy'. While he continued to play on sessions, he established himself on the Chicago club circuit, often in partnership with Junior Wells, whom he had met at the earlier 'Battle of the Blues' contest.

From 1965 the duo cut albums such as *Hoodoo Man Blues* (1965), *On Tap* and *It's My Life Baby* (1966), and *Southside Blues Jam* (1967) for Sam Charters' Vanguard label. While the first-named was the most impressive, these albums paved the way for *A Man and the Blues* and *This Is Buddy Guy* (1968) under just Guy's name. Later collaborations included *Buddy and the Juniors* (1970), which also featured pianist Junior Mance, and *Buddy Guy and Junior Wells Play the Blues* (1972). Although the partnership was dissolved in the early 1980s, Guy has gone from strength to strength: his tremolo-laden solos with lots of sustain echoed the drama of B. B. King's style, prompting luminaries such as Keith Richards and Jeff Beck to beat a path to Guy's Chicago club, Legends.

In the 1980s Guy released albums such as *Stone Crazy* (1981), *The Complete DJ Play My Blues* (1981), and *Ten Blue Fingers* (1985). However, during the 1990s a measure of consistency entered his recording schedule when he signed with the UK-based Silvertone label, where he cut albums such as *Damn Right I Got the Blues* (1991), *Feels Like Rain* (1993), and *Live! The Real Deal* (1996). While these albums are modern in their approach – featuring many friends and admirers – the technique and spirit in which they are executed recapture the spontaneity and *jeu d'esprit* of the way electric blues has always been played in Chicago.

JOHN LEE HOOKER

Although all this might suggest that Chess held the monopoly, they didn't because in 1953 the Vee Jay label came into being. While the latter built their reputation on vocal groups such as the Spaniels and The El-Dorados, as they were a black-owned label, they needed to ensure they appealed to the full sweep of the local population. So their contribution to the electric blues was the signing of John Lee Hooker and Jimmy Reed. Of the two, it was Reed who enjoyed greater immediate popularity but it is Hooker who has endured, enjoying a degree of financial independence and security that would have been unthinkable at the beginning of his career.

Hooker was born on 22 August 1917 in Clarksdale, Mississippi, and moved north to Detroit during the Second World War to get work on the automobile assembly lines. His musical career had started when his stepfather, William Moore, taught him how to play the guitar and together the two of them would play local dances. In 1931 he ran away to Memphis where he met Robert Junior Lockwood; he then moved to Cincinnati where he sang in gospel choirs for ten years. By the time Hooker arrived in Detroit in 1943, he was sufficiently clued up to realize that work on the assembly line need not impede his musical career and so he started to play in blues clubs and bars throughout the black ghetto around Hastings Street. In 1948 he was given the chance to record 'Boogie Chillun', which was leased to Modern in Los Angeles, and it became a good-sized hit. For the next half-dozen years or so, as Hooker's relationship with Modern prospered, the rhythmic, mesmerizing tapping of the foot on the sounding board with a fractured chord here and there characterized a string of records including 'Whistling and Moaning Blues' and 'Crawling Kingsnake' (1949), 'Roll 'n' Roll' and 'Let Your Daddy Ride' (1950), 'I'm in the Mood' (1951), 'It Hurts Me So' and 'Key to the Highway' (1952), 'Ride Til I Die' and 'Too Much Boogie' (1953), 'Shake, Holler, and Run' (1954), and 'I'm Ready' (1955).

Throughout his association with Modern, Hooker had moonlighted for any number of labels under different pseudonyms, but when he arrived at Vee Jay, he settled into a comfortable groove. Firstly he enlisted sidemen such as Jimmy Reed and guitarist Eddie Taylor, but he also took account of the folk or rural blues market by cutting albums such as *The Folk Blues of John Lee Hooker* (1959) for Riverside. However, it was the electric R&B that kept his popularity bubbling along with titles such as 'Troubles Blues', 'Dimples', and 'I'm Worried Baby' (1956), 'I'm So Excited' and 'Rosie Mae' (1957), 'I Love You Honey', 'Maudie', and 'Boogie Chillun' (1958), and 'Hobo Blues' (1959).

As R&B fell out of favour, Hooker left Vee Jay in 1964 and cut albums for Chess and the jazz label Impulse, before cutting *Live at Cafe Au Go-Go* (1967) with the Muddy Waters Band for ABC's Bluesway label. This was followed by two more albums – *Urban Blues* (1968) and *Simply the Truth* (1969) – for Bluesway, which sought to update the image of the blues and R&B by addressing contemporary issues such as the Vietnam war. This adaptability has stood Hooker in good stead subsequently, because early collaborations with groups such as the Steve Miller Band and Canned Heat ultimately paved the way for a series of albums in the late 1980s and 1990s. Featuring fans such as Bonnie Raitt, Eric Clapton, Pete Townsend, Robert Cray, Van Morrison, and Larry McCray, among others, albums such as *The Healer* (1989), *Mr Lucky* (1991), and *Don't Look Back* (1997) have won Hooker fresh admirers among a new and younger audience. While he may still cuss at the way his music has been exploited, he has lived to tell the tale and to reap some of the rewards. Many haven't.

JIMMY REED

Jimmy Reed was one of the many to fall by the wayside just as real financial security and appreciation were about to be his. For Reed's long, lean, sinuous boogie lines exerted as much influence on the impressionable youth of the UK during the late 1950s and 1960s as did Muddy Waters. This was manifest by the profusion of covers of Reed songs by British groups such as the Rolling Stones, the Pretty Things, the Animals, and Them.

Reed was born Mathis James Reed on 6 September 1925 in Leland, Mississippi. After moving to Chicago in 1948, he worked in a steel foundry in Gary, while working the club circuit. By the early 1950s he had jettisoned full-time work and had started to play with guitarist Eddie Taylor, whom he had known from his youth back in Mississippi. Making his debut in 1954 with 'High and Lonesome' for the local Chance label, he was spotted by the Brackens, the owners of Vee Jay, and promptly signed. From 1954 until Vee Jay went out of business, Reed made the charts with a string of hits that included 'You Don't Have to Go' (1954), 'Ain't That Lovin' You Baby' (1956), 'Honest I Do' (1957), 'Take Out Some Insurance' and 'Baby What You Want Me To Do?'(1959), 'Big Boss Man' (1960), 'Bright Lights, Big City' (1961), and 'Shame Shame Shame'. With Taylor playing bass and Reed playing guitar and harmonica, Reed avoided the implicit menace of bluesmen like Howlin' Wolf and John Lee Hooker. Moreover, Reed only used horns once; the rest of the time he slipped in a harmonica break, which contributed to the rural feel of his records. The difference was the electric guitar, which propelled his records as forcibly and insistently as a full-scale band. When Vee Jay went bust, Reed signed with ABC Bluesway in 1965, cutting albums such as *The New Jimmy Reed Album* (1967), but a combination of ill health and poor production militated against the success of these albums. Reed died in 1976 and, although nobody doubts the extent of his influence, he still seems to remain a peripheral figure, forever sidelined in importance by Muddy Waters and John Lee Hooker.

ELMORE JAMES

The final Chicago-based bluesman to exert a significant impact on the way R&B developed and later generations of guitarists was Elmore James. Like John Lee Hooker at the start of his career, James showed little inclination for tying himself contractually to a single record label; he just recorded for anyone who expressed interest. James therefore never had the stylistic continuity that allegiance to one specific label imparted and so there is a repetitiveness implicit in much of his output, but that doesn't alter the fact that his bottleneck slide guitar work was a significant influence, especially on the British blues-based bands of the 1960s.

James was born on 27 January 1918 in Canton, Mississippi, but moved to Chicago in 1953. Before making the move, James worked regularly with the second Sonny Boy Williamson (also known as Rice Miller), particularly on KFFA's radio show, *King Biscuit Time*, out of West Helena in Arkansas. This enabled him to get work as a DJ on WOKJ in Jackson, where he cut his first side for the local Trumpet label. It was 'Dust My Broom' (1952). Featuring Williamson, it owed a debt to Robert Johnson, but it quickly became James's trademark and would reappear throughout his career, sometimes under the alternative titles 'I Believe My Time Ain't Long' and 'Dust My Blues'. In 1953, after Trumpet, James cut 'I Believe' and 'Sinful Woman' for the Meteor label, which was run as a subsidiary of Modern by Lester Bihari in Memphis.

Once he had moved north, James's abrasive bottleneck style – which had fallen out favour since the blues plugged in – and raucous vocals soon found their niche on the club circuit alongside Muddy Waters and Howlin' Wolf. Shortly after his arrival, he cut 'Country Boogie' for the Chess subsidiary Checker. As his reputation flourished on the club circuit, where he was accompanied by pianist Johnny Jones and his cousin Homesick James on bass, James started to record for another Modern subsidiary, Flair. Here, for the only time in his career, he experienced some continuity, staying with the label for around two years, cutting sides such as 'Hawaiian Boogie', 'Strange Kinda Feeling', and 'Rock My Baby Right' (1954) and 'Standing at the Cross Roads', 'Dust My Blues', and 'Blues Before Sunrise' (1955).

For the remainder of his career, James recorded for the Chief (Vee Jay also issued these sides), Chess ('The Sun Is Shining', 1959), Bobby Robinson's Fire ('The Sky Is Crying', 1959), Enjoy, and Fury labels, but his style of playing was becoming increasingly outmoded as younger audiences looked for a greater degree of sophistication. In 1963 he died of a heart attack in Chicago. It was perhaps ironic that James – who had based so many of his songs upon the material of other bluesmen such as Robert Johnson ('Standing at the Cross Roads'), Robert Nighthawk ('Anna Lee'), and Tampa Red ('It Hurts Me Too') – should have acquired mythic status through groups such as John Mayall's Bluesbreakers, Fleetwood Mac, the Johnny Winter Band, and the Paul Butterfield Blues Band. However, it was not just white blues enthusiasts who looked to James for inspiration as his style is evident in the work of Hound Dog Taylor, Luther Allison, and J. B. Hutto.

As the electric blues were superseded in the affections of black record buyers by the smoother, swankier sounds coming out of Berry Gordy's Tamla Motown or the gospel-fuelled soul emanating from the Stax studios in Memphis, it fell to a new generation of white, college-educated kids – on both sides of the Atlantic – to keep interest in R&B and the blues alive.

chapter eight

DINAH AND THE R&B DIVAS

W HILE MAMIE SMITH'S 'CRAZY BLUES' was one of the first catalysts for the blues explosion of the 1920s, the contribution of gospel singers such as Sallie Martin, Clara Ward, and Mahalia Jackson to the development of R&B is incalculable. Not only did they threaten the male domination of the record industry, they also offered an example for others to emulate. While male vocalists such as Sam Cooke, Jackie Wilson, and Clyde McPhatter, among others, started their careers in choirs and then gospel groups, there was still resistance from some to the notion that working in the entertainment business was a suitable job for a woman. Of all the vocalists to pick up the gauntlet, Dinah Washington was perhaps the most important, providing a stylistic conduit between the gospel purity of Jackson and the earthy ribaldry of Big Mama Thornton, and in so doing, she provided the inspiration for generations of black vocalists from Ruth Brown to Nancy Wilson, from Diana Ross to Millie Jackson, and from Cassandra Wilson to Whitney Houston.

DINAH WASHINGTON

Dinah was born Ruth Jones on 29 August 1924, in Tuscaloosa, Alabama. After moving to Chicago, she started to sing in a baptist church on the South Side, accompanying herself on the piano. With her mother guiding her, she began touring the country and performing in churches. In 1939, after winning a talent contest at Chicago's Regal Theatre, she temporarily abandoned gospel in favour of appearing in night clubs. The next year she returned to gospel when she was hired by Sallie Martin, who was a partner of gospel composer Thomas A. Dorsey. For the next three years Ruth toured widely with Martin, acting as her assistant, accompanist, and protégée, and becoming a founder member of Martin's gospel group.

In 1943 Ruth was heard by booking agent Joe Glaser at Chicago's Garrick Bar and he alerted Lionel Hampton to the presence of this girl who worked in the washroom but was always trying to get up on stage to sing. After auditioning 'Evil Gal Blues' for Hampton, she got the job. Armed with a fresh identity – Hampton had insisted that she change her name to Dinah Washington – she was given the chance to cut 'Evil Gal Blues' and 'Salty Papa Blues' with Hampton's septet for Eric Bernay's jazz label, Keynote. Written, arranged, and produced by future jazz critic Leonard Feather, these sides might not have ignited the charts, but they certainly confirmed that Dinah had the grace and chutzpah to embrace any style.

While Dinah flourished in the Hampton band, recording dates were scarce and it was May 1945 before she was allowed back in the studios. With a similar arrangement as before, Dinah cut 'Blow Top Blues' but, frustrated by the lack of studio time, she left Hampton to embark on a solo career. Within weeks she had signed with the Apollo label. Backed by Lucky Thompson's All-Stars, which included bassist Charlie Mingus and vibraphonist Milt Jackson (he later co-founded the Modern Jazz Quartet), the sessions for Apollo took place in Los Angeles in December 1945. Cutting a variety of titles, including 'Wise Woman Blues', 'Rich Man's Blues', 'Blues For Day', 'Chewin' Woman Blues', and 'Pacific Coast Blues', Dinah confirmed that she had her own identity which made her instantly recognizable. Even when she took on jive novelty items such as Slim Gaillard's 'Me Voot Is Really Voot' and 'Me Voot Is Boot', her style was transcendent.

By the time she left Apollo for the fledgling Mercury label, which had opened at the end of 1945, Dinah had been dubbed 'Queen of the Blues' because of the success of Apollo sides on jukeboxes. At Mercury, as Shaw points out, she was treated like a jukebox, cutting over four hundred sides in a 16-year career and, of these, there were over fifty hits. These included 'Baby Get Lost' (1949), 'I Wanna Be Loved' and 'It Isn't Fair' (1950), 'Cold Cold Heart' (1951), 'Trouble in Mind' and 'Wheel of Fortune' (1952), 'Teach Me Tonight' and 'I Don't Hurt Anymore' (1954), 'I Concentrate on You' (1955), 'What a Difference a Day Makes' (1959), and 'This Bitter Earth' (1960). As the stylistic range of these titles suggests, Dinah excelled with the steamy R&B of tunes such as 'Baby Get Lost' but could give a perfectly good account of herself on pop tunes such as 'I Wanna Be Loved', which was also covered by the Andrews Sisters. However, the high points occurred when she dug back into her gospel background and cut tunes such as 'This Bitter Earth', which – as Ray Charles had done – fused elements of the secular and non-secular, resulting in a performance with virtually universal appeal. That was not all, for although Dinah's records were targeted initially at black audiences, it soon became clear that she could cross over to white audiences, and it wasn't long before she started to pack venues nationwide in concert and in cabaret. That was confirmed when 'What a Difference a Day Makes' hit *Billboard*'s Top Ten in 1959; four more releases went Top Thirty – 'Unforgettable' (1959), 'This Bitter Earth' and 'Loved Walked In' (1960) and 'September in the Rain' (1961).

Perhaps the greatest indication of her pop sensibility was her duets with Brook Benton – 'Baby (You've Got What It Takes)' and 'A Rockin' Good Way (to Mess Around and Fall in Love)' – which took the R&B charts by storm and lodged firmly in *Billboard*'s Top Ten. To this day, Dinah remains underrated: her ability to cover pop tunes, rock out on the steamiest R&B numbers, and to swing on the most complex jazz arrangement made her suspect. Nobody possessed that much talent or could be that malleable without incurring some cost. For Dinah, the cost was a hectic and torrid private life that resulted in at least six marriages and an early death in 1963 from an overdose of sleeping pills taken in conjunction with alcohol. There has never been any suggestion that this was anything but an accident.

ELLA MAE MORSE

Despite any reservations one might have about her individual performances or, perhaps, facets of her career, no other woman exerted quite the same influence as Dinah, but she was not the first to update her delivery of the blues and place it in the rather more risqué context of R&B. Ella Mae Morse, who was born in the same year as Dinah, came from Mansfield, Texas, a one-horse place south of Dallas. Her father led a local jazz band and the young Ella Mae made her debut not long after she reached puberty. Jimmy Dorsey, passing through Texas, spotted and recruited her, but she didn't last long. Dorsey's arranger Freddie Slack left the band to become pianist and arranger in Will Bradley's Orchestra, but left two years later to form his own trio. This led to dates in Los Angeles with vocalist Joe Turner and Slack decided to augment the trio to an orchestra and add a female vocalist. Slack was signed to Johnny Mercer's Capitol label and when he went into the studios, his female vocalist was none other than Ella Mae Morse.

The fruits of this collaboration – 'Cow Cow Boogie' (1942) – brought Capitol their first hit and announced the arrival of a new singing sensation. When the musicians returned to the studios later that year, Slack added guitarist T-Bone Walker and the sessions produced another hit, 'Mister Five By Five' (1942). Ella Mae sensed the big time just around the corner so she and Slack parted company. Unhappily, despite appearances in a couple of Universal movies and recording superb tracks such as 'Invitation to the Blues', Ella Mae could not revive her failing fortunes so she took the sensible decision to team up again with Slack for – among other things – 'The House of Blue Lights'. Ten years later it would have been called rock 'n' roll and no one would have batted an eyelid. However, in 1946 the mood was not quite that liberal – particularly when it came to nice, white gals from Texas extolling the pleasures of the flesh with such an unrepentant lasciviousness and verve. Eyebrows were raised, but that didn't stop the record from climbing the R&B charts although it never crossed over into pop. It was followed by 'Pig Foot Pete' and 'Pine Top Schwarz', but after getting married and having three children Ella Mae disappeared from sight.

In 1951 she re-emerged with covers of R&B songs such as 'Smack Dab in the Middle' and a predictable mixture of pop and country covers. No one was listening so she went back to her home in Palo Alto for another three years. Her next outing came in 1954 when she cut *Barrelhouse, Boogie and the Blues*, which was a sharp collection of covers of contemporary R&B material such as 'Money Honey'. Still no one listened and, by 1957, Ella Mae had become a footnote. In 1976 she made a comeback, playing dates on the Los Angeles club circuit, but her repertoire had softened with the passage of time and so not even Ella Mae could extract much raunchiness from songs such as 'Feelings'.

SISTER ROSETTA THARPE

Sister Rosetta Tharpe shared Dinah's gospel upbringing but seemed to relish the lack of sophistication in her vocals, which were complemented by the stinging ferocity of her guitar work. Born Rosetta Nubin on 20 March 1915 in Cotton Plant, Arkansas, she started her career singing gospel in church. Early on, though, she began to develop a bluesy strain to her vocal delivery that she combined with her abrasive guitar.

In 1938 she expanded her musical career by joining Cab Calloway's band and starting a solo career in gospel. While her earthy, uninhibited approach to both the guitar and singing was temporarily an asset in Calloway's band, a conflict arose over her continuing solo gospel performances so she left Calloway but returned to secular work two years later when she joined Lucky Millinder's band. With Millinder she cut a string of shouters such as 'Trouble in Mind', 'Shout Sister Shout', and 'That's All'. Although the stridency of her punchy licks on electric guitar foreshadowed rock 'n' roll by many years, she left R&B behind in favour of gospel. However, even as a gospel performer, whenever she made a major appearance she was always a show-stopper; her performance at the 1967 Newport Jazz Festival was, by all accounts, a case in point. In 1970 she suffered a stroke, resulting in the amputation of a leg, but she continued performing aided by crutches. She died on 9 October 1973 in Philadelphia.

HADDA BROOKS

Further emphasis as to Dinah's contribution lay in the sheer volume of material she needed to service her prolific output, which enabled young writers such as Hadda Brooks to gain wider recognition when Dinah recorded Brooks's 'A Slick Chick (on the Mellow Side)'. Hadda Hopgood was born on 29 October 1916 in Los Angeles. Learning to play the piano at the age of four, she graduated to playing for rehearsals at a dance studio when she was widowed in 1945. She met Jules Bihari, who was about to launch his Modern label with his brothers and he persuaded Hadda to consider a career as an entertainer.

Settling on the name Brooks for her professional career, her first release was the instrumental 'Swingin' the Boogie', which became Hadda's and the label's first hit. While she continued scoring with instrumentals, band leader Charlie Barnet suggested to her one night at an engagment at the Million Dollar Theatre that she sing for an encore. The ovation was rapturous and Hadda embarked on another phase of her career that would make her the first black woman to have her own TV show and give her a string of hits that included 'That's My Desire', 'I Feel So Good', 'Trust in Me', 'A Slick Chick (on the Mellow Side)', and 'Out of the Blue'. While her style was less in the manner of an R&B vocalist and more in the way of a 'torch' singer, her synthesis of jazz and blues made her the forerunner of entertainers such as Eartha Kitt and Lena Horne.

However, as rock 'n' roll took over, Hadda became sidelined and she moved to Europe and then Australia where she remained for the next 12 years. In 1987 Hadda came out of retirement for a series of cabaret dates in San Francisco, Los Angeles, and New York, and then the Rhythm and Blues Foundation gave her the prestigious Pioneer Award in 1993. Still performing and appearing in movies, Hadda cut the immaculate *Time Was When* for Virgin's Point Blank label in 1996.

RUTH BROWN

Of course, Dinah Washington wasn't the only female vocalist to forge a style that was uniquely her own. At Atlantic on the East Coast in New York, both Herb Abramson and Ahmet Ertegun were adept at spotting promising newcomers and nurturing them until they were ready to flower. Of these, Ruth Brown received – initially at least – red carpet treatment from Abramson and Ertegun after she was involved in a car accident in Chester, Pennsylvania, having made a verbal agreement with Abramson. As a consequence of that accident, Brown was hospitalized for a year, but Atlantic did pay her medical bills.

She was born Ruth Weston in Portsmouth, Virginia, on 30 January 1928, marrying trumpeter Jimmy Brown in the mid-1940s. In 1948, while working at the Crystal Caverns – a club run by Blanche Calloway – she made contact with Abramson. On her way to a performance at the Apollo in Harlem, she was involved in that fateful car accident. She was not to get into the recording studio for the next 12 months. When she did, she fully vindicated Abramson's and Ertegun's faith by knocking out a series of R&B sides that remain definitive. These included 'So Long' (1949), 'Someday', and 'Teardrops From My Eyes' (1950), 'I Know' (1951), '5-10-15 Hours' (1952), '(Mama) He Treats Your Daughter Mean' (1953), 'Somebody Touched Me', 'Oh What a Dream', and 'Mambo Baby' (1954), 'I Want To Be Loved' (1956), 'Lucky Lips' (1957), and 'This Little Girl's Gone Rockin'' (1958), all of which were monster R&B hits. Indeed, 'Lucky Lips' – composed by Jerry Leiber and Mike Stoller – and 'This Little Girl's Gone Rockin'', crossed over to *Billboard*'s national charts. As a result of this success Ruth was dubbed 'Miss Rhythm' and Atlantic was nicknamed 'The House That Ruth Built'. Despite the energy of her R&B sides and her ability to transcend the rock 'n' roll era, she still managed to retain some of the jazzier nuances in her delivery, but in 1962 she parted company with Atlantic after her hard rockin' style had become unfashionable.

From 1962 until 1976 she raised her children and worked in a variety of jobs, including driving school buses and cleaning. Since then she has begun to accrue some of the credit due to her, principally in the form of royalties backdated from her years with Atlantic; her quest to retrieve those royalties led to the formation of the non-profit-making Rhythm & Blues Foundation. In the 1980s she appeared variously in Allen Toussaint's off-Broadway musical *Staggerlee*, in John Waters' film *Hairspray* as 'Motormouth Mabel', and hosting *Harlem Hit Parade* and *Blues Stage*. In 1989 she won a Tony Award for her performance in the Broadway play *Black and Blue*, and *Blues on Broadway* earned her a Grammy. She is still a regular broadcaster on New York radio and her album *Fine and Mellow* (1992) is a tribute to her tenacity, proving that she still has ample zest for a business that had treated her pretty disgracefully.

LAVERN BAKER

For LaVern Baker the passage to the top of the tree was no less tortuous, but at least it didn't involve the discomfort of hospitalization. Born Delores Williams in Chicago on 11 November 1929, she made her debut in the local church choir when she was 12. By the time she was 17, she was a regular attraction at the De Lisa club where she was on a retainer for six months, becoming known as 'Little Miss Sharecropper'. Jerry

Wexler asserted in his autobiography, *The Rhythm and the Blues*, that 'she [LaVern] stood smack dab in the middle of the great tradition of Ma Rainey and Bessie Smith'. After being spotted by jazz musician Fletcher Henderson, she was signed to Columbia's OKeh subsidiary but a move to Detroit and to manager Al Green brought her a contract with King. At King, where she was backed by the Todd Rhodes Orchestra, she cut a couple of singles, 'Trying' and 'Lost Child', but even with extensive tours her career still failed to take off.

In 1954 she was signed to the Atlantic label by Ahmet Ertegun and Jerry Wexler, who produced her as if she were Esther Phillips or Etta James. Although he might not have been aware of it, Wexler fashioned the template for Aretha Franklin's 'I Never Loved a Man' and 'Respect' with 'Soul on Fire' and 'I Cried a Tear'. Between 1954 and 1963, Baker scored with a string of hits that included 'Soul on Fire' (1954), 'Tweedle Dee' and 'Bop Ting-A-Ling' (1955), 'I Can't Love You Enough' and 'Jim Dandy' (1956), 'I Cried a Tear' (1958), 'I Waited Too Long' (1959), 'Saved' (1961) and 'See See Rider' (1963). Although many of these were covered by white artists such as Georgia Gibbs, Baker had the dubious pleasure of seeing her style become the rage with the emergence of soul in the 1960s. Curiously, though, she wasn't able to adapt, despite cutting the excellent *I'm Gonna Get You* (1966) for Brunswick. Later she moved into retirement in the Philippines after falling ill while entertaining troops in Vietnam. She stayed for 22 years, returning to the US in 1991, where she recorded *Woke Up This Morning* (1991) with guitarist Cornell Dupree, among others. LaVern Baker died on 10 March 1997.

BIG MAMA THORNTON

Although Atlantic had LaVern Baker and Ruth Brown, Mercury had Dinah Washington, Modern had Etta James and Esther Phillips – the latter even spent time with Savoy – but Duke had Big Mama Thornton. Her career might appear to have revolved around one incident: in 1952 she recorded the first version of Jerry Leiber and Mike Stoller's 'Hound Dog', which is one of the most accurate distillations of the essential ingredients of R&B. Furthermore, Thornton's version embodies the spirit of rock 'n' roll, and when Elvis Presley came to cover it himself a few years later, his performance was – if anything – slightly better-mannered than Thornton's original. Although Big Mama Thornton was a blues singer in the same mould as Bessie Smith, she was able to make any necessary adjustments to her style, which transformed her into one of the great female shouters.

Born Willie Mae Thornton on 11 December 1926 in Montgomery, Alabama, she toured the South in the 1940s as a multi-talented entertainer, eventually settling in Houston, Texas, where she was signed by Don Robey to his Peacock label. At Peacock she cut sides such as 'Partnership Blues' (1951) and 'Mischievous Boogie' (1952) before being spotted by Johnny Otis, who featured her in his 1952 revue and suggested to Leiber and Stoller that she might be the ideal person to record their song 'Hound Dog'. After 'Hound Dog' she continued to record singles quite regularly and to tour with other Duke or Peacock artists such as Junior Parker, Clarence 'Gatemouth' Brown, Johnny Ace, and Bobby Bland.

In 1957 she moved to Los Angeles, where she performed regularly on the club circuit, but her days with Peacock were over as Robey had made the mistake of ripping off Thornton. During the 1960s she recorded for a variety of labels, including Kent, but her real audience was on campuses and the club circuit. And it was as a result of her success among young, white middle-class audiences that Arhoolie owner Chris Strachwitz recorded the albums *Big Mama Thornton in Europe* (1965) – featuring Buddy Guy and mouth-harp man Walter 'Shakey' Horton – and *Big Mama Thornton, Volume 2* (1966), on which she was backed by the Muddy Waters Band. During the 1970s she recorded little, but her sessions for Sam Charters' Vanguard label resulted in *Sassy Mama* (1975), which was notable for some stunning guitar work from Cornell Dupree. Shortly before her death in 1984 she confounded the popular belief, as 'Gatemouth' Brown's father woud have it, at least, that zydeco was vulgar, by recording *Live Together* with accordionist Clifton Chenier. Despite her lack of all-round appeal, Big Mama Thornton nevertheless exerted a huge influence on white vocalists such as Janis Joplin, Maggie Bell, and, more recently, Michelle Wilson.

BIG MAYBELLE

The same could be said of Big Maybelle, but she suffered from being signed to a record label – the Columbia subsidiary OKeh – that had little idea how to harness the innate power of her vocals, especially after rock 'n' roll drove all before it. Born Mabel Louise Smith on 1 May 1924, in Jackson, Tennessee, she sang in the choir of the Sanctified Church in Jackson as a child and in 1933 she won a talent contest. This led to stints with Dave Clark's Band and then Tiny Bradshaw's Orchestra, which kept her occupied until 1953 when she was signed by OKeh. Almost immediately she scored with 'Grabbin' Blues', 'Way Back Home', and 'Whole Lotta Shakin'' – later to be popularized by Jerry Lee Lewis and then countless British R&B outfits. While nominally she was a shouter in the tradition of the jump-band vocalists, her gospel background enabled her to turn in some sterling perfomances that were awe-inspiring in their tenderness.

However, record company problems aside, her dabblings with smack did not win her many friends and in 1956 she was signed to Savoy. At Savoy she managed just one hit – a reworking of the old blues standard, 'Candy' (1956) – before ducking out of sight, and she didn't trouble chart statisticians again until 1966 when she re-emerged with 'Don't Pass Me By' and again in the following year with a sulphurous version of '96 Tears', the proto-punk/garage classic of ? and the Mysterians. Although she too was lionized by white audiences towards the end of her career, causing her to be dubbed 'The Mother of Soul', the rigours of touring and her bad habits led to her demise on 23 January 1972.

ARETHA FRANKLIN

In modern times only one person has approximated, in terms of influence and vocal agility, the range of Dinah Washington and that person is Aretha Franklin. Those with a highly developed spiritual second sense might possibly aver that Franklin was ordained by a higher authority to continue where Dinah left off: when Dinah died, Aretha was three years into her career at Columbia with John Hammond. Although Hammond was to demonstrate a lack of understanding of how best to potentiate the talents of his charge, Aretha's mere presence in such august company was all Jerry Wexler at Atlantic needed when her contract with Columbia ran out. The rest is history. Not only did Aretha appear to step into Dinah's shoes but there was also the suggestion that it was a role for which she had been groomed ever since she first opened her mouth.

Aretha was born in Memphis on 25 March 1942, but her parents separated and she was brought up in Detroit by her father, Reverend C. L. Franklin, pastor of the New Bethel Church. However, Reverend Franklin was not just a local pastor in an inner city, for he had the ears of some of the most influential movers and shakers at work in the Civil Rights Movement. Indeed, it could be said that it was around his table that some of the plans and the ideology of the Civil Rights movement were formulated, with gospel singers such as Mahalia Jackson, Clara Ward, and Marion Williams offering their support to the political endeavours of charismatic figures such as Martin Luther King. And it was in this atmosphere that the young Aretha first learned how to hold a note. By the time she was 14, regular visitors to the house, such as Ward and Dinah Washington, had convinced Reverend Franklin that his daughter should cut an album of Clara Ward's hymns. Recorded live at the New Bethel Church, it was issued in 1956 on the Checker label – the Chess subsidiary; the same label had regularly issued albums of her father's sermons. In 1960 she moved to New York, where she recorded four songs, including 'Today I Sing the Blues';

these came to the attention of John Hammond at Columbia Records and he put her under contract.

Her first secular album, *The Great Aretha Franklin,* was released in October 1960. Apart from 'Today I Sing the Blues', which became an R&B hit, it failed to generate much enthusiasm. She remained with Columbia for six years, during which time she recorded some estimable tracks, including 'Operation Heartache' (1961), 'Running Out of Fools' (1964), and 'Cry Like a Baby' (1966), but major success eluded her, partly because Hammond – convinced that he had discovered Billie Holiday's successor – had her working with inappropriate material. When her contract was up, Hammond let her go and Jerry Wexler stepped in.

In January 1967 Wexler took Aretha down to Rick Hall's Fame Studios in Alabama and recorded 'I Never Loved a Man (The Way I Love You)' and the Chips Moman and Dan Penn composition, 'Do Right Woman'. Both featured the Muscle Shoals house band, which comprised Moman and Jimmy Johnson on guitars, Tommy Cogbill on bass, and Roger Hawkins on drums, with Aretha playing the piano, Spooner Oldham playing electric piano, and saxophonist Charlie Chalmers leading the horn section. It was the record that took up Ray Charles's baton, completing the cycle he had started when he recorded 'I Got a Woman', and the secularization of gospel had run its full course.

Since that day in 1967, Aretha has continued racking up hits, such as 'Respect', 'Baby I Love You', '(You Make Me Feel Like) A Natural Woman', and 'Chain of Fools' (1967), 'Think' and 'I Say a Little Prayer' (1968), 'Don't Play That Song' (1970), and 'Spanish Harlem' (1971), and it's worth noting that these were hits in *Billboard*'s national charts. No black woman had sustained such a run of success in the pop charts. Not even Dinah Washington. While there is little doubt that her work with Wexler was her supreme achievement, Aretha – like Dinah before her – is a transcendent figure: one might occasionally doubt the suitability of her song selection process, but that is a matter of taste. Aretha still presides – queen regnant – as different vocalists and performers scrap for the crumbs from her table. Not only were her singles huge commercial successes but also her albums were sustained artistic triumphs, giving the lie to the premise that the only useful purpose for an album was to gather together a string of singles. Albums such as *I Never Loved a Man* and *Aretha Arrives* (1967), *Lady Soul, Aretha Now!,* and *Aretha in Paris* (1968), *Soul '69* (1969), *This Girl's in Love With You* and *Spirit in the Dark* (1970), and *Young, Gifted and Black* (1972) proved conclusively to Tamla Motown artists such as Stevie Wonder and Marvin Gaye that the album really was the optimum format for any musical expression.

In March 1971 Aretha performed for three nights at the Fillmore West in San Francisco with Ray Charles, King Curtis, and Tower of Power. This could have been her nemesis: appearing in front of an atypical audience, made up of young, white middle-class kids at the home of the hippies in San Francisco was not a situation that would have occurred to many as being a good career move. That Aretha should have taken the day with flying colours – as the album of the event, *Aretha Live at the Fillmore West*, attests – was not surprising: quality is immediately recognizable. She also seemed to touch a nerve in both King Curtis and Ray Charles, enabling them to perform out of their skins. *Aretha Live at the Fillmore West* is one of those rare records that accurately elucidates the way in which gospel and R&B fused, becoming soul. Not long after this appearance on the West Coast, Aretha cut another live album, *Amazing Grace* (1972). Recorded at a church in the Watts district of Los Angeles and featuring James Cleveland and the Southern California Community Choir, it was her final collaboration with Wexler.

From 1973 until she left Atlantic, Aretha recorded with a number of different producers, including Quincy Jones ('Angel', 1973), Lamont Dozier – one-third of Motown's former production partnership, Holland, Dozier, and Holland – Curtis Mayfield and Arif Mardin ('Until You Come Back to Me (That's What I'm Gonna Do)', 1974). When she left Atlantic in 1980 she signed with Clive Davis's Arista.

This was the beginning of a new phase in her career, which would bring her to a significantly wider and younger audience. Although the hits were fewer, albums such as *Aretha* (1980) and *Who's Zoomin' Who?* (1985) demonstrated Aretha's ability to imbue a basic pop song with style and heart. Davis, like Wexler before him, provided Aretha with the support and guidance, teaming her with sympathetic producers such as Luther Vandross and Narada Michael Walden, who were able to write material specifically for her. Despite the strongly commercial slant to her records, in 1988 she recorded the double live gospel album *One Lord, One Faith* at the New Bethel Church, as a personal tribute to her father, who had died the previous year.

Doubtless there are those who would contend that her recent material could not hold a candle to her early Atlantic records. But 'The Voice' – so described by the state governor as 'one of Michigan's natural resources' – has retained its strength and her phrasing and timing are unimpaired by the passage of time, and although these days the new divas of soul are more likely to be Toni Braxton or Chaka Khan, their inspiration came from the intuitive performances of Aretha. From there, it is just a small matter of zillions of hours in the recording studios back to Dinah Washington's first sides with the Lionel Hampton Septet, cut literally a few months after Aretha's birth.

chapter nine

THE AVATARS
OF SOUL

AS THE STYLES OF MANY OF THE VOCAL GROUPS suggest, the church provided much of the galvanizing force as R&B slid seamlessly into the soul era but it was the efforts of three performers – Ray Charles, James Brown, and Sam Cooke – which cemented that transition. Moreover, each sought to control his musical destiny: Charles led – and still leads – his own orchestra and was one of the first black musicians to set up his own record label; Brown co-owned a music publishing company and a booking agency; and Sam Cooke, at the time of his death, had set up a record label that – judging from the talent on its roster, which included the Womack Brothers and the Soul Stirrers – would have become a major force in the US record industry.

While the prime motivation may well have been a perfectly natural desire to control and, therefore, to reap as many of the financial rewards as possible, there was the subtext of ridding themselves of the white man's shackles. And it is this facet of the transition from R&B into soul that is inseparable from racial issues: ever since the emergence of R&B in the 1940s, white performers had capitalized with anodyne cover versions. However, the combination of gospel and R&B was too powerful to replicate. Furthermore each man recognized that in gospel there were the vocal techniques that could be employed within a secular discipline. And 'discipline' is the key term here because Charles, with his Orchestra and backing vocalists, the Raelets, and Brown, with the Famous Flames, applied a musical discipline that appeared almost draconian in the carefully structured arrangements. As a consequence, both Charles and Brown were able to adapt the vulgarisms of R&B's basic form to their own ends, albeit in differing ways: Charles's orchestra paid more than a passing nod to the bands of Lionel Hampton, Buddy Johnson, Count Basie, and Duke Ellington; Brown, on the other hand, acknowledged the showmanship of Hampton, Calloway, and Jordan, while paying lip-service, at least, to the small groups of Johnny Otis. For Cooke the stylized crooning of Charles Brown and Nat 'King' Cole was the template, but the smooth delivery and vocal restraint were redolent of the Soul Stirrers. Through this trio of performers, R&B ventured into a more commercial, yet non-transferable, framework, which sowed the seeds – and developed the lingua franca – of soul.

RAY CHARLES

Raymond Charles Robinson was born in Albany, Georgia, on 23 September 1930, and started to learn spirituals and the blues from as early as three years old. When he was seven, he contracted glaucoma and became blind, and he was sent to study piano and clarinet at the Deaf and Blind School in Florida. By the time he was 16 he was earning his living playing in various bands in and around Florida. In 1948 he moved to Seattle, where his next-door neighbour was Quincy Jones, and formed the McSon Trio with guitarist G. D. McGhee and bassist Milton Gerred. In 1949 they signed with Jack Lauderdale's Downbeat Records, who released Charles's first published composition, 'Confession Blues'. The same year he changed his name to Ray Charles, while Downbeat changed their name to Swingtime. With Swingtime he released a spate of singles, including 'See See Rider' (1949), 'I'll Do Anything But Work', and 'All to Myself' (1950), until in 1951 he cut 'Baby, Let Me Hold Your Hand'. With Charles sounding uncannily like his idol, Charles Brown, he notched up his first hit. Although it was only medium sized, it was enough to persuade the owners of Atlantic – Herb Abramson and Ahmet Ertegun – to buy out his contract from Lauderdale for $2,500 in 1952.

Overnight the emphasis in his repertoire changed from a jazz-tinged flavour to a much harder R&B sound. Making his debut with 'Roll With My Baby', Charles echoed the current trends in R&B with the big beat horn notation provided by a bunch of session musicians. This was later followed by 'Mess Around', which had been written for him by Ahmet Ertegun. While 'Mess Around' has since become a classic of the genre, other titles such as Jesse Stone's 'Losing Hand' and Lowell Fulson's 'Sinner's Prayer' managed to fuse the secular and the non-secular with awe-inspiring arrangements that were as stark as they were appropriate. Even more to the point, all echoes of Charles Brown and Nat 'King' Cole had been eradicated from his vocal style, which was now fired by a gospel-laden fervour.

In 1954 he notched up his first hit single, 'It Should Have Been Me', which became his first big R&B hit, but his big move was just around the corner. In November 1954 he premiered his own hand-picked band, featuring the saxophonists Donald Wilkerson and David 'Fathead' Newman. As he was to say to Jerry Wexler, 'My theory was this, if I could find cats who could play jazz, I could fix it so they could play . . . rhythm and blues'. Apart from the two saxes, the band featured two trumpets, drums, bass, and piano. From these sessions, four titles – 'I've Got a Woman', 'Greenbacks', 'Come Back Baby', and 'Blackjack' (1954) – emerged to set the pattern for R&B and lay the ground rules for soul.

Over the next three years, Charles's brand of gospel-infused R&B stilled the carping comments of religious zealots who had been only too quick to condemn him for his 'sacrilege' in applying the forms of gospel to R&B: titles such as 'This Little Girl of Mine (1955), 'Hallelujah! I Love Her So' (1956), and 'Ain't That Love' (1957) crossed over into mainstream popularity. In 1957 his first album, *Ray Charles*, was released; it was followed in November by his first major hit, 'Swanee River Rockin' (Talkin' 'Bout That River)' (1957). The next year he appeared at the Newport Jazz Festival and his performance was recorded and released as *Ray Charles at Newport*. Then came the release of 'What'd I Say?' (1959), which, with its dynamic call-and-response vocals, sent the teenage rock 'n' roll enthusiasts into spasms of ecstasy. It didn't last long, though, for Charles always seemed to slip in and out of conjunction with what was deemed fashionable: *Soul Brothers*, with guitarist Kenny Burrell and vibraphonist Milt Jackson, recorded the same year, was as funky as they come but his new youthful following did not see it that way. In the meantime he had continued to expand the band, adding Hank Crawford on alto sax and Leroy 'Hog' Cooper on baritone. The biggest addition to the line-up was the Cookies, a three-girl vocal group led by Margie Hendricks, who were hired to add backing vocals for 'Lonely Avenue'; they never left and became the Raelets.

DAVID 'FATHEAD' NEWMAN

Charles always had a particular attribute that probably elevated him above normal mortals: he seemed to be aware from the outset that, in order to fulfil his musical aspirations, he needed to surround himself with the best. As a consequence, the key horn men in his line-up, David 'Fathead' Newman and Hank Crawford, both remained with him for over ten years. Newman was born in Fort Worth, Texas, on 24 February 1933, and started his professional career working with the guitarists T-Bone Walker and Lowell Fulson. In 1954, during a stay in Texas, Charles heard Newman and recruited him for his embryonic band. For Charles the addition of men raised on jazz and the blues meant he had the best of both worlds as and when the bubble burst on R&B, for he was already looking to develop other aspects of his musical persona. With Newman and Crawford he was able to present a band that had the versatility and acumen to win over anybody. So powerful was the combination that Newman remained with him until the mid-1960s when he launched a solo career. Despite being out of Charles's band, Newman's albums, such as *Fathead: Ray Charles Presents David Newman* (1968) and *Newmanism* (1974), still bore the imprint of Charles's influence. Furthermore, the experience accrued from working with Charles enabled him to develop a profitable career as a session man. In recent years Newman's work has slowed down, but in 1989 he re-established the old partnership with Hank Crawford on *Night Beat*.

HANK CRAWFORD

With Hank Crawford, Charles found an alter ego. Jerry Wexler has speculated that had Charles played the horn, he would have sounded very similar to Crawford, who – within months of joining Charles – had risen through the ranks to become Charles's co-arranger and amanuensis. Hank was born Bennie Crawford on 21 December 1934 in Memphis, Tennessee, and studied at the University of Tennessee. Hired by Charles in 1958 as the baritone horn man, he moved to alto when 'Hog' Cooper was found in Dallas. As with the best arrangers, Crawford had the knack of writing notation that fitted individual strengths and styles: each player had his own voice and no one's musical identity was subsumed. However, Crawford remained committed to a hard-edged R&B sound, softened only by a distinctive tonal purity.

By 1961 Crawford had signed a solo contract with Atlantic, cutting albums such as *More Soul* (1961), *From The Heart* (1962), *True Blue* (1964), *Mr Blues* (1967), and *Double Cross* (1968). In 1964 he left Charles to concentrate on session work with Esther Phillips, among others, but carried on working regularly with Newman. During the 1970s Crawford signed with Kudu, a division of Creed Taylor's CTI labels. While Crawford tended to draw much of his repertoire from contemporary writers, his group comprised some of New York's finest; these included guitarists Eric Gale, Cornell Dupree, and Hugh McCracken, the late Richard Tee on keyboards, bassists Ron Carter and Chuck Rainey, drummers Bernard 'Pretty' Purdie and Steve Gadd, and the Brecker brothers on horns. In common with Newman, Crawford has slowed down of late, but he still does sessions with Aretha Franklin, among others, and keeps his hand in with the occasional album such as *Roadhouse Symphony* (1986) with the indefatigable Dr John.

In 1959 Charles signed a three-year contract with ABC-Paramount, although Atlantic retained the rights to his recordings, which enabled them to reissue his earlier material at whim, most notably *The Genius of Ray Charles* (1960) and *Ray Charles in Person* (1960). For Charles, the point at issue was not so much the amount of money he could earn, but rather that he needed greater artistic control over what he recorded and what was released. With ABC, he was able to set up his own music publishing company, Tangerine, and was no longer constrained creatively: he was able to embrace other styles of music at will.

His first ABC album, *The Genius Hits the Road* (1960), was novel in that all the song titles related to US state names; James Brown would later run a name-check of cities and towns on his touring itinerary on 'Night Train'. However, it has to be remembered that up to the 1960s, pop or R&B albums were viewed simply as a means of gathering singles together with perhaps the occasional B-side thrown in for good measure. Albums featuring a dozen or so songs of equal merit or importance did not exist at that time. When standards such as 'Georgia on My Mind' were included on his albums, though, Charles was able to breathe fresh life into them, putting a completely different spin on the tried and trusted.

While Charles's popularity with black and white audiences continued to grow, he showed little inclination to rest on his laurels. Cutting *Genius + Soul = Jazz* (1961), with arrangements by Quincy Jones, an old chum from his early years, he demonstrated his intention of keeping alive his interest in the traditions of the big-band sound. Remarkably, one of the songs, 'One Mint Julep', crossed over to become a substantial hit. However, it also illustrated another facet of Charles, for although he had never been much of a writer, he was a great arranger. And Hank Crawford was still a fine collaborator, but Charles's insistence on using Quincy Jones illustrated the lengths to which he was prepared to go to crystallize hitherto unexplored areas of his musical vision. And to that same end, he hooked up with writer Percy Mayfield, in whom he found a writer who was able to blend the emotional conviction of the blues with the spiritual commitment of gospel. Mayfield could also bring an intensity to his songs that was perhaps lacking in others because, at the height of his popularity, he had been involved in an horrific road accident that had left him with extensive facial scars.

PERCY MAYFIELD

Mayfield was born in Linden, Louisiana, on 12 August 1920, and was brought up in Houston, Texas. After moving to Los Angeles in the 1940s he started to compose for Jimmy Witherspoon but was persuaded to cut some of the material himself, including 'Half Awake' and 'Two Years of Torture'. This led to a contract with Specialty. Almost immediately he scored with the pleadingly haunting 'Please Send Me Someone to Love'

(1950). Within two years, Mayfield was one of the best respected and most popular vocalists on the West Coast and other hits followed, such as 'What a Fool I Was', 'Cry Baby', 'The Big Question', and 'Lost Love'. After the accident he continued recording, but with little success.

After Charles set up Tangerine and was casting around looking for fresh writers, he happened upon Mayfield. With songs such as the massively successful 'Hit the Road, Jack', 'Hide Not Hair', and 'Danger Zone', Charles fashioned a series of hits that bridged the gap between R&B and soul. Indeed, such was the success of the partnership that Mayfield became one of the first signings to Tangerine when Charles set up the record label division in 1962. Curiously, though, Mayfield's own recordings lacked the confidence of his earlier output and albums such as *My Jug and I* (1962) sounded old-fashioned. Although he managed to keep recording for different labels such as Brunswick and RCA, Mayfield gradually slipped into obscurity until 1982, when he was coaxed out of retirement for a European and US tour. Sadly, it was a short-lived return to the high-life for he died on 11 August 1984.

After the success of his Mayfield collaborations, Charles sparked considerable controversy by recording *Modern Sounds in Country and Western Music* in 1962. Featuring songs such as 'I Can't Stop Loving You' and 'You Don't Know Me', many fans castigated Charles for selling out to gain country enthusiasts. Naturally there was nothing further from his mind: having been raised in the South, country music had dominated the radio during his upbringing so it was a natural source of inspiration. Furthermore, before leaving Atlantic, Charles had made his intentions quite clear by covering Hank Snow's 'I'm Movin' On' and it had been a sizeable hit into the bargain; additionally, there had long been a tradition among R&B performers of covering country material, with Bullmoose Jackson and Ivory Joe Hunter being prime examples. Perhaps what grated with Charles's longtime admirers was the use of lush, swirling string arrangements. Whatever the feelings of his detractors, Charles returned with a sequel, *Modern Sounds in Country and Western Music, Volume 2* (1963). It featured another brace of hits, 'Your Cheating Heart' and 'Take These Chains From My Heart', and both albums set the pattern for later country soul artists such as Percy Sledge and James Carr.

While Charles remained a front-runner stylistically through the 1960s – an inspiration to more than can possibly be enumerated here – the success and the toll taken by continuous touring gradually began to erode the trail-blazing base of his operation. His record label was not a commercial success. Certainly his own records fulfilled most obligations, but Tangerine was never to become a force to be reckoned with as an independent. Furthermore, as first Crawford and then Newman left, Charles showed that, while he might be able to hold the reins of an orchestra, the whole creative process of keeping a band on the road, working to its full potential, was another matter entirely. As a consequence, the ideas that had made his early records so appealing began to dry up and, increasingly, Charles found that it was his past glories that drew the audiences.

Since the release of *Ingredients in a Recipe For Soul* (1963), which featured one of his final enormous hits, 'Busted', the consistency has been found wanting; even so, albums such as *The Volcanic Action of My Soul* (1971) showed that he still has the muscle when he wants to use it. More significantly, his better performances – on record at least – have been in supporting roles: a duet with Aretha Franklin at the Fillmore West in 1971; the recording of George Gershwin's *Porgy and Bess* with Cleo Laine in 1976; and, in 1989, a contribution to Quincy Jones's *Back on the Block*. Charles still displays the knack of the true genius: just when you think he's all washed up, he cuts an album, *My World* (1993), that is – almost – as good as anything he's ever done. As if to confound the sceptics even more, a tour with Van Morrison in 1996 showed Charles at his spritely best and Morrison sounding slightly diffident in the august shadow of his idol.

JAMES BROWN

To this day Ray Charles spends a large part of the year touring. However, in comparison with James Brown, Charles seems like a pipe and slippers man because Brown has been dubbed 'The Hardest-working Man in Show Business'. Now, since modesty has never been Brown's strongest suit, it is not inconceivable that he came up with this description himself. What is certain, though, is that it ceased to apply on 17 December 1988, when a South Carolina judge sentenced James Brown to six years in prison on a variety of charges, including possession of illegal drugs, resisting arrest, and carrying firearms without a licence; a career that had spanned 33 years thus ground to a temporary halt.

In his heyday, Brown combined the flamboyant showmanship of Little Richard with the musical nous of Ray Charles; he was a fine, instinctive writer, who used words to supplement the rhythm. Certainly he emoted with every ounce he could muster in a manner that was firmly grounded in gospel, but his forte was adapting slogans that would fit into the rhythmic patterns. In common with Charles, though, he had a propensity for hiring sidemen who could play virtually anything – be it jazz, R&B, or the blues. Without the contribution of musical directors such as Nat Jones and, later, Pee Wee Ellis, it is a moot point whether Brown would have had the technical expertise – or musicianship – to produce the records that have laid the foundations for funk, rap, swingbeat, and hip-hop.

Born in Augusta, Georgia, on 3 May 1928, Brown was raised in rural poverty by an aunt. In 1949 he was convicted of petty theft and incarcerated at the Alto Reform School for four years before obtaining an early release. He joined the Gospel Starlighters, which included Bobby Byrd. Gradually Brown started to take control of the Gospel Starlighters and changed their name to the Famous Flames. In 1955, on a routine visit to Macon, King A&R man Ralph Bass heard one of Brown's demos and ran him to ground at a local club. Taking Brown up to Cincinnati, Bass signed him to Federal, a subsidiary of King. As Bass was later to recall, when Syd Nathan heard Brown's debut, 'Please Please Please', he described it as 'a piece of shit'. However, later on Nathan was even heard plugging the record for distributors so it can't have been that bad. However, as Bass went on to say, 'Brown was ahead of his time. He sang gospel to an R&B combo with a really heavy feeling'.

Breaking out almost immediately, 'Please Please Please' hit the R&B Top Ten in 1956 and crossed over to become a pop hit as well. For the next two years, titles such as 'Messing With the Blues' failed to repeat that initial triumph. In 1958 he finally struck again, this time with 'Try Me'. While it seemed more in keeping with something that Little Willie John might have recorded, the lyrics may have been directed at his fans and Syd Nathan, as this had been his tenth effort to repeat the success of 'Please Please Please'. The following year, having signed with Ben Bart, the owner of the booking agency Universal Attractions, Brown took the 'James Brown Show' out on the road and began a practice that would earn him the sobriquet of 'The Hardest-working Man in Show Business'. Furthermore he ensured that, whenever he was to play a new venue, the local radio stations and record shops knew about it well in advance so that his records were promoted remorselessly.

With the pattern now established, Brown set about consolidation by releasing a new single every couple of months. While some such as 'I'll Go Crazy' (1960), with its stop-and-start riffing, and the Five Royales' 'Think' (1960), with its hectoring delivery, intimated the direction in which he was moving, others such as the Dominoes' 'The Bells' and 'Prisoner of Love' (1963), which had been a hit for Perry Como and Billy Eckstein, seemed tokenistic in their attempt to crack the mainstream. Even so, 'Night Train' (1962), with its recitation of city names on the tour schedule, effectively showcased the extent to which Brown and the band drew their propulsive thrust from the R&B bands of the 1950s. In 1962 he released *Live at the Apollo*. While Ray Charles had been breaking new barriers with the release of properly conceived albums, *Live at the Apollo* showed that it was possible to capture the bare excitement of a stage show.

In 1964, eager to capitalize on the success of *Live at the Apollo*, Brown formed his own production company, Fair Deal, with Ben Bart and sent some new recordings to the Smash label, a subsidiary of Mercury. Brown – like Charles and his record label and music publishing company, Tangerine – was clearly making a serious effort to retain complete control of his business interests. Of course, Syd Nathan realized that losing Brown would make substantial inroads into the profitability of his empire, and so injuctions were served and Brown remained with King, but not before Nathan had acceded to Brown's demands for a higher royalty rate and greater artistic control. This need for greater control had been made apparent with one of the sides for Smash, 'Out of Sight' (1964). Featuring the now trademark juddering bass line and punctuated by staccato blasts from the horn section, it was the rhythmic intensity of guitarist Jimmy Nolen that opened the door for the dance-orientated funk of the 1970s.

From that point onwards, Brown bestrode what was now described as 'soul' with a string of hits that included 'Papa's Got a Brand New Bag' and 'I Got You (I Feel Good)' (1965), and 'It's a Man's, Man's, Man's World' (1966). In 1967 there were more crucial changes: following the replacement of Nat Jones by Alfred 'Pee Wee' Ellis as Brown's chief musical collaborator and the arrival of drummer Clyde Stubblefield, Brown's blend of funk and R&B reached its apogee with 'Cold Sweat'. By 1971 the Famous Flames had mutated into the JBs, featuring a funkier horn section with players such as Fred Wesley, Maceo Parker, and St Clair Pinckney. The benefits of the reorganization were quick to materialize with hits such as 'Get Up, Get Into It, Get Involved' and 'Soul Power', epitomizing Brown's sound. In the meantime he parted company with King, setting up the People record label, which he licensed to Polydor for worldwide distribution. This change gave him the real control over his affairs that he had long sought, enabling him to record long-term collaborators such as Bobby Byrd.

Since the early 1970s, Brown has dabbled with film scores such as *Black Caesar* and *Slaughter's Big Rip-Off* (1973) but the number of hit records has decreased. However, his influence remains as keen as ever and nowhere is this more apparent than in the volatile atmosphere of clubland, where by the 1980s his earlier records were being sampled and remixed by DJs. Despite his spell in jail – he was released in April 1991 – Brown has returned to the relentless touring schedule. Although his stamina shows signs of letting up, his commitment and enthusiasm are as focused as ever.

SAM COOKE

Although both Charles and Brown still work extremely hard, Sam Cooke's rise to stardom was as meteoric as his fall from grace was cataclysmic. Born in Clarksdale, Mississippi, on 22 January 1931, and one of eight children, his career started in church when he was nine, forming the

Singing Children with two of his sisters and a brother. By 1950, after a spell with the Highway QCs, he became lead tenor of the Soul Stirrers. Ever since their formation in the early 1930s, the Soul Stirrers had been revered for their pioneering work in gospel, but discord had set in among the ranks as material such as 'Jesus Hits Like the Atom Bomb' pointed to a progressively more secular route. When Cooke arrived in 1950, the drift towards a non-spiritual interpretation accelerated as he demonstrated his ability to whip up a frenzy among the congregation with such traditional pieces as 'Touch the Hem of His Garment' and 'Nearer to Thee'.

Cooke remained with the group until departing for a solo career at the suggestion of 'Bumps' Blackwell, the head of A&R at Specialty, who encouraged him to record some 'pop songs' . The first, 'Lovable' – under the pseudonym of Dale Cook, so as to avoid offending Cooke's gospel admirers – flopped and they reverted to plain Sam Cooke. He then cut 'You Send Me' (1957), with a white female chorus to broaden its appeal, but Art Rupe was so unimpressed that he allowed Cooke and Blackwell to pull out of their contracts and take the tape elsewhere. Eventually it was released on a small Los Angeles label, Keen. Selling over a million copies, it was the first of eight consecutive hits for the label that included '(I Love You) For Sentimental Reasons' (1958), 'Only Sixteen' (1959), and 'Wonderful World' (1960). Not only did Cooke demonstrate his skill as a writer, having co-written 'Wonderful World' with Lou Adler and Herb Alpert, but he also retained the melismatic vocal stylings that suggested his gospel links were still intact. This was the beginning of a style that was as warm as it was sensuous because Cooke dispensed with the florid embellishments of style so often a concomitant of gospel. Furthermore, these pop songs – for that's all they were – were distinguished by a lyrical purity and a directness that were intended to cross racial barriers into the white pop market. As his reputation blossomed, he was soon the toast of the Los Angeles club circuit, where his overt sexuality became a magnet for whites as well as blacks.

In 1960 Cooke's contract with Keen expired and he signed with RCA for a guaranteed minimum of $100,000. While this seems a trifling amount in comparison with the big bucks routinely handed out these days, it has to be set in context: RCA had acquired Elvis Presley's contract less than five years previously for a very conservative $35,000. Because RCA considered they were lining up their own Nat 'King' Cole, Cooke was duly partnered with the production team of Hugo and Luigi. Never afraid to swamp even the most moderate performers with lavish string arrangements, Hugo and Luigi had a field day with him. Somehow Cooke managed to transcend the lush arrangements, bringing a strong gospel feel to hits such as 'Chain Gang' (1960), 'Cupid' (1961), 'Twistin' the Night Away' and 'Bring It on Home to Me' (1962), and 'Another Saturday Night', 'Frankie and Johnny', and 'Little Red Rooster' (1963). Indeed, it could be argued that in spite of the arrangements, lyrically Sam Cooke was moving ever closer to the roots of the black experience.

In 1961, as his popularity continued to flower, he set up the SAR label with his manager and confidant, J. W. Alexander. With SAR, the object of the exercise was to nurture young talent or to provide a haven for those who might not get another opportunity. In this respect, Cooke was far better equipped to deal with the frustrations of running a record label than either Ray Charles or James Brown. For one thing, Cooke was a fine songwriter and producer, but the other key point was that he wasn't interested in spending his time trailing across the continent with a band in tow; he was quite happy just to play Las Vegas and the affluent supper-club circuits of New York and Los Angeles. This, in turn, would have provided him with the wealth to develop his own record company in much the same way as Berry Gordy was doing with Tamla Motown in Detroit.

Whatever Cooke's long-term goals may have been, these quickly turned to nothing on 11 December 1964 when he was shot and killed in Los Angeles by the manageress of a motel. In the years since his demise, rumours have abounded surrounding the circumstances. Speculation that his business interests had become so substantial that he was treading on the toes of organized crime was one line, but then it could have been as mundane as the official reports would have it: he came on strong to the wrong person, at the wrong time, and paid for it. What is certain is that one of his final recordings, 'A Change Is Gonna Come' (1964), possessed a prophetic poignancy as civil unrest began to grow throughout the US, causing attitudes – superficially at least – to change towards black people. Furthermore, Cooke – along with others such as Clyde McPhatter, Jackie Wilson, and Jesse Belvin – opened the door for the 'sweet soul ballad', which has influenced everyone from Bob Marley to Dennis Brown, Otis Redding to Al Green, and Marvin Gaye to Luther Vandross. As for SAR, Alexander didn't have the heart to continue, and so he closed it down. However, Cooke, Brown, and Charles tore up the rule book, paving the way for other black artists such as Prince and producers such as LA and Babyface to establish their own record labels that would reflect and facilitate their own endeavours.

chapter ten

THEY CALLED
IT ROCK

I N PINPOINTING THE TRANSITION FROM R&B to rock 'n' roll, the
only real distinction seems to lie in the iconography: cars joined sex
and drinking as the prime suspects. For many the distinction was
purely semantic. Fats Domino had been playing with some success
since the early 1950s; when rock 'n' roll replaced R&B as the buzz
phrase, Domino became inextricably associated with this style: no longer
was he described as R&B, he was dubbed a rock 'n' roller. As Domino's
producer and arranger Dave Bartholomew was moved to observe, 'rock 'n'
roll and R&B are the same thing, but they [the whites] stole it from us [the
blacks]'. Johnny Otis – a white man – says much the same thing. So rock
'n' roll was less to do with a style and was rather the product of a good marketing man's fevered imagination: in this instance that marketing man was
Alan Freed. Rumour has it that Freed attempted to copyright the term; here
he was a bit slow on the uptake because registering it as a trademark would
have been far more lucrative.

However, for all the assertions that rock 'n' roll was exclusively a by-
product of black music, there are grounds for suggesting that country music
played as big a part in the genesis of rock 'n' roll as R&B. This, too, needs
clarification because nowadays the country-influenced strain of rock 'n'
roll is dubbed 'rockabilly'. At its peak no such distinction was drawn, for
Elvis and Carl Perkins were routinely lumped together with Little Richard
as purveyors of the all-encompassing rock 'n' roll genre. Furthermore, it
would be a mite too simplistic to suggest that just the black performers
brought R&B to the party and white performers brought country: Chuck
Berry was heavily influenced by country music, and Elvis Presley was as
influenced by the blues as by country. The real point at issue, though, is

that from the rock 'n' roll era, a range of artists and performers who, quite reasonably, might have described themselves as R&B musicians became purveyors of rock 'n' roll as distinct from R&B. Semantics, again? Perhaps, but the case for Little Richard would be that he adapted the potency and emotional commitment of gospel to rock 'n' roll.

While musically there were few intrinsic differences between R&B and rock 'n' roll, those that did exist were glossed over by marketing men or, more importantly, producers. Both Leiber and Stoller and George Goldner were experts, in their own way, in taking R&B vocal groups and adapting their sound to meet the requirements of rock 'n' roll. And so it was that the dominant R&B musicians to bestride the rock 'n' roll artists arena benefited from producers or label owners who were far-seeing enough – or just that cute – to master the cross-generational and cross-racial imagery of rock 'n' roll. If one wishes to be absolutely brutal about it and perhaps over-simplistic: those who were perceived as rock 'n' roll artists were those who were signed to record labels that had the distribution to make the records available nationally. Lew Chudd at Imperial in Los Angeles knew perfectly well that Fats Domino's appearances in a variety of films such as *The Girl Can't Help It* could do more to stimulate record sales than any number of appearances on Dick Clark's *American Bandstand* could achieve. Similarly, it was common knowledge at Chess that appearances on the Alan Freed *Moondog Balls* would stimulate record sales.

Therefore it was producers such as Dave Bartholomew, Johnny Vincent, and Allen Toussaint in New Orleans, 'Bumps' Blackwell in Los Angeles, and the Chess brothers – Phil and Leonard – with Willie Dixon in Chicago, who turned R&B into rock 'n' roll because they worked with labels that had the financial clout and distribution to ensure that records became hits. Companies such as Bobby Robinson's group of labels and Atlantic on the East Coast also exerted an influence but both were inclined towards a more purist view: Robinson was already enjoying some success with a brand of up-town R&B that would generate attention as soul, but he adopted the traditional expertise of the label owner by issuing specific songs to gain a place in the market rather than attempting to develop an artist. As for Atlantic, they remained firmly on the periphery of rock 'n' roll, with groups such as the Coasters and the Clovers being their principal standard-bearers.

However, New Orleans, Los Angeles, and Chicago were the hot spots. Quite why New Orleans should have found itself at the cutting edge is something of a mystery. Certainly the cosmopolitan mixture of races and creeds rendered it less susceptible to the streamlined mercantilism of the music industry in New York and Los Angeles. Its position as the birthplace of jazz gave it an unmatched kudos, but the prime consideration was the *laissez-faire* attitude among the Crescent City's musical community.

This made it an environment that was altogether more stimulating and more susceptible to off-the-wall ideas, in spite of the South's legendary racist attitudes.

FATS DOMINO AND DAVE BARTHOLOMEW

The roots of rock 'n' roll in New Orleans can be traced back to 1949 when Lew Chudd, the owner of Imperial, went to New Orleans on a talent-scouting mission to hear a young, fat, black kid whom Dave Bartholomew had told him about. Bartholomew had served in the army and played trumpet with Duke Ellington's band, before setting himself up in New Orleans with his own band and as a talent scout for Chudd. According to Bartholomew, Domino came by a club where Bartholomew was working and asked to sit in with the band. And that was the start of Domino's career.

Known as Fats because of his corpulent girth, Antoine Domino was born on 26 February 1928 in New Orleans. When in his teens, he learned to play the piano from his uncle, Harrison Verrett, and adopted the boogie-woogie style of Albert Ammons combined with the florid, rococo shadings of Professor Longhair and the driving rhythm of Amos Milburn. In 1945 he joined Billy Diamond's Combo until, in 1949, he hooked up with Bartholomew. Working with Bartholomew, Domino cut his first record, 'The Fat Man', in 1950. While it was credited to both Domino and Bartholomew, it was basically a reworking of 'Junkers Blues'. It immediately hit the R&B Top Ten, starting a pattern that would continue until the late 1950s. Using musicians from Bartholomew's band – which included bassist Frank Field, drummer Earl Palmer, guitarist Walter 'Papoose' Nelson, and horn men Lee Allen, Herb Hardesty, and Alvin 'Red' Tyler – and recording at Cosimo Matassa's J&M Studios, this was essentially the set-up that remained in place until the end of the 1950s.

With a driving piano-style and slightly nasal vocals, Domino became synonymous with New Orleans rock 'n' roll through a succession of hits that included 'Every Night About This Time' and 'Rockin' Chair' (1951), 'Goin' Home' (1952), 'Goin' to the River' and 'Please Don't Leave Me' (1953), and 'You Done Me Wrong' (1954). Quick to see the need to stay in the public eye, in 1951 Domino started a pattern of touring constantly, which would continue throughout the 1950s and early 1960s. With a touring band that was drawn from the same nucleus of session musicians, Domino was thereby able to replicate the sound of the records on stage, which did his quest for national acceptance no harm whatsoever. That acceptance finally came in 1955 with 'Ain't That a Shame', another Domino and Bartholomew collaboration – which was covered by Pat Boone

– but, as Shaw succinctly points out, Domino became a rock 'n' roller 'not through a change of style, but through the acquisition of a mainstream audience and his choice of repertoire'.

Over the next six years he notched up more than thirty-five Top Forty hits, including 'I'm In Love Again' and 'Blueberry Hill' (1956), 'Blue Monday' , 'I'm Walkin'', and 'Valley of Tears' (1957), 'Whole Lotta Loving' (1958), 'I Want to Walk You Home' and 'Be My Guest' (1959), and 'Walkin' to New Orleans' (1960). While the round of touring helped establish him in the mainstream, the routine covers of his material did not work against him, as Domino's version of 'I'm in Love Again' easily outsold the Fontane Sisters' cover. Although it can be said that covers by the likes of the Fontane Sisters and Pat Boone offered scant contest, Domino had another ace up his sleeve: he – like Louis Jordan, the Mills Brothers, and the Ink Spots – had no problem in embracing Hollywood, and consequently his appearances in highly exploitative (of rock 'n' roll, that is) films such as *The Girl Can't Help It* (1956), *Shake, Rattle and Roll* (1956), *Jamboree* (1957), and *The Big Beat* (1958) actually worked to his advantage.

Although Domino became a putative victim of the changing face of popular music in the early 1960s and had to change label in 1963, moving to ABC, he was more a victim of circumstances as New Orleans' celebrated red-light district was cleaned up and the once-flourishing club circuit went into decline. The net result was that many of the musicians who had worked sessions and clubs moved to Los Angeles or New York in search of regular gainful employment. So far as Domino was concerned, his high profile as a recording artist and performer enabled him to become a regular in cabaret in Las Vegas. Despite the paucity of new recordings, Domino remains active to this day and, as recently as 1979, he returned to the studios – this time to Marshall Sehorn and Allen Toussaint's Sea-Saint studios in New Orleans – to cut *Sleeping on the Job*.

SMILEY LEWIS

As Domino's success spiralled into the mainstream, it attracted others such as Smiley Lewis and Shirley and Lee. Lewis was typical of the New Orleans journeyman: good writer, guitarist, and arranger. Lewis was born Overton Amos Lemons on 5 July 1913, in DeQuincy, Louisiana, and his career began in the 1930s when he started playing the club circuit, first as a soloist and then heading a trio. In 1947 he made his recording debut for the DeLuxe label at the J&M Studios, but it was not until he signed with Lew Chudd at Imperial that he started to make an impact. Backed by Bartholomew's band, Lewis adopted a jump style on titles such as 'My Baby Was Right' (1951) and 'Growing Old' (1952), but by the time he got round to cutting 'The Bells Are Ringing' and 'Gumbo Blues' (1952), he was totally in thrall to Domino and the prevailing New Orleans idiom. While he was influenced by Domino, it did work both ways, because Lewis's version of 'Blue Monday' predated Domino's and Domino was also to cut his own version of Lewis's biggest hit, 'I Hear You Knocking'. Domino wasn't the only one to latch on to Lewis as a good source of material because Elvis covered Lewis's 'One Night', using it most memorably in his 1968 TV special, *Elvis*, when he went out on stage to prove to his doubters that he could still cut the mustard. Despite his talent and ability, Lewis never achieved the fame that was his due, and after Imperial was sold to Liberty in the 1960s, Lewis went on to record for a string of labels before dying of cancer on 7 October 1966.

SHIRLEY AND LEE

With Shirley and Lee, Bartholomew demonstrated how such a potentially bland formula as a 'boy-and-girl' duo could exact a level of excitement and musical excellence that were unthinkable in its white counterparts. Shirley Pixley and Leonard Lee were both natives of New Orleans, who happened to cut a demo at J&M, which came to the attention of Eddie Mesner at Aladdin. Backed by Bartholomew's usual crowd of session men, their debut, 'I'm Gone' (1952), combined novelty value with a hard-hitting urgency that invoked the call-and-response idioms of gospel. The novelty value was continued with a series of songs in the 'Work With Me Annie' mould, chronicling the ups and downs of Shirley and Lee's ongoing courtship. These included 'Shirley Come Back to Me' and 'The Proposal' (1953) and 'Lee Goofed' (1954). If these were good, solid fare, others such as 'Feel So Good' (1955), 'Let the Good Times Roll' (1956), and 'Rock All Night', 'Rockin' With the Clock', and 'I Feel Good' (1957) predicated the symmetry of rock 'n' roll and R&B. In particular, 'Let the Good Times Roll' achieved the impossible in eclipsing Elvis's 'Heartbreak Hotel' and 'Hound Dog' in *Billboard's* annual *Honor Roll of Hits* while remaining an implausibly good record. After the collapse of Aladdin, they lost their way somewhat as later sides for Imperial confirm. Why that should have happened is another of those impenetrable mysteries. After moving to Los Angeles, Shirley quickly found work with others from the Crescent City's session elite – such as Jessie Hill, Harold Battiste, and Mac Rebennack – before surfacing in 1975 under the name of Shirley and Company with a monster disco hit entitled 'Shame Shame Shame'. Lee died in New Orleans on 26 October 1976. Ten years later, Shirley secured half the royalties from Lee's family for 'Let the Good Times Roll'.

Etta James casts a
long dismissive look
at some Wallflowers
– they must be
drinking coke

Koko Taylor's tour
schedule is as hectic
as it ever was
(Courtesy of Alligator Records)

Not to be trifled with,
Lavern Baker gives
the finger
(Michael Ochs Archive)

Billed as Miss
Rhythm, Ruth Brown
gives a practical
demonstration of
her talents
(Michael Ochs Archive)

Better known for
his guitar work
Clarence 'Gatemouth'
Brown is a dab hand
with the fiddle
(Courtesy of Alligator Records)

Before opening up
his vocal chords,
Bobby 'Blue' Bland
was B.B. King's
driver/valet
(Courtesy of Warner Bros)

Dr John, also known as Mac Rebennack, has turned his hand to singing themes to TV sitcoms
(Courtesy of Warner Bros)

Formerly a member of The Dominoes, Jackie Wilson shows how to testify
(Michael Ochs Archive)

King Pleasure and The
Biscuit Boys indulge in
some youthful pranks
to alleviate the tedium
of a photo shoot
(Courtesy of Jim Simpson/
Big Bear Management)

Roomful of Blues
have featured such
august personalities
as Duke Robillard in
their line-up
(Courtesy of Rounder Records)

Stevie Ray Vaughan with
Double Trouble knocked his
competitors out of the sky
(Courtesy of Epic Records)

ART RUPE AND 'BUMPS' BLACKWELL

While Chudd and Bartholomew were two of the first to recognize and develop the New Orleans potential in R&B, others such as Art Rupe, the owner of the LA-based label Specialty, was not far behind. The following story gives an idea of the symmetry – and competitiveness – that existed between the two record bosses. When Chudd went to see Fats Domino, he had originally gone to the Crescent City to see Lloyd Price. Chudd was so bowled over by Fats that he didn't get round to seeing Price, but Bartholomew suggested that Rupe, who was also on the trail of Domino, should sign Price instead.

Rupe was strategically well-placed to develop into rock 'n' roll. He had set up the Jukebox label in 1944 with the express purpose of developing R&B acts; it became Specialty in 1946. While his most prestigious R&B act was Roy Milton, he had had success with the Sepia Tones (on Jukebox) and the archetypal R&B record, 'Shuffleshuck', by Jimmy Liggins and His Drops of Joy, featuring a screaming horn solo. The following year Rupe had expanded to take in the very lucrative gospel market, signing the Soul Stirrers, featuring an ultra-smooth Sam Cooke, and the Swan Silvertones. In 1952 he went to New Orleans with his A&R director, 'Bumps' Blackwell. Blackwell's career had started during the 1940s when he played in a band with Ray Charles and Quincy Jones, but after studying composition in Hollywood, he moved to Specialty as an arranger and producer.

LLOYD PRICE

Despite Rupe and Blackwell's failure to sign Domino, Lloyd Price turned out to be a pretty good substitute. Price was born in Kenner, Louisiana, on 9 March 1933 and started his career in 1950, performing and writing jingles for one of New Orleans many radio stations – WBOK. After signing to Specialty, he was hustled into the J&M Studios. Legend has it that Rupe – who was producing the session – got so frustrated at Price's inability to come up with anything worthwhile that he was going to abandon the session, at which point Price pulled 'Lawdy Miss Clawdy' out of the hat. Apocryphal, or not, it's a nice tale. Additionally, there's a further irony in that the piano introduction is reputedly none other than Fats Domino – so at least Rupe got round to recording the 'Fat Man', even if it was only in an auxiliary capacity. With Fats heading up Bartholomew's regular crew, 'Lawdy Miss Clawdy' is pure rock 'n' roll and it was 1952. Raucous as it comes, this was the template for the Little Richard and Larry Williams sides, many of which were cut in the same New Orleans studios. Even so, Rupe and Blackwell captured the sound perfectly, enabling them to replicate the feel and the sound of New Orleans' sides back on the West Coast. After the success of 'Lawdy Miss Clawdy', Price failed to build on it – giving the impression that 'Lawdy Miss Clawdy' was a flash in the pan – but titles such as 'So Long', 'Tell Me Pretty Baby', and 'Ain't It a Shame' were perfectly reasonable. Price then joined the US Army in 1953 and turned that to his advantage by forming a band and spending his time touring South-east Asia entertaining the forces.

After three years, he was discharged and settled in Washington, DC, where he formed the KRC label. While titles such as 'Hello Little Girl' and 'How Many Times' failed to register, the self-penned 'Just Because' (1957), which was leased to ABC-Paramount, demonstrated Price's knack for assessing the mood swings of popular taste. The follow-up, 'Stagger Lee' (1959), went to number one across the country. If there were any doubts about his shrewdness and entrepreneurial zeal – he was, after all, one of the first black American musicians to form his own production company and record labels – these were quickly silenced when he cut another version of 'Stagger Lee' especially to be broadcast on Dick Clark's *American Bandstand*, because the prevailing view was that the original tale of revenge and murder was considered too risqué for prime-time television. However, later titles such as 'Where Were You (On Our Wedding Day)?', 'Personality', 'I'm Gonna Get Married', and 'Come Into My Heart' (1959) and 'Lady Luck', 'No Ifs, No Ands', and 'Question' (1960) were somewhat unprepossessing, despite their success.

By 1963 Price's hit-making days were gone, but he continued developing his business interests, spotting a young Wilson Pickett in the Falcons, whom he signed to another of his labels, Double L. During the late 1960s he founded a club and another label – both called Turntable – which led to an association with boxing promoter Don King. Although there are many question marks about the overall quality of work in Price's career, 'Lawdy Miss Clawdy' was a benchmark and it still sounds pretty good to these ears.

LARRY WILLIAMS

While Price exerted an influence through 'Lawdy Miss Clawdy', it was his nous about the music industry that paid dividends. For it was Price who suggested to Rupe and Blackwell that they should sign both Larry Williams and Little Richard. Williams was born in New Orleans on 10 May 1935. After moving to San Francisco in 1953, he formed the Lemon Drops, backing artists such as Percy Mayfield and Roy Brown. In 1955 he returned to New Orleans and worked for Price as his valet for a spell, before Price convinced Rupe that he should sign Williams. His first outing was a cover of Price's 'Just Because', but that was followed a string of frantic, rock 'n' roll classics such as 'Short Fat Fannie' and 'Bony Moronie' (1957), and 'Slow Down', 'Bad Boy', and 'Dizzy Miss Lizzy' (1958). Although many have dismissed these sides as derivative, the instrumental arrangements were of a comparable quality to those of Little Richard or, indeed, anyone else who recorded under the auspices of Bartholomew at New Orleans' J&M Studios. In 1959 he was busted for possession of drugs, with the result that he disappeared from public view for a time. On his return in 1964 he teamed up with Johnny 'Guitar' Watson and they toured the UK in a revue called *The Larry Williams Show*, which was recorded and released by producer Mike Vernon. When he went back to the US, he worked with the OKeh label as a producer, where he recorded some tracks with erstwhile label-mate Little Richard. Resuming his partnership with Watson, they cut a version of 'Cannonball' Adderley's instrumental 'Mercy Mercy Mercy' (1967), to which they added lyrics.

Throughout his career there had been the suggestion Williams was involved in drugs and prostitution, so it was no particular surprise when he was found shot dead in his Cadillac in the garage of his house in Laurel Canyon, California, on 2 January 1980. The official verdict was suicide.

LITTLE RICHARD

As for Little Richard, it was at the suggestion of Lloyd Price that he sent a demo to Art Rupe in Los Angeles. At the time Little Richard was washing dishes in a Greyhound bus station in Macon. After Rupe heard the demo he agreed to sign him, but not before he had bought out Little Richard's existing contract with Don Robey's Peacock label.

Born Richard Wayne Penniman on 5 December 1935 in Macon, Georgia, Little Richard was one of 12 siblings. Having spent his childhood singing gospel in a church choir, he started his career in medicine shows in 1950 before securing a deal with RCA. Although these early sides – 'Every Hour', 'Get Rich Quick', 'Why Did You Leave Me?', and 'Please Have Mercy on Me' (1952) – were bluesy in character, they could not mask his flamboyant nature, which was apparent in the piano style adapted from another New Orleans performer, Esquerita, and the strong gospel feel in his inflexions. In 1953 he moved to Houston and, with the Tempo Toppers, he recorded for Peacock. It is perhaps worth noting that, at this juncture, Robey's Peacock label was tending to specialize in gospel so Robey and his producer, Joe Scott, must have spotted something in Little Richard's delivery that would fit into the label's image, because as Robey asserted, 'rhythm and blues was felt to be degrading, low, and not to be heard by respectable people'.

After moving to Specialty Records, Little Richard toured briefly with the Johnny Otis Show but in 1955 he started to record at Cosimo Matassa's studios with 'Bumps' Blackwell producing. While Blackwell used the same body of session musicians as Bartholomew, the results could not have been more different. One fundamental difference though, was that Little Richard came from gospel, while Fats had come from New Orleans jazz. Between 1955 and his conversion to religion in October 1957 Little Richard made a series of records that changed the face of popular music: 'Tutti Frutti', 'Long Tall Sally', and 'Rip It Up' (1956), and 'The Girl Can't Help It', 'Lucille' , 'Jenny, Jenny', and 'Keep A-Knocking' (1957); then later 'Good Golly Miss Molly' and 'Ooh! My Soul' (1958), and 'Kansas City' (1959). In common with Domino, Little Richard had no scruples about appearing in films either, as performances in *The Girl Can't Help It* (1956), with Jayne Mansfield, and *Don't Knock the Rock* (1957), with Bill Haley, confirmed.

The precise reasons for Little Richard's subsequent ordination are steeped in controversy, for he has not survived into the 1990s without being a master of his own PR. What is certain is that his grasp of gospel ensured a safe passage to his ordination at Oakwood Theological College in Huntsville, Alabama, as a minister for the Seventh-Day Adventists in 1958. Thereafter, from 1959 until 1962, he recorded gospel, including sides for Mercury with Quincy Jones producing. In 1962 he returned to the arena with a comeback tour of the UK, where he headlined a concert at the Cavern Club in Liverpool, featuring Cilla Black, Gerry and the Pacemakers, and the Swinging Blue Jeans. This led to further tours of the UK and Europe the following year with groups such as the Beatles, the Rolling Stones, and the Everly Brothers. In 1964 Little Richard signed with the Chicago-based Vee Jay label, re-recording his greatest hits as well as a few tasty morsels such as 'I Don't Know What You Got, But It's Got Me' (1965). This, for instance, was anomalous, as the histrionics of Wilson Pickett and the declamatory style of James Brown were sweeping all before them, but Little Richard just couldn't cast off the mantle of rock 'n' roll. So, if he couldn't slot into what was described as soul, his only alternative was to trade on his past glories. And he did. And still does – no award ceremony is quite complete without Little Richard, espousing the gospel according to Penniman. For all his assertions that rhythm and blues meant nothing to him as he grew up, those early Specialty sides are another link in the chain: for doubters, 'Keep A-Knocking' is a close approximation of the Louis Jordan classic 'Open the Door, Richard'.

JOHNNY VINCENT AND EARL KING

Although Bartholomew and Blackwell were the most successful at reaping the rewards that New Orleans had to offer, Johnny Vincent epitomized the latent opportunism of the rock 'n' roll era. Born Vincent

Imbragulio of Italian extraction, he changed his name to Johnny Vincent, working as a distributor before joining Specialty in 1952 as Head of A&R for the southern states. In this capacity Vincent discovered and signed a youthful guitarist called Earl King. While King was never to achieve national distinction, he has become an integral part of the New Orleans club scene and session circuit. Signed in 1952, King's early records such as the self-composed 'Trick Bag' and 'Let the Good Times Roll' illustrated an unpremeditated gutsiness. While King failed to win many admirers beyond New Orleans, Vincent stuck with him, signing him to his own Ace label, which he had set up in Jackson in 1955 although he continued to do his recording in New Orleans. With Ace, records such as 'Those Lonely, Lonely Nights', 'It Must Have Been Love', and 'My Love Is Strong' confirmed New Orleans' separateness from the mainstream of R&B and rock 'n' roll. Despite King's abilities as a composer, Vincent was not averse to claiming a slice of the composer's royalty. As Vincent was certainly no benevolent society, they parted company and King was signed to Imperial by Bartholomew in 1959, where he recorded a version of Guitar Slim's 'The Things I Used To Do' (1962) that easily bears comparison with the original. Throughout the 1960s King was a key member of the session fraternity, working with some of the Crescent City's finest such as Mac Rebennack, Lee Dorsey, and the Meters. Now he seems to have acquired that long-overdue status as one of New Orleans' most venerated survivors as albums such as *Glazed* (1986), with Roomful of Blues, and *Sexual Telepathy* (1990) and *Hard River to Cross* (1993) attest.

HUEY 'PIANO' SMITH

Another to join Vincent at Ace was Huey 'Piano' Smith. With Smith, Vincent had an original, cast in a similar mould to that of another New Orleans stylist, Professor Longhair. Smith's piano style managed to harness the rolling boogie-woogie of Albert Ammons and pitch it somewhere between Fats Domino's and Little Richard's, so in a sense Smith's style owed more to the traditions of New Orleans than either Domino's or Little Richard's. Born on 10 October 1924 in New Orleans, he joined Guitar Slim's trio as pianist in 1949; soon after, he joined the serried ranks of session musicians working out of Cosimo Matassa's studios, backing artists such as Little Richard, Smiley Lewis, and Lloyd Price. In 1955 Vincent suggested he cut sides under his own name, but as Smith's voice lacked confidence, he formed the Clowns, with Bobby Marchan, Junior Gordon, and Roland Cook. Between 1957 and 1958 this combination cut 'Rockin' Pneumonia and the Boogie Woogie Flu' (1957) and 'Don't You Just Know It' and 'High Blood Pressure' (1958). Emblematic of New Orleans R&B,

Smith was distinctive while possessing a mainstream potential. Furthermore, with a lead vocalist in Bobby Marchan, he had in his group one of the best-known eccentrics on the New Orleans music scene. Despite Marchan's penchant for transvestism, which could not have set him in particularly good stead with the racist majority, he had recorded solo sides for Vincent such as 'Little Chicken Wah Wah' (1955), but when he joined the Clowns his impassioned falsetto brought a pitch of real hysteria to the mumbo jumbo of 'Rockin' Pneumonia and the Boogie Woogie Flu' and 'Don't You Know Yockomo'.

When Marchan left in 1959 to resume his solo career, he fared slightly better than Smith as he scored a minor hit with a revival of Big Jay McNeely's 'There Is Something on Your Mind' (1960) for Bobby Robinson's Fury label. It turned out to be fleeting and, after working with Joe Tex's producer, Buddy Killen, he concentrated on live work on the local club circuit. So far as Smith was concerned, he failed to excite popular opinion when he signed to Imperial in 1960, and so he toured with three different groups – the Pitta Pats, the Hueys, and the Clowns. After a brief spell with the Atlantic subsidiary Cotillion in 1970, he retired and became a Jehovah's Witness. For Vincent the 1960s brought little recompense for his unstinting labours, although the success of Frankie Ford ('Sea Cruise', 1959) and Jimmy Clanton should have stood him in good stead to deal with the lean years. After Clanton's final hit 'Venus in Blue Jeans' in 1962, Vincent closed down Ace.

ALLEN TOUSSAINT

While producers and label owners managed to extract fresh ideas from local talent, establishing a network of artists that would make New Orleans synonymous with rock 'n' roll, they also – probably unwittingly – set up a breeding ground for other producers and musicians. Although many of these would pass their days in the relative obscurity of the recording studio, seldom achieving much beyond the immediate locales, some such as Allen Toussaint were able to develop careers as producers as well as those of writers and session musicians. Toussaint had the benefit of youth on his side: R&B and rock 'n' roll were just as much a part of his heritage as jazz, the blues, and gospel. Within that, as Toussaint pointed out, 'New Orleans had always tended to stick by the old ways of doing things: they had resisted the arrival of the electric bass, preferring instead to keep on using the stand-up string bass'. There was still the possibility of taking the traditions of that heritage and updating them to fulfil a wider potential; in that respect Toussaint continued the process that Bartholomew had pioneered.

Born on 14 January 1938 in New Orleans, Toussaint joined Snooks Eaglin's band before replacing Huey 'Piano' Smith in Shirley and Lee's touring band. Hired by Bartholomew as a session pianist and arranger, he worked with Smith, Fats Domino and Lloyd Price, and even arranged 'Walkin' With Mr Lee' – the instrumental by horn man Lee Allen. Despite all this activity behind the scenes, Toussaint emerged centre-stage, cutting his first solo album, *The Wild Sounds of New Orleans* (1958), under the name of Al Tousan. Although it was entirely instrumental, it showed Toussaint's allegiance to Professor Longhair and also served notice that he was a fine writer, penning titles such as 'Java', which was given a wider airing by trumpeter Al Hirt in 1963.

Slipping back into an auxiliary role, he was hired by Joe Banashak of the Minit label in 1960 to become the house producer and arranger. 'When the label was set up', Toussaint recalls, 'Joe and Larry [McKinley] were expecting Harold Battiste, who was working for Specialty, to become their in-house producer and so I played piano for the auditions'. Here he worked with performers such as Ernie K-Doe, Aaron Neville, Smiley Lewis, Chris Kenner, and Irma Thomas, providing a fillip for some careers, a launching pad for others and, in a couple instances, their only real stab at glory.

ERNIE K-DOE AND CHRIS KENNER

For both Ernie K-Doe and Chris Kenner, it was to be a real stab at glory. K-Doe was born Ernest Kador Jr in New Orleans in 1936 where his father was a minister in a Baptist Church. After singing gospel in his youth, he moved to Chicago and recorded for the United label, before returning to New Orleans as a member of the Blue Diamonds. In 1955 he left the Blue Diamonds for a solo career after recording 'Honey Baby' (1954) for the Savoy label. His next stop was Specialty for a slight, but curious, imitation of Little Richard on 'Do Baby Do', which was followed by 'Tuff Enough' (1958) for Ember. In 1960 he was rediscovered by Toussaint and promptly signed after changing his name. While 'Mother-In-Law' (1961) was nine parts novelty – the catchy tune with Benny Spellman's bass repetitions underpinned by a rumbling piano – it was sufficiently humorous to place it in a similar context to Leiber and Stoller's playlets for the Coasters. K-Doe proved to be a one-hit wonder as subsequent releases such as 'I Cried My Last Tear', 'Pop-Eye Joe', 'A Certain Girl', and 'Waiting at the Station' failed to generate much interest. After recording for Duke with producer Willie Mitchell, K-Doe resorted to live work around New Orleans.

As for Chris Kenner, his career was beset by personal problems that involved occasional run-ins with the authorities, but it was through Toussaint that he managed to win some recognition with a series of classics that included 'Land of 1000 Dances', 'Something You Got', 'How Far?', and 'I Like It Like That' (1961). While his vocal style was developed initially through singing gospel, he later broadened his scope to encompass R&B but retained a gospel phrasing throughout his career. Despite the on-off nature of his career, 'Land of 1000 Dances' is one of the real landmark records of the Crescent City.

THE NEVILLE BROTHERS

Despite these one-hit wonders, Toussaint possessed an eagle eye for potential and through the Neville Brothers, he latched on to four siblings – Aaron, Art, Charles, and Cyril – who have endured in vastly differing circumstances to the present day. The first brother to stake his claim was Art, in 1954, when he joined the Hawketts, cutting 'Mardi Gras Mambo' for Chess, which was a local hit. Utterly typical of New Orleans R&B, it made no attempt to embrace the mainstream and somehow illustrated that even youngsters from New Orleans were aware that their musical heritage had little to do with what was going on in the rest of the country. By 1957 Art had joined Lee Diamond's band, cutting 'Cha Dooky Doo' and 'Ooh Wee Baby' before recording a handful of solo singles with Specialty.

Art joined the navy in 1959, while Aaron was incarcerated for six months for stealing a car. When he came out of prison, Aaron signed a solo deal with Toussaint and his first record, 'Over You' (1960), turned into a moderate R&B hit. When Art was discharged from the navy, he joined the Hawketts before teaming up with Toussaint to cut 'All These Things' (1962) for another of Joe Banashak's labels, Instant. At this point the brothers converged, forming the Neville Sounds – with the exception of Charles, who had moved to New York to become a member of Joey Dee and the Starliters.

In 1966 Aaron signed with the Parlo label and cut the haunting 'Tell It Like It Is' (1967); the follow-up, 'She Took You For A Ride', was in stark contrast with its up-tempo shuffling rhythm. In 1968 Aaron and Cyril left the Neville Sounds to form the Soul Machine; Art and the remainder of the group – 'Ziggy' Modeliste (drums), George Porter (bass), and Leo Nocentelli (guitar) – then became known as the Meters.

Between 1968 and 1970 Toussaint and Marshall Sehorn used the Meters as their house band at the Sea-Saint studios, backing Lee Dorsey, Betty Harris, and Irma Thomas. Furthermore, Toussaint and Sehorn decided to record the group in their own right as an instrumental group, in an attempt to emulate the success of Booker T. and the MGs in Memphis. It proved a wise move as 'Sophisticated Lady', 'Cissy Strut', and 'Ease Back' (1969), and 'Look-Ka Py Py' and 'Chicken Strut' (1970) stretched out to win national popularity for the group's style. With this new-found acceptance, a certain amount of discord erupted, culminating in the group's separation from Toussaint and the eventual formation of the Neville Brothers. Through the 1980s and 1990s the Neville Brothers have retained an authentic R&B style that is effectively non-transferable and impossible to replicate, with albums such as *Fiyo on the Bayou* (1981) and *Neville-ization* (1984).

LEE DORSEY

After doing his national service between 1963 and 1965, Toussaint teamed up with Marshall Sehorn to mastermind the revitalized career of Lee Dorsey and to develop the career of Irma Thomas. Although both artists were to be associated with what was now being described as soul, even the New Orleans interpretation of it was still distinct from its regional counterparts. Toussaint continued to write and produce, and his work with Dorsey particularly established a firm financial footing for all his later endeavours.

Dorsey, a native of Portland, Oregon, had had a moderately successful career as a boxer during the 1950s, when he was known as 'Kid Chocolate'. After national service he moved to New Orleans and started a recording career with Joe Banashak, cutting 'Lottie Mo' (1960). Through Banashak, he was placed with producer Harold Battiste by Toussaint. Released through Bobby Robinson's Fury label, 'Ya Ya' (1961) and Earl King's 'Do Re Mi' (1962) both found an audience. However, the Fury label shut up shop and Dorsey was left high and dry. Three years later, Toussaint took him under his wing and signed him to the Bell subsidiary Amy. The resulting records included 'Ride Your Pony' (1965) and 'Get Out of My Life, Woman', 'Confusion', 'Working in a Coalmine', and 'Holy Cow' (1966). From 1967 his records became increasingly less successful but his reputation as a performer flourished. After the release of *Yes We Can Can* (1970), he went into semi-retirement and looked after his car-repair shop until 1980. He died of emphysema on 1 December 1986.

IRMA THOMAS

The other Toussaint signing to transcend stylistic changes in popular taste was Irma Thomas. Today Irma remains a potent reminder of New Orleans' recent past, appearing regularly at the local prestigious Jazz and Blues Festival. Although over the years she has worked with many different producers and embraces some of the notional values of what soul is all about, she combines gospel and the blues and jazz and R&B in a heady mix that is entirely characteristic of New Orleans.

Starting her career in 1958, Irma moved on to the Minit label in 1962, where she recorded 'Ruler of My Heart' and 'It's Raining' with Toussaint before scoring her biggest hits with the soul classics 'Wish Someone Would Care' and 'Time Is on My Side'. She was then unable to gain any continuity with a succession of record labels as she moved to Chess, Capricorn, and a variety of independent labels. During the 1980s, she at last managed to secure some sort of consistency with Rounder, recording albums such as *The New Rules* (1986), *The Way I Feel* (1988), and *Simply the Best* (1991).

DR JOHN/MAC REBENNACK

One other performer linked with Toussaint, whose career has run parallel but with much less commercial success, is Dr John – or, officially, Mac Rebennack. Another disciple of Professor Longhair, Rebennack has been as responsible as Toussaint for elevating the traditions of New Orleans R&B to its current high standing because he has consistently championed the less populist aspects of the city's musical heritage.

Born Malcolm John Rebennack on 12 November 1940 in New Orleans, by 1957 he had established a reputation for himself as a session musician, working with Shirley and Lee, Lloyd Price, Archibald – who had cut one of the first versions of 'Stagger Lee' – Snooks Eaglin, Guitar Slim, and Smiley Lewis. Despite his youthfulness, he had already started talent-scouting for Johnny Vincent at Ace and producer Huey Meaux. In 1958 he issued 'Storm Warning', after co-writing 'Lights Out' for Jerry Byrne (1958). In 1962 he went to Los Angeles, as the New Orleans session circuit was beginning to dry up and he became highly sought-after as a session musician by producers such as Phil Spector, H. B. Barnum, and Harold Battiste. Over the next three years he established a fresh identity as Dr John Creaux, the Night Tripper, fusing the traditional sounds of New Orleans R&B with West Coast rock. In 1968 he released *Gris Gris* for Atco, the Atlantic subsidiary; although it failed to sell in large quantities, it attracted a substantial following among the cognoscenti – or, more accurately, tripped-out hippies. Over the next three years he released three more albums until in 1972 he returned to his roots, recording *Gumbo*. Comprising R&B standards, mostly originating from New Orleans, it was produced by Jerry Wexler and provided him with his first hit, 'Iko Iko' (1972). The next album, *In the Right Place* (1973), continued where its predecessor left off but this time it featured new material, confirming Rebennack's song-writing skills, with 'Right Place, Wrong Time' and 'Such a Night' being exemplars of the New Orleans sound. After more albums, including *Desitively Bonnaroo* (1974), with Toussaint producing and the Meters providing accompaniment, Rebennack's health began to fail but the quality and eclecticism of his output has not let up.

Throughout the 1970s Toussaint continued producing and writing for other artists but his solo career underscored the unwritten agenda of New Orleans, maintaining a balance between lyricism through songs such as 'Southern Nights' and the cultural heritage of the city through his musical *Stagger Lee*; this sense of perspective informed the supervision of the soundtrack of Louis Malle's film *Pretty Baby*. Although he still maintains the Sea-Saint studios in New Orleans, his credentials have caused many such as the Band, Robert Palmer, and Paul Simon to come a-knocking at his front door.

While New Orleans had its own style – perhaps even vernacular – for interpreting R&B, and then rock 'n' roll, Chicago too had its own unique approach. Although the Windy City should have been a barometer because of its location in the Midwest, reflecting the trends of the rest of the country, the reality was that Chicago bucked those trends. With a population that comprised immigrants from Eastern Europe and migrant Blacks from the South, Chicago was the embodiment of a cosmopolitan society. And that was reflected in the idiosyncratic nature of the record business, with the two principal purveyors of R&B – Chess and Vee Jay – denoting that mix.

While both labels had been front runners in establishing a form of R&B that drew from the rural roots of the blues, artists such as Muddy Waters, Sonny Boy Williamson, Lowell Fulson, Howlin' Wolf, John Lee Hooker, and Jimmy Reed adapted by utilizing electrified instruments. Therefore, although these artists were still playing the blues as such, the amplification of electric guitars gave them a power and thrust that were in stark contrast to those of their antecedents. However, while Vee Jay managed to embrace the coming of rock 'n' roll by signing vocal groups such as the Dells, the Spaniels, the El-Dorados and, much later, the Impressions, Chess lagged behind with just the Moonglows. That is, until they signed Chuck Berry and Bo Diddley.

CHUCK BERRY

Both Southerners by origin, Chuck Berry and Bo Diddley were the mavericks that the Chess brothers needed to push them into the rock 'n' roll era. Of the two, Berry was more clearly of the R&B tradition than of the blues, by alluding to country as well as to the sly humour of Louis Jordan. However, it was Berry's guitar work that was particularly at odds with prevailing trends because he used the single-string soloing techniques favoured by T-Bone Walker and the late jazz guitarist Charlie Christian. These elements, combined with a readiness to utilize the imagery of rock 'n' roll, made Berry an innovator.

Born in St Louis, Missouri, on 18 October 1926, Berry formed a trio with drummer Ebby Harding and pianist Johnnie Johnson in St Louis in 1952, while employed as a hairdresser. After working the chitlin' circuit, they wound up in Chicago in 1955, where Berry – after being rejected by both Vee Jay and Mercury – met Muddy Waters, who suggested that they might get a deal with the Chess brothers. Berry made his debut with a country song called 'Ida Red' but Leonard Chess directed him to rewrite the song and turn into something more approachable. The result was 'Maybellene'. Though 'Maybellene' was the template for Berry's career, it took the influence of Alan Freed to get the ball rolling, for which he was fulsomely rewarded with a co-writing credit. While 'Maybellene' was melodically based on 'Ida Red', Berry turned it around and into a love song where the car was the star. With later titles such as 'Roll Over Beethoven' (1956) and 'School Day', 'Oh Baby Doll', and 'Rock and Roll Music' (1957), Berry continued to highlight the concerns and preoccupations of adolescence. This was a million miles from the personalized reflections of the blues, but added to this were the plangent, roller-coaster guitar licks that made the pop music of white contemporaries sound feeble and insipid.

As rock 'n' roll became more recognizable as a form and not just a passing fad, Berry's songs continued to cross racial divides. Berry states in his autobiography that in 'Johnny B. Goode' he had wanted to sing 'There lived a coloured boy named Johnny B. Goode', but what he ended up singing was 'There lived a country boy named Johnny B. Goode'. This was not mere tokenism; it suggested the awareness that within the context of rock 'n' roll being an essentially ephemeral commodity, it possessed that capacity to influence as well as entertain. So Berry was commercially canny enough to realize that songs such as 'Carol' and 'Sweet Little Sixteen' (1958) and 'Almost Grown' and 'Back in the USA' (1959) had a universality in their appeal. However, while his records sold in their thousands, Berry's performance of 'Sweet Little Sixteen' at the Newport Jazz Festival (later featured in Bert Stern's film *Jazz on a Summer's Day*) emphasized the extent to which, as a performer, he could both retain his artistic integrity and command a huge audience.

Meanwhile, there was always the suggestion that the authorities would not allow the minds and morals of the young to be corrupted for too long by all this rock 'n' roll stuff. Elvis was quickly packed off into the army and Berry was arrested and charged with violating the Mann Act in July 1959. He had brought a girl from Texas to work as a cloakroom attendant at his night club in St Louis but fired her when he was told she was working as a prostitute. She went to the police and confessed to them that she was only 14; Berry was charged with transporting a minor over a state line for immoral purposes. At first the charge was quashed, but the prosecutors hounded him until they secured a conviction on 28 October 1961, when he was sentenced to two years in prison. Unlike Elvis, though, who could be seen to be endorsing the 'American way of life', Berry became that much more associated with the mood of disaffection among the nation's youth. This was not restricted to the US alone because, although Berry was in prison, Chess managed to sustain and develop his reputation in the UK too by issuing sides such as 'Memphis Tennessee' (1963).

When Berry emerged from prison in 1964, he picked up where he had left off with titles such as 'Nadine (Is It You?)', 'No Particular Place to Go', and 'You Never Can Tell' (1964). The first two were chart successes, proving that Berry flew in the face of prevailing trends because contemporaries such as Fats Domino had become outmoded by the movement away from R&B and rock 'n' roll towards soul. For this Berry could thank the wave of US and British bands that had grown up on his music and were now seeking to emulate him with their own spirited endeavours. It was not to last, however, because groups such as the Beach Boys, the Beatles and the Rolling Stones developed their own musical identities. While Berry gradually slipped from view, despite albums such as *Live at the Fillmore Auditorium* (1967), backed by the Steve Miller Band, *Back Home* (1970), and *San Francisco Dues* (1971), he continued to be a source of inspiration for successive generations of rock bands. In 1972 he teamed up with the Faces for a concert at the Manchester Arts Festival and then recorded *The London Chuck Berry Sessions*, which featured the Faces as well as members of the Rolling Stones. From these sessions, Berry scored his biggest hit ever with a cover of Dave Bartholomew's 'My Ding-A-Ling' (1972). Leeringly suggestive, 'My Ding-A-Ling' recalled the innuendo-laden output of Jordan and Cab Calloway.

In later years Berry toured constantly but was seemingly at odds with himself, as well as his admirers, creating a picture of a lonely, embittered man with a massive chip on his shoulder. Even Berry's long-time pianist and occasional collaborator, Johnnie Johnson, has been moved to suggest that working with Berry is not the easiest of jobs.

BO DIDDLEY

While Berry may well have felt aggrieved by the way fate dealt with him, his label-mate at Chess – Bo Diddley – has aged gracefully with a sly twinkle in the eye, safe in the knowledge that while he may have been ripped off, used, and abused, he had a bit of a laugh at everyone's expense as well. Bo Diddley took the simple bump-and-grind shuffle beat, with a heavily distorted guitar and loads of tremolo (anticipating, incidentally, Jimi Hendrix), and applied to that a lyrical thrust that owed as much to Louis Jordan as to Jerry Leiber and Mike Stoller.

Bo Diddley was born Elias Bates on 30 December 1928, in McComb, Mississippi, but was adopted by his mother's cousin and raised on Chicago's South Side. Assuming the family name, McDaniel, he started to play the violin and learned to box, before taking the nickname 'Bo Diddley' and playing guitar on street corners. By 1951, in tandem with local hero and mouth harpist Billy Boy Arnold, he had become a fixture on the South Side's flourishing club circuit.

In 1955 he signed to the Chess subsidiary, Checker, because, as he told critic Lenny Kaye, 'everybody else slammed the door in my face'. After cutting 'Bo Diddley', with its accentuated Latin-American shuffle beat, which was mainly due to Jerome Green's maracas and Frank Kirkland's drumming, Bo Diddley's material was the antithesis of Berry: where Berry's lyrics were couched in the vernacular of teenage America, Bo Diddley used the blues or the language of the street – indeed, there is a declamatory facet to his style that is echoed by the gangsta rappers. However, where Bo and Chuck were in complete concord was in the frenetic energy of their performances and this, combined with their appeal for black as well as white audiences, enabled both to cross over from R&B into rock 'n' roll. Despite all this, Bo Diddley never managed to achieve a level of record sales comparable with Berry's. Much of this can be attributed to the fact that Bo Diddley remained at heart a Chicago bluesman and his band, comprising Kirkland, Green, Arnold, and pianist Otis Spann – later augmented by Bo Diddley's half-sister, The Duchess, on second guitar – was geared from the outset to clubs and bars, not the packaged tours of the rock 'n' roll circuit.

Even so, over the next five years Bo Diddley recorded titles such as 'Bring It to Jerome' and 'Pretty Thing' (1955), 'Diddy Wah Diddy', 'Who Do You Love?', and 'Cops and Robbers' (1956), 'Hey Bo Diddley' (1957), 'Say Man' (1959), and 'Roadrunner' (1960), which were as inspirational as Berry's to British and American groups in the 1960s. Still touring, Bo Diddley's sense of humour and distrust of the music industry as such has enabled him to accept his lot philosophically, but his influence should not be underrated.

In the long term, despite the influence of Chicago and New Orleans on the way the future of rock 'n' roll eventually unravelled, the streamlining of record production by the major labels in Los Angeles and New York ensured that much of the stuffing would be knocked out of rock 'n' roll. It also meant that, although the influence of Berry and Domino on later generations of musicians was significant, R&B and rock 'n' roll were destined to become staging posts in the evolution of popular music. While some musicians were to be only too literal in their interpretation of their original inspiration, others were able to develop new styles. The key point remains that, with the dawning of the 1960s, R&B's golden era was coming to its close.

chapter eleven

WHO PUT THE BOMP?

BY 1954 THE R&B VOCAL, or doo-wop, groups had achieved a plateau that obviated any inherent novelty value. Although Leiber and Stoller and the Coasters would take the concept of novelty to another level, this did not stop more groups forming, but it ensured that those that did would be seeking the middle-ground market between R&B and pop. This would later be described as 'rock 'n' roll', but that still remained a catchphrase of telephone-directory-thumping DJs. However, what became more frequent was the incidence of the one-hit wonder. Although that was to become a very 'rock 'n' roll' concept in itself – cut a record and bang it out with maximum publicity – the intensity of the competition ensured that good material with a crossover potential was at a premium and that, consequently, fewer groups were able to build and sustain a career. While producers such as George Goldner would soon get hip to the idea of forming groups – or labels, come to that – just to record a song, groups such as the Harptones, the Crows, and the Jewels all came together with stars in their eyes and their hearts set on careers. Unfortunately all three groups failed to establish themselves.

THE HARPTONES AND GEORGE GOLDNER

The Harptones were formed in Harlem by pianist and arranger Raul Cita as the Harps. Influenced by the Five Keys and the Swallows, the group played throughout New York and New Jersey until they were heard by promoter Leo Rogers, who persuaded them to sign to Morty Craft's Bruce label. Changing their name to avoid confusion with a similarly named outfit from Virginia, the group never achieved any significant sales. Their debut, 'Sunday Kind of Love' (1953), produced by Goldner, acquired classic status almost immediately locally with lead vocalist William Winfield's dreamy tenor making the group something of a cause célèbre in Harlem. The group's follow-up, Cita's 'My Memories of You' (1954), was another hit on the East Coast but still the group failed to break out nationally. Although this failure was partly due to the inability of the Bruce label to market their records satisfactorily beyond the eastern seaboard, there were stylistic differences in the Harptones' delivery that made them sound just too smooth for Midwestern and West Coast tastes. After cutting several more singles, including a sumptuous version of Ivory Joe Hunter's 'I Almost Lost My Mind' (1955), they moved on to the Philadelphia-based Essex label for 'I'll Never Know', and then to Sam and Hy Weiss's Paradise label for a brace of singles – 'Life Is But a Dream' and 'It All Depends on You' (1955) – before hooking up with George Goldner's Rama label.

Now Goldner was tarred with the same brush as Leiber and Stoller: entrepreneurial by instinct, combined with an innate feel for a good song. The downside, though, was that Goldner was temperamentally incapable of concentrating on the job in hand: as soon as he had put together some cash, he was off at the race track or the casino, trying to get rid of his bankroll as quickly as possible. It has to be said that he was very successful at this. Consequently, time and again, he would form labels and cut some records, only to have to sell the label on to bail himself out of debt. So it was that when the Harptones signed to Rama in 1956, Goldner was on a roll, having achieved spectacular success with the Crows and the Cleftones.

With the Harptones, Goldner just could not repeat his winning ways and after three singles, including 'The Masquerade Is Over' (1956), the Harptones moved on to record for other small indies such as Andrea and Raven. Despite their lack of national success, the group's stock on the East Coast remained high and this was confirmed in 1956 when the group's baritone, Billy Brown, died at the tender age of 20: his funeral was attended by so many thousands that a casual observer might have concluded that a much-loved civic dignitary had passed away. While the group plodded on, cutting more singles for Goldner's Gee label ('Cry Like I Cried', 1957), Warwick ('No Greater Miracle', 1959), and Companion ('What Will I Tell My Heart?', 1961), among others, the group disbanded in 1964. Clearly Winfield was so impressed by the attendance at Brown's funeral all those years before that he opened his own funeral parlour – which, apparently, thrives to this day. In the meantime he has re-formed the Harptones for the occasional revival and, in 1982, Winfield and Cita got together to cut *Love Needs* for the Ambient label. While some of the material, such as Jackson Browne's 'Love Needs a Heart', seemed at a glance out of place, Winfield's tenor and Cita's arrangements were as superior as ever.

THE CROWS

If George Goldner failed to take the Harptones to the top, it was not through want of trying or lack of pedigree because Goldner had established his credentials in 1954 with the Crows' 'Gee'. 'Gee' is one of a handful of records whose significance has been debated long and hard by rock 'n' roll historians. Was it, as Philip Groia asserts in *They All Sang on the Corner*, 'the first recording of black street-corner singing to transcend the realm of R&B into the white pop market'? Probably not, because that fails to take into account the influence of either the Mills Brothers or the Ink Spots: the street-corner vocal groups were as much a synthesis of the jubilee gospel vocal group style, the Mills Brothers, and the Ink Spots. Charlie Gillett, in *The Sound of the City*, points out that '"Gee" was an original composition and had a quick dance rhythm' and was therefore distinct from the Orioles' 'Crying in the Chapel', which had charted the previous year. While both these points are well founded, the most obvious consideration is that 'Gee' was George Goldner's first big hit and, while the Crows themselves might have had aspirations to long-term stardom – they made an abortive attempt to crack Las Vegas – Goldner knew that songs were the key to success: find the song and then find a group to record it – the personalities were secondary. This inversion was crucial in the notional transition from R&B into rock 'n' roll. While the group went on to cut several other token singles for Goldner, such as 'Heartbreaker' (1953) and 'Untrue' and 'Miss You' (1954), they wound up their career with 'Mambo Shevitz' for the Tico label in 1955.

THE CLEFTONES

Although Goldner might not have had much intention of developing the Crows' career, he was sufficiently grateful for their hit to name his next record label, Gee, after it. He signed the Cleftones – who had started to sing while at Jamaica High School in Queens, New York, as the Silvertones – in 1955 and they made their debut with 'You, Baby, You', which had been written by the group's second tenor, Berman Patterson. Despite this streak of independence – their follow-up, 'Little Girl of Mine', was an R&B Top Ten hit and was co-written by lead vocalist Herbert Cox and Goldner, or, more likely, Goldner was just claiming a credit as the label proprietor – they did not make a significant impression until 1961 when they covered Hoagy Carmichael and Frank Loesser's standard, 'Heart and Soul'. In between times they cut a succession of likeable titles such as 'String Around My Heart' and 'Why Do You Do Me Like You Do?', but the group themselves seemed to have a clear enough view of the prospects of long-term success to develop careers elsewhere: one member wound up at IBM as a technician and another worked as a computer analyst. However, they continued to work the circuit into the 1970s, but only at weekends.

FRANKIE LYMON AND THE TEENAGERS

If the Cleftones took a very relaxed view of stardom, another of Goldner's protégés, Frankie Lymon, was totally in awe of it. Born on 30 September 1942, in Washington Heights, New York City, Lymon joined the vocal group the Premiers in 1955. Formed on the streets of Harlem, the group comprised Lymon, Jimmy Merchant, Sherman Garnes, Herman Santiago, and Joe Negroni. Richard Barrett, a talent scout for Goldner, spotted them singing on a street corner, and they were auditioned and signed to the Gee label. Barrett himself was no stranger to the vicissitudes of the record industry for he, too, had once been a member of a group called the Valentines. While the Valentines had recorded several singles on the Rama label, such as 'I Love You Darling' (1955) and 'Don't Say Goodnight' (1956), Barrett had sorted himself out a cosy niche within the Goldner organization.

As the discoverer of the Premiers, Barrett encouraged them to change their name to that of the Teenagers and they made their debut with 'Why Do Fools Fall in Love?'. According to legend, it was written by Lymon after reading a poem. Not surprisingly, Goldner claimed a songwriting credit, which has been replaced with Morris Levy's name; Levy acquired most of Goldner's assets before the latter's death in 1970. In the pantheon of rock 'n' roll history 'Why Do Fools Fall In Love?' is significant for two main reasons. The first is the fact that Lymon was a mere 14 years old when the song came out, which established a precedent of turning children into pop stars, but this is not the place to debate the moral dilemmas posed by this practice. The second reason is that this was one of those rare occasions when an original version of a rock 'n' roll song comfortably outsold the cover; in this case the perpetrator of the cover was Gale Storm. With the success of 'Why Do Fools Fall In Love?', Frankie Lymon and the Teenagers became stars of stage and TV overnight, earning around a thousand dollars each for appearances at the Brooklyn Paramount and on *The Ed Sullivan Show*. The group's tours to London saw them indulging in such high jinks that they were thrown out of a succession of hotels, although London hoteliers at that time might well have taken exception to the smallest misdemeanour and it is not recorded whether they established the time-honoured habit of hurling television sets from bedroom windows.

While their UK tour was deemed a success and later records such as 'I Want You to Be My Girl' , 'I Promise to Remember', and 'The ABCs of Love'

(1956) and 'I'm Not a Juvenile Delinquent' and 'Baby, Baby' (1957) possessed a hectic urgency, the breaking of Lymon's voice signified the start of a downward spiral: now there was little to separate them from all the other vocal groups. Lymon embarked on a solo career at the end of 1957, but 'Goody Goody' was destined to be his final success and his career hit the skids. After three years in the wilderness, Lymon returned with a cover of 'Little Bitty Pretty One', but having acquired a heroin problem in the meantime, the writing was on the wall for him. On 28 February 1968, at the grand old age of 25, with a new contract from Morris Levy's Roulette under his belt and having spent the preceding years in poverty, Lymon had a celebratory shot of heroin in the bathroom of his grandmother's flat. It was his last, and time for Lymon to check into the big rehab clinic in the sky.

LITTLE ANTHONY AND THE IMPERIALS

While Frankie Lymon and the Teenagers scaled the rickety ladder of fame and fortune, Goldner and Barrett had come upon another young hopeful. Anthony Gourdine was another New Yorker; born on 8 January 1940, in 1955 he joined the DuPonts, who were engaged by Alan Freed to appear at one of his gigs at the Brooklyn Paramount. The DuPonts performed and were swiftly consigned to the bargain bins after cutting just the one single, 'Prove It Tonight' (1955), for the Royal Roost label. Gourdine, however, graduated from Brooklyn High and joined the Chesters. At this juncture the Chesters featured Tracy Lord, Ernest Wright, Clarence Collins, and Glouster Rogers. When Goldner heard Gourdine, the cash registers started to ring as he saw another Lymon in the making. Changing their name to Little Anthony and the Imperials at the suggestion of Freed, the group were signed by Barrett to the End label in 1958.

With their debut, 'Two People in the World', the straight harmony vocal was offset by Gourdine's wailing falsetto before giving way to a fairly unimaginative lead vocal from Gourdine. It was all right but nothing to get worked up about, and so DJs started to play the other side, 'Tears on My Pillow'. Anthony's crying lead vocal fulfilled Goldner's every dream that here might be someone capable of taking over Frankie Lymon's mantle. With hindsight, the recording endures to this day as one of Goldner's greatest achievements. Fortunately for Anthony he didn't follow Lymon's path, but instead settled for the quiet life on the oldies circuit – not before he had racked up a number of other hits that included 'A Prayer and a Jukebox' and 'Shimmy, Shimmy Ko-Bop' (1960).

After a brief stint as a soloist, Gourdine re-formed the group, with Sammy Strain replacing Lord and signing to Teddy Randazzo's DCP label. Adapting to the coming of soul and the chart domination of Tamla Motown, they scored a few more hits that included 'I'm on the Outside (Looking In)' and 'Goin' Out of My Head' (1964) and 'Hurt So Bad', 'Take Me Back', and 'I Miss You So' (1965). While more lean years followed, the group continued working the club and oldies circuit until 1969 when they cut 'Better Use Your Head' for United Artists, which became a hit in the UK in 1976. Still active as Little Anthony and the Imperials on the cabaret and oldies circuits, Gourdine has come full circle by recording a gospel album, *Daylight* (1980), as well as working with Nancy Wilson on *A Lady With a Song* in 1989.

JAMES SHEPPARD

In some instances Goldner did not need to venture very far to search out fresh talent: sometimes it just fell into his lap. The Heartbeats, led by James Sheppard, were signed to the Hull label in 1955 where they cut three smooth and mellow ballads, 'Crazy For You', 'Darling How Long', and 'People Are Talking'. What happened next was almost, as Dave Marsh asserts, an early instance of 'the concept single', but spread out over a number of years through a series of releases. Therefore what we have is not so much a concept, more a way of life – for the group's fourth release was 'A Thousand Miles Away'. The story goes that Sheppard's girlfriend had moved from Queens to Texas, inspiring Sheppard to pen this paean to separation and long-distance love. The saga had begun with the group's debut, 'Crazy For You', continuing through 'Darling How Long' and 'People Are Talking', and culminating with the magnificent 'A Thousand Miles Away', which made the R&B Top Ten. At this juncture, the Hull label turned up its toes temporarily as Goldner came on the scene and snapped it up, assigning the Heartbeats to the Rama label. Sheppard continued to write about his aspirations and dreams, with 'Wedding Bells', 'Everybody's Somebody's Fool', 'Tormented', 'When I Found You', and 'After New Year's Eve'. By this time doo-wop and vocal groups were fast approaching their sell-by date and – let's be honest about this – doo-wop was not the medium that would spring to most minds as being the ideal vehicle for recounting the trials and tribulations of one's emotional turmoil. Sheppard was undaunted, as Goldner moved the group from Rama to Gee to Roulette. Still the saga continued with 'Down On My Knees' and 'One Day Next Year', but the group disbanded for a time.

In 1961 Sheppard put together a new group, Shep and the Limelites. He even steered clear of Goldner and went back to a revived Hull label. This new chapter opened with 'Daddy's Home' (all students of the genre will know that 'A Thousand Miles Away' had concluded with the words 'Daddy's coming home soon') and continued through 'Three Steps to the Altar', 'Our Anniversary', 'What Did Daddy Do?', and 'I'm All Alone'

(1962) and 'Remember Me'. However, with 'Daddy's Home' Sheppard had adapted to the mood swings of fashion, replacing the doo-wop stylings of the earlier records with the gospel inflexions implicit in 1960s soul. Although it was a massive hit, reaching number two nationally, the full impact of Sheppard's autobiographical sequence was never properly acknowledged. The group disbanded and re-formed in 1969 for the revival circuit, but Sheppard was found bludgeoned to death in a car park on Long Island on 24 January 1970; his assailant was never discovered.

THE CHANTELS

While Goldner's activities were blatantly opportunist, he was not averse to giving groups a break: he was, after all, a very serious gambling man and the philosophy of 'nothing ventured, nothing gained' described his entrepreneurial spirit more accurately than anything else. It is hardly surprising, therefore, that it was Goldner who gave the Chantels their first break. In 1956 the rock 'n' roll scene was a male-dominated arena; although R&B vocalists such as LaVern Baker, Ruth Brown and Etta James offered some threat to this domination, the vocal group, too, was almost exclusively a male preserve. One exception was the Teen Queens – Rosie and Betty Collins – who had some success with 'Eddie My Love' for the Bihari Brothers' RPM label.

The situation changed with the emergence of the Chantels. Formed in New York in 1956 and comprising Arlene Smith, Lois Harris, Sonia Goring, Jackie Landry, and Rene Minus, they sang together in the choir of St Anthony of Padua in the Bronx. Using doo-wop groups such as the Cadillacs and Otis Williams and the Charms as their template, they were signed to the End label by Richard Barrett, where they immediately made an impression with Smith's 'He's Gone'. Featuring Smith's doom-laden lead vocal over simple piano, bass, and drum accompaniment, Barrett bathed it with echo, causing one to think that perhaps Phil Spector's Wall of Sound was not as ground-breaking as many had assumed. In 1958 they broke out with a national hit 'Maybe', written by Smith and Barrett. Dave Marsh, in *The Heart and Soul of Rock 'n' Roll,* describes 'Maybe' as 'virginity personified as an unwelcome condition'. After two more singles, 'I Love You So' and 'Every Night (I Pray)' (1958), Arlene Smith left to be replaced by Annette Smith from the Veneers. The group changed labels, moving to Carlton, while retaining Barrett as producer, but 'Look in My Eyes' and 'Well I Told You' (1961) were their final hits.

Arlene Smith launched out on her own, signing with the Big Top label, where she worked with Phil Spector. Despite her prowess as a writer and arranger, her solo career never took off. Since then she has taught in a primary school in New York and performed in aid of under-privileged children. While their success was limited, the Chantels created the mould for later all-girl vocal groups such as the Shirelles and the Marvelettes and, of course, Spector's protégées.

THE CADILLACS

Although the entrepreurial zeal of Goldner and Leiber and Stoller was a catalyst for rock 'n' roll as we know it, groups such as the Cadillacs, the Penguins, the Jewels, the Chords, and the Cadets achieved a notional zenith as the rock 'n' roll era dawned. While they were inevitably destined to compete with more established outfits such as the Orioles, the Dominoes, the Drifters, the Charms and, later, the Coasters, each group in its own way contributed to the pre-eminence of the vocal group in the mid-1950s, despite a consensus that rock 'n' roll had superseded R&B; in fact, as many have constantly pointed out, the two genres were inseparable.

The Cadillacs were one of the first to draw inspiration from car manu-facturers for their name. More significantly, though, they were inheritors of a pure R&B tradition as pioneered by the Orioles. They passed their entire recording career with the Josie label, a subsidiary of Jubilee, which was owned by R&B specialist Jerry Blaine. Making their debut with the ballad 'Gloria' in 1954, they followed this with similarly even-tempoed numbers such as 'Wishing Well' and 'Down the Road'. In 1955, after working at the Apollo – where their slick choreography and snappy dressing won almost as many admirers as their material – they scored with 'Speedo'. This was basically a jump tune with a close-mouthed, 'blow' harmony, as developed by the Moonglows, but the Cadillacs with Earl Carroll – later of the Coasters – achieved more distinction for the manner of their delivery. In addition, they moved the modus operandi of the vocal group into another dimen-sion, for it was the precision choreography and outré uniform that were to become the trademarks of Berry Gordy's Tamla Motown, although the snap-py tunes didn't harm.

Later titles such as 'Zoom' (1956), 'Sugar, Sugar' (1957), a revival of the Hollywood Flames' 'Buzz, Buzz, Buzz' (1958), and 'Cool It Fool' (1959) saw them adopt the novelty playlet approach of Leiber and Stoller but they had too little commercial appeal; they even reprised the exploits of 'Speedo' in 'Speedo Is Back' (1958). They then became embroiled in a battle between Esther Navarro, who had nurtured them in their formative years, and label owner Blaine over who had rights to the group name. The net result was two groups working as the Cadillacs. Nobody won and the group disband-ed but 'Speedo' remains a glowing testament, as do all those immaculate dance routines with impossible steps.

THE PENGUINS

If the Cadillacs got a raw deal, the Penguins suffered the ignominy of cutting one of the best doo-wop songs of the period, 'Earth Angel' – Jesse Belvin's 'Earth Angel' – only to have it covered by at least a dozen other groups, most notably a particularly feeble version by the Crew Cuts. Still a seminal doo-wop record in the same way that the Marcels' 'Blue Moon' has come to be synonymous with the era, it transcends genre and style.

Formed at LA's Freemont High School alongside other groups such as the Medallions and the Dootones, the Penguins were signed to Dootsie Williams's Dootone label. After scoring with 'Earth Angel', they cut a number of other romantic ballads such as the uncompromisingly titled 'Love Will Make Your Mind Go Wild' and 'Kiss a Fool Goodbye' (1955). Then, after recording 'Dealer of Dreams' for the label, they were taken in hand by the arranger and lawyer turned manager Buck Ram, who got them a deal with Mercury: the Platters were also part of the package. While the Penguins achieved a certain local favour with songs such as 'Be Mine Or Be a Fool' and 'Devil That I See', the group's calling card was indisputably 'Earth Angel' and so they re-recorded it in 1956 for Mercury. Although the Penguins continued into the 1960s, the Platters had Buck Ram's undivided attention and were now reaping their rewards on the international cabaret circuit. The Penguins, for their part, gradually drifted apart and eventually broke up.

OTHER GROUPS ON DOOTONE

As a footnote, the sales from 'Earth Angel' enabled Dootsie Williams's other groups – the Medallions, the Cufflinks, the Meadowlarks, and the Dootones – to keep going for much longer, but with little national success. The Medallions, led by Vernon Green, were also graduates of Freemont High and scored a local hit with 'The Letter', but they overplayed their hand with their constant references to cars: 'Buick '59' was fine, but ''59 Volvo' and 'Pushbutton Automobile' stretched the credibility just a mite too far. The Cufflinks thought they had winners with the ballads 'Guided Missile' and 'Lawful Wedding' (1957) but they were wrong. The Meadowlarks, led by Don Julian, recorded at first for the Modern subsidiary RPM, cutting two singles: 'Real Pretty Mama' and 'LSMFT Blues' (1954). Both were upbeat tunes with jump-style arrangements, but when the group moved to Dootone, they became local celebrities with their ballad 'Heaven and Paradise'. Several other fine ballads followed, including 'This Must Be Paradise' and 'Blue Moon'; they continued into the 1960s when Julian, now calling the group the Larks, scored with 'The Jerk' (1965). The Dootones' claim to fame rested solely on the lightly likeable 'Teller of Fortune' (1955).

THE CHORDS

Although the Crew Cuts proved to be the Penguins' nemesis, the Chords might have harboured similar ill feeling, but there was little reason for it because their only hit, 'Sh-Boom', was a product of the era and serendipity played the larger part in its success. Formed at school in the Bronx out of three other groups – the Tunestoppers, the Keynotes, and the Four Notes – the Chords were inspired by groups such as the Ravens and the Orioles and were accustomed to practise their vocalizing on street corners until they were spotted by talent-agency scout Joe Glaser in just such a location. 'Sh-Boom' utilized the vernacular and jive of the street by adopting the soft, sibilant sounds in contrast with the harder consonants for metre. It was a basic form of scat and it was probably this that Glaser heard on the street corner. Glaser took the group round to Jerry Wexler at Atlantic and the record was cut with basic instrumentation and issued on Atlantic's Cat subsidiary as a B-side to a cover of Patti Page's 'Cross Over the Bridge'. DJs immediately started playing 'Sh-Boom' instead. Although the Crew Cuts' anodyne cover climbed to the very top of the charts, the Chords can't have been too displeased with their Top Ten showing. After cutting a further two records, 'Zippity Zum' and 'A Girl to Love', they changed their name to the Chordcats and then, inevitably, to the Sh-Booms. However, later records for labels such as Vik, Roulette, and Atlantic failed to create a stir and they disbanded in the late 1950s. They re-formed in the 1960s for the benefit of oldies' shows, at which they continued to play until the death of tenor Claude Feaster in 1981.

THE CADETS

The Cadets represented the Bihari Brothers' attempt to beat other labels at their own game, for the group recorded covers of popular R&B sides. However, they took things a step further because their uptempo numbers were cut for the Modern label, while the ballads were put out under the name of the Jacks on the RPM label. This was a moderately successful ploy as they could rely on a 'house' style and just tailor the material accordingly, so Nappy Brown's 'Don't Be Angry', the Marigolds' 'Rollin' Stone', the Willows' 'Church Bells May Ring', and the Jayhawks' 'Stranded in the Jungle' (1956) all got the treatment. Indeed, they didn't stop there – they even stuck a cover of 'Heartbreak Hotel' out as a B-side and cut 'Annie Met Henry' (1956) as their contribution to the Hank Ballard 'Annie' saga. All were vindicated when 'Stranded in the Jungle' hit the national Top Twenty. In their guise as the Jacks they were less successful, but no less enterprising as they covered the Joe Williams and Count Basie classic 'Smack Dab in the Middle' and the Feathers' 'Why Don't You Write Me?'. However, there can have been few illusions about their potential longevity, as lead singer Aaron Collins knew full well from sisters Betty and Rosie, who had enjoyed fleeting success as the Teen Queens; the group's bass singer, Will 'Dub' Jones, went on to greater things with the Coasters.

THE IMPRESSIONS

From post-1955, with the rock 'n' roll era fully under way and the jump-inflected R&B becoming more and more a thing of the past, the most successful vocal groups were well established. Increasingly those that emerged were white groups magpie-ing elements of the sound and presenting an homogenized version. This was not to say that no black groups achieved any success, for the Coasters and the Drifters were approaching their zenith, creatively speaking, but this was tailored to encompass a pop sensibility. Jerry Leiber and Mike Stoller and George Goldner had shown that they were more than able to tap accurately into a mood that would not alienate black record buyers, but would also enthuse a new generation of white kids. With doo-wop beginning to be passé, the predominant strains to be heard in black vocal groups were those of gospel laced with a hard-edged user acceptability. Perhaps the most enduring group to emerge were the Impressions. Combining the rhythmic urgency of the jump groups with a heavy gospel inflexion in the vocals, the Impressions were one of the first to anticipate the swing from R&B and rock 'n' roll into soul. They were formed in 1957 when three of the five members of the Tennessee group, the Roosters – Sam Gooden and the brothers Arthur and Richard Brooks, who had been raised in Chattanooga – moved to Chicago, where they were joined by Jerry Butler and Curtis Mayfield. While both Butler and Mayfield had been members of the Northern Jubilee Gospel Singers since they were kids, they had gone their separate ways as teenagers with Butler joining the Quails and Mayfield the Alphatones. When they joined up with the Roosters, they came to the attention of Ewart Abner and Calvin Carter at the local Vee Jay label. Changing their name to the Impressions, they auditioned for Vee Jay and made their debut with 'For Your Precious Love'. Firmly rooted in the gospel tradition, Butler sermonized, but the song was resolutely secular in its lyrical content. However, such was the enthusiasm of Vee Jay to get the record on the market, they credited it to Jerry Butler and the Impressions. As Butler was later to say, 'I just split because I saw this was getting to be a problem where we were busy worrying about who was getting top billing'. After Butler's departure for a solo career, he was replaced by another ex-Rooster, Fred Cash.

With Butler out of the picture, the group slipped gradually out of sight. Butler meanwhile continued to work with Mayfield, who was employed at Vee Jay as a session guitarist and writer; with Impressions manager Eddie Thomas they set up a music publishing company, Curtom, around this time. Although Butler had to wait two years before his next hit, he continued to demonstrate in his work the sentiments he later outlined to *Rolling Stone* magazine that 'C&W and black popular music – blues and rhythm and blues . . . stay around because they talk about everyday situations; they talk about true-to-life things'. While Mayfield co-wrote and arranged many of Butler's hits, such as 'He Will Break Your Heart' (1960) and 'Find Another Girl' and 'I'm A-Tellin' You' (1961), Butler was not above taking popular titles of the day such as 'Moon River' (1961) and 'Make It Easy on Yourself' (1962) and fashioning them to his ends.

In the meantime, Mayfield re-formed the Impressions in 1961 and moved to New York, where he secured a contract with ABC-Paramount and scored with 'Gypsy Woman'. The next three singles got no further than the lower reaches of the charts, and so Mayfield, Gooden, and Cash returned to Chicago, retaining the name of the group and leaving the Brooks brothers behind. On their arrival Butler gave Mayfield some advice: 'You're not writing about what you live'. Mayfield took the advice to heart and responded with with 'It's All Right' (1963). This was the first of many hits that included 'Talkin' About My Baby', 'I'm So Proud', 'Keep On Pushin'', and 'You Must Believe Me' (1964), 'Amen' and 'People Get Ready' (1965), 'You've Been Cheatin'' (1966), and 'We're a Winner' (1968). All these songs addressed with greater adroitness than probably ever before the disparity between the living standards in black and white communities, while combining the muscular urgency of R&B with a soulful integrity.

In the meantime, Mayfield's gifts as a writer were becoming more widely acknowledged as he started to produce material for others. As Mayfield was later to remember, 'some of the songs I wrote just couldn't work for the Impressions, and so I was only too happy to give them a chance somewhere else'. Among those to benefit were Major Lance, who ran up a string of Mayfield-penned hits between 1963 and 1964; these included 'The Monkey Time' and 'Hey Little Girl' (1963) and 'Um, Um, Um, Um, Um, Um' (1964). Other beneficiaries were Jan Bradley with 'Mama Lied' (1964), Gene Chandler with 'Just Be True' and 'What Now' (1964) and 'Nothing Can Stop Me' (1965), and The Fascinations with 'Girls Are Out to Get You' (1966). While many of these reflected the growth in popularity of Tamla Motown and the concomitant swing towards a user-friendly blend of pop-soul, Mayfield's roots grounded them firmly in the traditions of gospel and R&B.

Although Butler's career had suffered a bit of a nosedive, 'Need to Belong' (1964) and a number of duets, such as 'Let It Be Me' (1964) and 'Smile' (1965), with Betty Everett, kept him afloat until Vee Jay went bankrupt in 1966. Butler signed a fresh contract with Mercury, becoming known as the 'Iceman', a nickname coined by Philadelphia DJ George Woods. Through the remainder of his career, his work became progressively smoother as the hard-edged R&B was replaced by a blend of pop and soul. This was exemplified in his association with Philadelphia producers Kenny Gamble and Leon Huff, who oversaw a sequence of hits that included 'Never Give You Up' and 'Hey, Western Union Man' (1968) and 'Only the Strong Survive', 'Moody Woman', and 'What's the Use of Breaking Up?' (1969). After Gamble and Huff left to start up their own record label in 1970, the partnership was dissolved. Butler, with the backing of the music publishers Chappell's, set up the Songwriter's Workshop to encourage the development of young writers. Although he has not had the success of his early years, Butler has continued touring and working, appearing with Curtis Mayfield in 1983 at a commemorative reunion to celebrate the 25th anniversary of the formation of the Impressions.

When the Impressions' contract with ABC expired in 1968, Mayfield set up a record label out of the Curtom music publishing company. After singles such as 'Fool For You' and 'This Is My Country' (1968) and 'Choice of Colours' (1969), Mayfield left the group in 1970 to pursue a solo career. Retaining a healthy interest in the group's activities, he even nominated his successor, Leroy Hutson. While the output from his solo career was patchy, Mayfield – as he had done many times – charted a course that was to be emulated by many of Tamla Motown's most creative and brightest stars. His solo debut *Curtis* (1970) was funkier than anything he had previously attempted with the Impressions, although he still used string arrangements where appropriate. With 'Move On Up' (1970), Mayfield combined his deep sense of compassion with a muscular urgency because throughout America a ground swell of social unrest and ill feeling prevailed in the wake of Martin Luther King's assassination. Using his lyrics to reflect what was going on around him was nothing new for Mayfield. Since the mid-1960s, with titles such as 'Keep On Pushin'', 'People Get Ready', and 'We're a Winner', Mayfield had consistently sought mediation and understanding instead of the prevailing tide of militancy and intolerance.

The following year Mayfield performed at New York's Bitter End – a venue more regularly associated with folk singers and the like. With Mayfield pursuing a line of social comment in his songs, the Bitter End was an appropriate place for him to touch down, given the number of performers such as Bob Dylan, Joan Baez, Paul Simon, and Randy Newman who had previously graced its stages. Featuring a small back-up band, Mayfield demonstrated on the resulting album, *Curtis Live!,* that he was as in touch with his roots as he was aware of what was going on in the world around him. Over the next two decades Mayfield remained one of the few to be able to adapt the songs that had made him famous to reflect changes in climate – both social and musical. Still cutting records regularly and writing as prolifically as ever, he worked with others including Aretha Franklin, Donny Hathaway, Barbara Mason, and June Conquest, while contributing soundtracks for films such as *Superfly* (1972), *Claudine* (1974) with Gladys Knight and The Pips, and *Let's Do It Again* (1974) with the Staple Singers, and made a plethora of appearances on TV specials.

While some performers from the 1950s had become alienated from the new brigade of rappers, Mayfield – forever the peacemaker – bridged the divide, cutting a re-make of 'Superfly' with Ice-T in 1990. Later that year, on 13 August, a lighting rig was blown over at an outdoor festival in Brooklyn: it struck Mayfield on the base of his neck, breaking it, and paralysing him from the neck down. Despite his immobility, Mayfield – in common with the heavily sampled James Brown – remains a conduit between the vocal groups of the 1950s and the new generation of rappers and hip-hoppers. As recently as 1993 Chaka Demus and Pliers revived 'She Don't Let Nobody' to spectacular effect.

THE SHIRELLES

In addition to the Impressions, the other vocal group to exert an influence on the swing from R&B into soul and pop-soul was the Shirelles. Now there might well be those who raise an eyebrow at the suggestion that such a group can be regarded within the context of R&B. However, as Jerry Butler has already noted, R&B 'talks about everyday situations' and for the Shirelles there was a knowingness to their songs that reflected as accurately as any one of their contemporaries the ups and downs of adolescence. This is not the world of the teenage fantasy in a TV sitcom where bedroom walls are covered in posters of teen idols and crushes are routinely dealt with; this is the world where girls get pregnant at 14 or 15 and perhaps are thrown out of their home for being sluts. With that in mind, songs such as 'Tonight's the Night' (1960) and 'Will You Love Me Tomorrow?' (1962) take on a 'should I or shouldn't I?' resonance.

Formed at school in Passaic, New Jersey, in 1957 as the Poquellos, they changed their name to the Shirelles. In 1958 they were persuaded by a schoolfriend, Mary Jane Greenberg, to audition 'I Met Him on a Sunday', which they had written themselves, for Greenberg's mother, Florence, who owned the Tiara label. It was leased to Decca and became their first hit. With this minor triumph behind her, Florence Greenberg formed Scepter Records with writer and producer Luther Dixon, who had been a member of a vocal group called the Four Buddies. In 1959 the Shirelles covered the Five Royales' 'Dedicated to the One I Love': while Pauling's famous guitar lick from the original had disappeared, it was replaced with a soprano obligato. At a time when female groups were in short supply – only the Chantels had managed to make much headway in this male-dominated market – the Shirelles started to chart a course with Dixon that resulted in a string of hits, including 'Tonight's the Night' (1960), 'Mama Said' (1961), 'Will You Love Me Tomorrow?', 'Baby It's You', and 'Soldier Boy' (1962), and 'Foolish Little Girl' (1963).

With their arrival they started a flurry of activity at high schools the length and breadth of the country, as girl groups inundated record labels with requests for auditions. For the Shirelles, things ran less smoothly because a legal tussle ensued between the group and Scepter in 1964, which would not be resolved until 1967: their earnings had not been paid into their individual trust funds as originally agreed. Once that problem was resolved, they were free to record where they liked, but in 1967 girl groups were on the wane. However, this did not apply at Tamla Motown in Detroit, where Berry Gordy Jr had charted the progress of the Shirelles and signed up his own troupe of girl groups from the surrounding housing projects. These included such familiar names as the Supremes, Martha and the Vandellas, the Marvelettes, and the Velvelettes. By following the example of two groups, the Impressions and the Shirelles, Gordy developed the template for Tamla Motown and in the process created one of the dominant sounds of pop music in the 1960s.

THE ISLEY BROTHERS

Although many of the groups Gordy signed were local kids who had worked in local vocal groups in the 1950s, most were ingénues. The one notable exception and the one group that remained substantially true to its roots was the Isley Brothers, despite the gloss that Motown applied to all its acts. Drawing their inspiration from gospel, the four brothers – Rudolph, Ronald, Vernon, and O'Kelly – performed in local churches throughout Cincinnati. After the death of Vernon in a road accident around 1956, they disbanded, but started to work together again at the request of their parents. Moving to New York in 1957, they recorded 'An Angel Cried' for the Teenage label, before signing with George Goldner's End label. For once in his life, Goldner was unable to capitalize and the Isleys started to build a reputation on the strength of their live performances at venues such as the Apollo and the Chicago Regal. Frantic and chaotic on stage, they worked themselves into the type of frenzy more readily associated with religious fervour. At one of their shows at the Howard Theatre in Washington, DC, they were seen by Howard Bloom of RCA records. He signed them there and then. However, his mistake was to turn them over to producers Hugo and Luigi. Their debut, 'Turn to Me' (1959), was all right, but anyone who had seen one of their shows would have thought, 'Must try harder'! Naturally, it failed to sell. The follow-up, though, 'Shout' (1959), was the antithesis of its predecessor. Raucous and frantic, it embodies the spirit of R&B at its most potent with the gospel-style call-and-response of the chorus demonstrating the extent to which the non-secular was shaping the future of contemporary black music: Dave Marsh says that it 'starts where "What'd I Say" finishes' and he's not wrong. What makes it even more remarkable is the context in which it appeared: rock 'n' roll being replaced by anodyne balladeers and teen idols, while the black vocal groups were beginning to embrace a wider pop sensibilty. Selling over a million copies, it is as perfect a slice of R&B as one could hope to find; moreover, it entered the repertoires of many R&B-inspired groups such as Joey Dee and the Starliters and the Chambers Brothers and, of course, Scotland's very own Lulu – for whom it has become her trademark.

After 'Shout' the brothers cut 'Respectable', but they couldn't see eye to eye with Hugo and Luigi and so they moved on to Atlantic, where they were teamed with Jerry Leiber and Mike Stoller. Four singles later, they were on the move once again, this time to Scepter subsidiary Wand. After one single they recorded 'Twist and Shout' (1963). While popular belief would have it that they cut the original version, that honour can be claimed by a group called the Top Notes; the producers on that occasion were Jerry Wexler and Phil Spector. But it was the Isleys' version that drew the plaudits. Written by Phil Medley and Bert Russell (the pen name of producer Bert Berns), 'Twist and Shout' has become a standard. Drawing its inspiration from the extraordinary popularity of dances that were sweeping the US, 'Twist and Shout' was the means of expression instead of the logistics of execution. Although it is a singular record, there is something lacking that makes it inferior to the earlier 'Shout'. For all that, it is still a great record for the time and later artists such as the Mamas and the Papas, Bruce Springsteen and, especially, the Beatles would demonstrate in wildly differing ways the extent to which R&B affected their own personal interpretation and expression.

Despite the Isleys' level of success, record labels found them a hard act to cope with: if they were described as an R&B outfit, they could be perceived by audiences as out of date, and if they were described as a soul band, a visit to one of their concerts would scotch that appellation just as quickly. Consequently they chopped and changed labels with increasing regularity. Indeed, they terminated their arrangement with United Artists on the grounds that they were told to record 'Surf and Shout'. They resolved the situation by forming their own label, T-Neck, and cutting 'Testify' with guitarist Jimi Hendrix. In 1964, after putting T-Neck on the back burner and having another stint with Atlantic, they signed with Motown. Here they underwent the sea change that had eluded them for years: they abandoned R&B in favour of the smoother blend of pop and soul that was now *de rigueur*. While the Motown songwriting and production partnership of Eddie Holland, Lamont Dozier, and Brian Holland provided them with high-quality material such as 'This Old Heart of Mine', 'I Guess I'll Always Love You', and 'Behind a Painted Smile' (1966), it lacked urgency and that element of chaos.

After re-establishing T-Neck, they reverted to the frenetic blend of R&B and gospel that characterized their early years and *It's Our Thing* (1969) sold over two million copies in the US and established the group with rock audiences in the process. During the 1970s the group's output oscillated between the soft soul of 'That Lady' (1973) and 'Harvest For the World' (1976) and the funky dynamism of their live shows, which were enlivened by the earlier recruitment of younger brothers Ernie on guitar and Marvin on bass, and cousin Chris Jasper on keyboards. While these additions drew the Isleys into line with other practitioners of rock-slanted funk and R&B such as Sly and the Family Stone and George Clinton's Funkadelic and Parliament collective, they have never been averse to criticizing social order or political systems with songs such as 'Fight the Power' (1975) and 'Send a Message' (1987).

In 1984 Chris Jasper and Ernest and Marvin Isley left to form their own group, Isley Jasper Isley, amid considerable acrimony, but the rift was resolved and they rejoined the group in 1990. The 1990s have been mixed, with vocalist and arranger Angela Winbush marrying Ronald, while O'Kelly succumbed to a heart attack in 1986 and Rudolph followed him in 1995. However, a new generation of rappers has been keen to endorse the Isleys' inestimable contribution by sampling them and in 1996 the Isleys worked with writers and performers R. Kelly and Keith Sweat. With Kelly they found themselves back in the Top Ten with 'Down Low (Nobody Has to Know)'.

With their appeal across generations and transcending styles and gen-res, the Isleys continue to prove that R&B is the legitimate antecedent of contemporary styles such as swingbeat and hip-hop. But that was far in the future, for the 1960s beckoned and with it the black vocal group slipped inexorably towards obsolescence. Except at Tamla Motown, of course.

chapter twelve

REVIVAL

A
S THE 1950s GAVE WAY TO THE 1960s, there was a mood of optimism abroad in the US: John Kennedy was in the process of securing the Democratic Party nomination to run in the up-and-coming presidential election. Few had any doubts that he would eventually become president, and that his youthful outlook would usher in a new phase of diplomacy and even improve the lot of black Americans. Furthermore, rock 'n' roll had confirmed that it was, indeed, here to stay, although some of its brightest hopes had foundered: Buddy Holly died in a plane crash in 1959 and Elvis Presley was still in the army.

Theoretically, opportunities were limitless. Some of the first to recognize the commercial potential of this new mood of optimism were the major record labels and they set about discovering 'new Elvises' and 'new Buddy Hollys' with commendable zeal. The only real problem with these role models was that Holly had been a quirky writer from Texas with spectacles and Elvis a country boy from the South. However, in Pat Boone the majors thought they had a role model that would typify the innate wholesomeness of the US and prove to the kids that, 'Yup, there's nothing wrong with rock 'n' roll'. The great difficulty lay in the fact that singers such as Bobby Vee, Johnny Tillotson, Frankie Avalon, and Fabian all lacked that essential element of rock 'n' roll: rawness. And it really didn't matter how many times Fabian curled his lip, he just did not possess the earthy authenticity of Elvis.

It wasn't all bad news, though, for at New York's songwriting factory in the Brill Building on Broadway, dozens of young writers such as Carole King and Howie Greenfield, Burt Bacharach and Hal David, Jeff Barry and

Ellie Greenwich, Barry Mann and Cynthia Weil, among others, were busy confecting little slices of magic that articulated the hopes and aspirations of teenagers in a language they understood. So it was to these writers that producers such as Jerry Wexler at Atlantic and Luther Dixon at Scepter looked for material for, respectively, groups such as the Drifters and the Shirelles.

In the Midwest, Chicago labels such as Chess were having a hard time realigning their artist roster to correspond more accurately with contemporary tastes because their biggest star, Chuck Berry, was under a cloud for suspected immoral activities and Bo Diddley was too close to R&B to be marketable on a wide scale. At Vee Jay things looked slightly better, where the Impressions, now led by a young writer, guitarist, and producer called Curtis Mayfield, were beginning to cut records that had 'crossover' potential. The real action, though, was centred around Motor City, Detroit, where another young writer and producer called Berry Gordy was beginning to lease records to the majors from his own group of labels, known collectively as Tamla Motown.

Out in LA, the story was, again, no different. At Modern, the Bihari Brothers started to repackage the contents of their vaults, reissuing them as albums on their bargain basement Crown label; and Art Rupe demonstrated singular prescience by closing down the Specialty label in 1959, as he couldn't be bothered with Little Richard's tantrums or Larry Williams's demands.

By the end of 1960, R&B had been given a face-lift, a manicure, and a nice new haircut. So Muddy Waters and John Lee Hooker had no alternative but to go back to the club circuit, Jimmy Witherspoon turned to jazz with Count Basie, Amos Milburn became a hotel clerk, but most just retired or adapted. Ike Turner managed to adapt. So did James Brown. And, of course, independent producers such as George Goldner and Jerry Leiber and Mike Stoller kept their eyes skinned for fresh talent. However, it did seem in the US that the only person with something new to offer was a young producer by the name of Phil Spector, because Spector knew his way around a recording console the way most know their way home. Using girl groups such as the Shirelles as his template, Spector found the Crystals a few months after they were formed and signed them to the Philles label, which he had established with Lester Sill, a consultant at the music publishers Screen Gems. Then after selecting appropriate material, he recorded them using every device at his fingertips: the process he later described as the 'Wall of Sound'. This is not the place to go into the enormous impact that Phil Spector was to have, but he and a couple of other young producers called Bert Berns and Jerry Ragavoy were, for the time being, the New York whizz kids.

EARLY R&B IN THE UK

On the other side of the Atlantic, in the UK, the music industry was under-going a curious sea change, the impact of which few could possibly have foretold. Briefly, pop music in the UK had always been a pale alternative to its American counterpart. The BBC was the only broadcasting company transmitting to the British Isles, apart from Radio Luxembourg, which only broadcast late at night and the reception was appalling. Therefore the BBC seemed to hold the monopoly over tastes in popular music and they laboured under the strange misapprehension that Tommy Steele and Ann Shelton were the acme of cool. In fact, British audiences never experienced rock 'n' roll as an indigenous musical form. It was second-hand by the time it reached the UK and those who had aspirations to be rock 'n' roll stars were merely looking to imitate their American counterparts.

However, there was the club circuit, catering to both jazz and folk audi-ences, and there were coffee bars. And it was in the jazz clubs that R&B began to take root. Traditional jazz had tended to be sustained by a bunch of musicians such as Ken Colyer who had taken the styles of New Orleans big-band jazz and adapted them to smaller, more malleable formations. Similarly Humphrey Lyttelton provided a training ground for mainstream players such as Tony Coe and Kathy Stobart. However, Chris Barber's band was a catalyst for not only did he help develop skiffle – perhaps the only indigenous by-product of R&B – but he also brought over such revered fig-ures as Sonny Terry and Brownie McGhee, Louis Jordan, and Muddy Waters to tour Britain. They remained essentially 'cult figures', though, despite being lauded by the cognoscenti and few people deserved that appellation more than Alexis Korner.

ALEXIS KORNER

Korner dominated the embryonic blues and R&B circuits in the UK throughout the early 1960s, enjoying a sort of 'Mr Fixit' role as well as being a father figure for scores of young musicians: groups such as the Rolling Stones, Manfred Mann, the Graham Bond Organisation, Cream, Led Zeppelin, and Free were formed, more or less, in his living room.

Korner was born on 19 April 1928, in Paris, France, and was raised in France, Switzerland, and North Africa before settling in London just as the Second World War broke out. After learning boogie-woogie from Jimmy Yancey records, he joined Chris Barber's band as a guitarist, then in 1952 he joined Ken Colyer's offshoot skiffle band, which included Lonnie Donegan among its number. As the 1950s progressed, Korner, in tandem with mouth-harp man Cyril Davies, began to emulate Muddy Waters by performing with amplified equipment and, by 1957, guitarist Jeff Bradford had joined them. From this starting point, Blues Incorporated came about in 1961, featuring musicians such as Paul Jones, who would later front Manfred Mann, and Brian Jones and Mick Jagger, who would co-found the Rolling Stones. It was a floating collective that appeared to be mutually supportive, while Korner presided over all, offering enthusiasm and encouragement to his protégés. Although the repertoire of Blues Incorporated drew heavily from Muddy Waters' catalogue, Korner's acoustic guitar work recalled Lonnie Johnson and Big Bill Broonzy and his compositions reflected his enthusiasm for Charlie Mingus and 'Cannonball' Adderley. In 1962 Davies left the group over musical differences; in this case the differences were real enough because Davies was a blues purist. He formed his own R&B All Stars, which had a similar membership policy to that of Blues Incorporated, but died in 1963 from leukaemia. By 1963 the beat-group boom to which Korner had contributed so much was up and running and its momentum threatened to engulf all in its torrent; it wasn't confined to London either. In Liverpool, the Beatles had been formed out of the remnants of an R&B group called the Quarrymen; in Belfast George Ivan Morrison had founded Them; Manchester had the Hollies; Newcastle had the Animals and so it went on. However, London was the mecca for the blues-based bands, and clubs such as the Bag O'Nails, the Flamingo, and the Marquee flourished, as groups such as the Rolling Stones, the Graham Bond Organisation, Manfred Mann, John Mayall's Bluesbreakers, the Yardbirds, Long John Baldry and the Hoochie Coochie Men, the Pretty Things, Georgie Fame and the Blue Flames, the Spencer Davis Group, and Zoot Money's Big Roll Band nightly trod the boards, playing material that had been made famous by musicians such Muddy Waters, John Lee Hooker, Howlin' Wolf, and T-Bone Walker. As Korner's charges grew in their wealth and fame, he was increasingly left to his own devices and always sounded genuinely pleased that he had been able to nurture talent and to help give the music he loved a wider currency.

STAX, AMERICAN STUDIOS, AND FAME

Meanwhile, back in the US, American musicians looked on in disbelief as groups of scruffy, long-haired, disreputable louts from London landed and talked – with completely incomprehensible accents – about how the blues had changed their lives. However, the American record industry had experienced a shot in the arm – well, two actually. Firstly, Bob Dylan had arrived on the scene, galvanizing a wave of enthusiasm for folk music, but, secondly – and more significantly within this context – Memphis had undergone a radical change as two local business people, spotting the wealth of local talent, had decided to form their own label, Satellite. It would later be renamed Stax.

In 1958 brother and sister Jim Stewart and Estelle Axton, who were white, founded Satellite to record local black talent for black audiences. Stewart was born in Middleton, Tennessee, in 1930 and after graduating from Memphis State University went into banking. In his spare time he played fiddle in a Western swing band and even recorded the country tune 'Blue Rose' in 1957. In 1958 the partners formed Satellite and were joined by Chips Moman, a white session guitarist from LaGrange, Georgia, who gradually became Satellite's in-house producer; the label's house band comprised Estelle's son Packy, Steve Cropper on guitar, and Donald 'Duck' Dunn on bass and were known as the Royal Spades; Cropper and Dunn went on to become the core of Booker T. and the MGs.

In 1960 Stewart leased a disused cinema on East McLemore Avenue for a $1000 per month. One of their first visitors was a local DJ at radio station WDIA called Rufus Thomas, whose daughter Carla was beginning to work as a vocalist. A deal was struck whereby a song – 'Cause I Love You' – that Stewart had composed would be cut by Carla, and Rufus would put the word about. John Richbourg at Nashville's WLAC, which had a predominantly black audience, agreed to get behind the record in exchange for a percentage of the royalties. After selling fifteen thousand copies locally, it came to the attention of Jerry Wexler, who leased it from Stewart for $1000 for national release on Atlantic. That was the beginning for the label, although in 1961 they had to change its namel; they chose 'Stax', which was a combination of the first two letters of their surnames – Stewart and Axton.

With signings such as William Bell and Otis Redding, Stax began to develop the sound of Southern soul. Although its roots in R&B were evident, soul used the emotional commitment of gospel, but in a secular format. The arrangements were built around the house band of Booker T. and the MGs, who were supplemented by the brass of the Mar-Keys. Throughout the latter half of the 1960s, Stax accumulated a roster of artists that included Eddie Floyd, Sam and Dave, Johnnie Taylor, Carla Thomas, Albert King, and Rufus Thomas, although the loss of Otis Redding in 1967 in a plane crash was a major blow.

In 1965 Stewart had enlisted the services of Al Bell as head of promotion. With Bell in place Stewart had a man who was quite prepared to use his blackness in the same way as Motown's Berry Gordy: to inspire racial loyalty. (It is ironic that Motown built its success on its crossover appeal.) In 1968 Stewart signed a deal with Gulf & Western, the owners of Paramount Records, and it was the beginning of the end for Stax. Despite major success with Isaac Hayes, the label closed in 1976 after a series of severe errors of judgement that resulted in its going bankrupt. Berry Gordy had, over a corresponding period, built Tamla Motown into the largest black-owned corporation in the US.

CHIPS MOMAN AND AMERICAN STUDIOS

What was most significant about Stax, though, was that although its output was aimed at black markets, many of the writers and session musicians were white. Their success had the knock-on effect of causing others such as Chips Moman and Rick Hall to set up similar operations. Moman, in particular, was a good example of how attitudes changed. Briefly he left Stax to set up his own studio, American, in late 1962 after a bitter argument with Stewart. As a settlement Stewart gave Moman $3000, which he used to set up and open the studio at 827 Thomas Street in 1964. Between 1964 and 1971, the American Studios turned out a succession of hits for artists such as James Carr, the Box Tops, Oscar Toney Jr, Bobby Womack, Joe Tex, Joe Simon, and Elvis Presley. While the house band comprised such luminaries as guitarist Reggie Young, Moman also attracted writers of quite staggering ability, such as Dan Penn and Spooner Oldham, who were able to cross the barriers of pop and soul and country with complete ease. In 1972, in a fit of pique, Moman shut down the studio in Memphis and reopened it in Atlanta; his wrath was caused by a reluctance on the part of the musical establishment to give him any credit for his achievements. It turned out to be a false move. In 1975 he moved to Nashville and set up studios on Music Row.

RICK HALL AND FAME

Rick Hall at FAME had been a member of a country group, Carmol Taylor and the Country Pals, where he met Billy Sherrill. By 1958 both he and Sherrill had left their respective groups to form the Fairlanes, which featured Dan Penn. In 1959, FAME (Florence Alabama Music Enterprises) was launched. At first it was sited above a drugstore belonging to the father of a local songwriter, Tom Stafford. Word got around and local white musicians such as Oldham, Penn, Roger Hawkins, David Hood, and Jimmy Johnson started knocking on the front door asking for work. In 1961 Hall had his first hit, 'You Better Move On' by Arthur Alexander, which was shortly covered by the Rolling Stones. With the royalties Hall set up the FAME studios in neighbouring Muscle Shoals. From this assortment of inexperienced musicians, he assembled the first of several versions of the house band and was the catalyst for the songwriting partnership that Penn formed with Oldham. Over the next ten years the steady stream of artists and producers willing to pay Hall's costs grew from a trickle to a torrent: Aretha Franklin, Wilson Pickett, Joe Tex, Clarence Carter, Etta James, Irma Thomas, Ted Taylor, Candi Staton, and Laura Lee.

In 1969, Johnson, Hood, and Hawkins, who had been the nucleus of FAME'S house band, moved and set up their own operation, Muscle Shoals Sound studios, in nearby Sheffield. Hall soldiered on for a while, but soul in the way that Hall treated it was beginning to lose some of its gloss. Additionally he was being offered sacks of cash to produce pop artists such as the Osmonds, Paul Anka, and Bobbie Gentry. In 1974 he closed FAME.

NEW INTERPRETERS OF THE BLACK EXPERIENCE

In a sense, the explosion of interest in Southern soul as instigated by a bunch of white guys was a corollary of the British beat-group explosion during the corresponding period. There was a basic difference, however: in Muscle Shoals and Memphis white guys were playing with black guys and helping them to realize a different interpretation of the black experience. On the other hand, the beat-group explosion in the UK was fuelled by a desire to create something new out of a form that already existed. Curiously, when white American collegiates formed bands, they strove at first to replicate the sound of their heroes but quickly recognized that this brand of orthodoxy actually did no one any good and so, as with the British groups, American blues-based bands such as the Paul Butterfield Blues Band, the Blues Project, Canned Heat, and the Electric Flag put their own spin on the blues. From a social point of view, miscegenation was still reviled in the South of the early 1960s and segregation remained a matter of course, but the attitude propounded by white musicians was 'if you don't like it, shove it'.

The heritage of blues and R&B music increasingly came to be nurtured by white college graduates. And to add insult to injury, these same blues-based groups – such as Canned Heat and Paul Butterfield in the US, and the Yardbirds, John Mayall's Bluesbreakers, and Fleetwood Mac in the UK, among others – took bluesmen such as Sonny Boy Williamson, John Lee Hooker, Muddy Waters, and Howlin' Wolf, to name but a few, out on tour with them. Whether Muddy Waters felt he was being patronized is difficult to know, but John Lee Hooker has always expressed the sentiment that white groups ripped off the blues and its practitioners. In the South black musicians appeared to enjoy the freedom of collaborating with white musicians on an equal footing, but racism was endemic and leopards don't change their spots: they merely fade with the passage of time. However, two guitarists who seemed to embody the reciprocal relationship that ostensibly existed were Taj Mahal and Ry Cooder. While they have played together occasionally, they share an almost sociological attitude towards music, examining it through whatever facet is currently engaging their curiosity. There are few genuine polymaths kicking around in rock 'n' roll land.

TAJ MAHAL

Born Henry St Clair Fredericks on 17 May 1942 in New York City, Taj Mahal is the son of an arranger. His opening shot was the initially shelved, but now much lauded, Rising Sons' sessions, which featured guitarists Cooder and Jesse Ed Davis and Spirit drummer Ed Cassidy. After the group disbanded, Taj settled on a solo career that initially took root on the West Coast club circuit and then he cut *Taj Mahal* (1967) for Columbia; his band included Davis, bassist Gary Gilmore, and drummer Chuck Blackwell. The result was a rich, but meditative, introduction to the country blues. The follow-up, *The Natch'l Blues* (1968), was similarly affectionate but broadened the terms of reference to include the blues in its upbeat, uptown, urban configuration. This was followed by Taj's perspective on the blues and R&B. Entitled *Giant Step/De Ole Folks at Home* (1969), the former was electric and brassy, while the latter was acoustic and mellow. Thereafter Taj rang the changes, incorporating Latin, African, and Caribbean rhythms on self-penned titles, as well as on traditional blues, folk songs, and spirituals.

RY COODER

Ry Cooder – born Ryland Cooder on 15 March 1947 in Los Angeles – started his career as a session guitarist and worked with Captain Beefheart on the early sessions for the Buddah label that resulted in the classic *Safe As Milk* (1967) album. In 1970 he cut his debut, *Ry Cooder*, which featured a mix of blues and hillbilly, livened up by a smattering of obscure R&B songs such as 'Pig Meat'. If his debut was eclectic, the follow-up, *Into the Purple Valley* (1971), which featured a profusion of R&B obscurities and wry social comment, showed a masterful and original hybrid that transcended simple classification. Some of his most memorable work has been reserved for others, particularly on soundtracks such as *Performance,* where the slide guitar work on 'Memo From Turner' is gritty and grainy, and for the Rolling Stones on their cover of Robert

Johnson's 'Love in Vain' on *Let It Bleed*. As if to emphasize the symbiotic relationship that exists with Taj, both have collaborated on separate occasions with V. M. Bhatt, the Indian mohan vina (a type of guitar that Bhatt had designed) specialist.

THE RISE OF ROCK

Despite the contributions from the iconoclastic Taj and Cooder, the initial enthusiasm for the blues began to wane in the late 1960s as white kids were more interested in all things pyschedelic, and bands such as Blood, Sweat and Tears and Paul Butterfield in the US and John Mayall's Bluesbreakers and Keef Hartley in the UK added horn sections to their existing line-ups, making them more recognizable as R&B outfits. Unfortunately many of them chose to write their own material, some of which had clearly been written while intoxicated or in an altered state of awareness. Only two groups, the Band and Creedence Clearwater Revival, seemed up to the task of appraising their roots and applying their own vision to their interpretations. The Band's *Moondog Matinée* (1973), with Robbie Robertson's immaculate guitar work, featured Sam Cooke's 'A Change Is Gonna Come' and Bobby Bland's 'Share Your Love With Me'. John Fogerty and Creedence Clearwater Revival took classics such as Screamin' Jay Hawkins's 'I Put a Spell on You', Dale Hawkins's 'Suzie Q', and Elvis Presley's 'My Baby Left Me' and used these to develop a churning, riff-based synthesis of R&B and rockabilly. However, such was the excellence of Fogerty's original material that Creedence were viewed, as were the Band, as commentators on the changing pace of contemporary American styles, although both, through their R&B covers, show a nostalgic affection for the music that informed their upbringing.

At the beginning of the 1970s in the UK, there was a wide-scale turn around: the blues boom had gradually evolved into a form of heavy rock that seemed to depend for its survival on the lead guitarist's ability to regurgitate as many cliché-ridden solos as possible, for as long as possible. This heralded an entirely new sub-genre known as 'heavy metal'. Many of the guitarists – such as Jimmy Page in Led Zeppelin, Jeff Beck, and Eric Clapton – whose careers had been grounded in the blues boom, now needed to explore fresh avenues. Along the way there were casualties as well: Jimi Hendrix died in 1971 and the immensely promising guitarist of Free, Paul Kossoff, was to die in 1976 before his talent fully matured. Elsewhere there were a plethora of groups such as Yes and Supertramp that were purveying what was grandiosely described as 'progressive rock' to the masses.

In the US, things were almost no different: both Janis Joplin and Jim

Morrison died uncomfortably early. Joplin in particular had the voice to become one of the greatest white blues singers of them all. While her early recordings with Big Brother and the Holding Company had lacked finesse, her second solo album, *Pearl* (1971), issued posthumously, suggested a vocalist with the range to match the passion. By now 'rock' music – a pejorative term if ever there was one – was big business. Few had any illusions about it and, as if to bang another nail in the coffin of what had been condescendingly known as the 'Woodstock Generation' (after the eponymous festival), groups chose venues according to the size of their egos. Sports arenas and large tracts of sprawling countryside in the backwoods became the chosen stage for bands such as Led Zeppelin and the Rolling Stones. Nevertheless, it should be noted that the Rolling Stones with *Exile On Main Street* (1972) had confidently predicated their R&B roots by adding saxophonist Bobby Keyes, trumpeter Jim Price, organist Billy Preston, Dr John on keyboards, and a host of backing vocalists such as Shirley Goodman, who had scored with *Let the Good Times Roll* in 1956 as one half of the duo Shirley and Lee.

Elsewhere, although Stax was still flourishing – just – Rick Hall was recording the Osmonds and Muscle Shoals Sound studios was recording white bands such as Traffic, the Rolling Stones, Boz Scaggs, and Rod Stewart. Although these musicians had espoused their love of R&B, their sound lacked the wholeheartedness and rough and ready vulgarity of R&B in its first flush of youth. There was one exception, for the Boz Scaggs sessions featured the wunderkind guitarist Duane Allman of the Allman Brothers Band. Led by brothers Duane and Gregg, the band had the passion and commitment to continue playing their fiery brand of R&B without suffering any compromises: Duane's slide guitar work was – and is – a sound for sore ears. However, his death in 1971, followed by that of the band's bassist, Berry Oakley, soon after, put paid to that as the group was progressively riven with strife.

In the meantime, soul had not been entirely usurped because over in Memphis at the old Sun studios on Union Avenue, trumpeter and producer Willie Mitchell had revived the Hi label, which, during the 1950s, had been basically a country label. Now it had become the home of Al Green and a crop of other soul singers such as Ann Peebles, O. V. Wright, Syl Johnson, and Otis Clay. In the north, Motown had relocated to Los Angeles, and over in Philadelphia two songwriters and producers, Kenny Gamble and Leon Huff, with the assistance of producer Thom Bell, had set up the Philadelphia International label in 1970. With funding from Columbia, Gamble and Huff built a roster of artists that included the O'Jays, Harold Melvin and the Blue Notes, and Billy Paul. Throughout the 1970s the Sound of Philadelphia was characterized by percussive dance rhythms offset by lush, swirling string arrangements. Although Gamble and Huff wrote a percentage of the material themselves, writers such as Gene McFadden and John Whitehead and Bunny Sigler were key contributors. However, by 1975 the Sound of Philadelphia had been reduced to a formula for the dance floor, although it would still generate a number of fine records such as McFadden and Whitehead's 'Ain't No Stoppin' Us Now'. By the middle of the 1980s, Gamble and Huff had returned to their former independent status as Gamble & Huff Records.

THE NEW INDEPENDENT LABELS

In the early 1970s, the one genuine spark of an R&B revival seemed to rest in the hands of a new wave of independent labels. Owned by enthusiasts, labels such as Alligator, Rounder, Malaco, and Arhoolie had adopted similar tactics to those of their antecedents in the 1940s and 1950s, by employing the services of musicians, writers, and producers who had been effectively marginalized as the music industry became big business. The only alternative to this monopoly was to establish independent labels that offered continuity to their roster of artists as well as promotional and, perhaps, emotional support. This was a world away from the attitudes of label owners such as Syd Nathan, Don Robey, and Herman Lubinsky, who had always maintained that the financial risk they incurred enabled them to assume as many of the artist's rights as possible. Alligator was, and remains, one of the strongest blues and R&B labels anywhere. It is perhaps not surprising that it was set up by a Chicagoan, Bruce Iglauer, who was raised on the blues emanating from the clubs and bars of the city's South Side. Although born in Wisconsin, Iglauer set up Alligator after spending several years working for Bob Koester – owner of Delmark Records and the famous Jazz Record Mart. Iglauer heard Hound Dog Taylor and the House Rockers, liked them, and cut an album with them, which he sold from the trunk of his Chevvy. Since those days Iglauer has built up a roster that includes Koko Taylor – who had one of Chess's final hits with Willie Dixon's 'Wang Dang Doodle' – Little Charlie and the Nightcats, Lonnie Brooks, Corey Harris, W. C. Clarke, and Fenton Robinson; and those who have recorded for him in the past include Professor Longhair, Clarence 'Gatemouth' Brown, and Luther Allison, among others.

The success of Iglauer's activities may well have contributed to the development of a new generation of black and white bluesmen who were reaching maturity as the 1960s folk and blues revival was beginning to take off. Similarly, the festival circuit had also begun to get into its stride so access to the great bluesmen of the 1940s and 1950s was far easier than it had been the first time around. This meant that, rather than having to depend on records, young players such as J. Geils, Duke Robillard, the Vaughan brothers – Stevie Ray and Jimmy – Bonnie Raitt, harmonica player Delbert McClinton, Bruce Springsteen, NRBQ (New Rhythm and Blues Quartet), and Robert Cray, among others, were able to get to grips with the essential joy and enthusiasm of R&B on a first-hand basis.

Although predecessors such as Paul Butterfield, Mike Bloomfield, Al Kooper, Steve Katz, Steve Miller, and Elvin Bishop had managed later on in their careers to play with their idols, initial exposure had been restricted to records. Furthermore, the rigours of constant touring had taken its toll, with both Butterfield and Bloomfield passing away prematurely, aged 45 and 37 respectively. Of them all, Elvin Bishop has managed to hang around longer than most. He started his career in Chicago in 1965, playing guitar on the club circuit until being recruited by Paul Butterfield. With Butterfield's Band, Bishop and fellow-guitarist Mike Bloomfield cut a number of albums including *East West* (1966), which anticipated the genus of the bluesy, twin lead-guitar band of the 1970s and 1980s as practised especially by Southern boogie bands such as Lynyrd Skynyrd, the Marshall Tucker Band and, of course, the Allman Brothers Band. After leaving Butterfield, Bishop moved to the Bay Area on the West Coast and cut albums for Fillmore auditorium supremo Bill Graham, until in 1976 he scored with 'Fooled Around and Fell in Love' (1976) for the Capricorn label – home of the Allman Brothers. In recent years his output has been on the lean side, but a deal with Alligator will probably see him making more trips to the studio.

THE J. GEILS BAND

Of the revivalists with a genuine feeling for the spirit of R&B and the blues, the J. Geils Band became the critics' darlings for a spell at the beginning of the 1970s. Formed by guitarist Jerome Geils in Boston in 1969 with Magic Dick (harmonica), Peter Wolf (vocals), Seth Justman (keyboards), Danny Klein (bass), and Stephan Jo Bladd (drums), the J. Geils Band initially invited comparisons with the Butterfield Band. Gradually, however, they edged away from the purist style of Butterfield by juxtaposing Bobby Womack's 'Looking For a Love' and Smokey Robinson's 'First I Look at the Purse' with John Lee Hooker's 'Serves You Right to Suffer'. What with Wolf's extrovert antics on stage and Magic Dick's harmonica ranged against the chunky chords of Geils, the group came close to breaking down some of the long-held views among purists that the blues was not something to be taken lightly. In other words, they drew from the same enthusiasm and showmanship that had rendered R&B distinct from the blues back in the late 1930s and early 1940s.

Over the next few years or so, albums such as *Morning After and Full House* (1972), *Bloodshot* and *Ladies Invited* (1973), and *Monkey Island* (1977) demonstrated their ability at combining the raucousness of R&B with the zip and style of contemporary rock. Inevitably, as they grew more successful, they started to rely more and more upon writer Justman. Increasingly, though, Justman led them further away from their roots, penning hits such as 'Centrefold', 'Freeze Frame', and 'Angel in Blue' (1982) but these only served to nibble away at the very foundations of the band, rendering them ultimately as directionless and potentially anodyne as 99 per cent of the other rock acts toiling from one venue to the next. By 1984 Wolf had jumped ship for a solo career and the group eventually split up completely. With Wolf out of the picture, Geils and Magic Dick returned to their blues roots and by the 1990s they had established themselves on the festival and club circuits, while putting out albums such as *Little Car Blues* (1992) and *Bluestime* (1994) for the independent Rounder group of labels.

DUKE ROBILLARD

No less influential, but certainly less flamboyant in his interpretation of R&B, was Duke Robillard. Hailing from Providence, Rhode Island, Robillard has developed a guitar style that is indicative of his wide-ranging influences from the blues styles of B. B. King, T-Bone Walker, and Guitar Slim to the jazz styles of Charlie Christian and Tiny Grimes. Inspired by Buddy Holly, Duane Eddy, and Chuck Berry, he built his first guitar while at high school and formed Roomful of Blues in 1967. As the group's reputation took hold, they accompanied artists such as Professor Longhair, Helen Humes, Red Prysock, and Earl King. In 1977 Roomful of Blues cut their debut album, *Roomful of Blues*. Featuring titles such as 'Duke's Jazz', 'Still in Love With You', and 'Stormy Monday', the influence of Walker and horn men Johnny Hodges and Lester Young shone with luminous clarity. The follow-up *Let's Have a Party* (1979) had a harder, more metallic sound, showing allegiance to Albert Collins, Pee Wee Crayton, and Johnny 'Guitar' Watson. In 1980 Robillard left Roomful of Blues and did stints with Robert Gordon and the ex-Muddy Waters sidemen, the Legendary Blues Band. After cutting solo albums such as *Swing* (1987) with Scott Hamilton, which re-created the jazzy roadhouse style of the 1930s and 1940s, and *Too Hot to Handle* (1989), he was recruited to replace Jimmy Vaughan in the Fabulous Thunderbirds for the excellent *Walk That Walk, Talk That Talk* (1991). In 1995 he cut one of the definitive R&B revival albums for Virgin. Entitled *Duke's Blues*, it features a small brass section comprising two saxes and a cornet. And as he so eloquently put it in early 1996:

'When I cut *Duke's Blues*, I wanted to get the sound and spontaneity of the records I heard when I was growing up. There's an immediacy that jumps out of the grooves that only happens when you cut things live and with a minimum of rehearsal.'

Despite the absence of Robillard, Roomful of Blues have flourished where others such as NRBQ have become slightly formulaic. Recent albums such as *Turn It On, Turn It Up* (1995) and *Under One Roof* (1997) possess a raucous vulgarity that doesn't compromise their essential enthusiasm. Furthermore the group's original material is beginning to juxtapose seamlessly with the occasional cover such as 'Smack Dab in the Middle' or 'Danger Zone'. Similarly the Fabulous Thunderbirds filled a gap in the US market for a white blues band that was authentic in its dissemination of the Chicago West Side style of R&B. Formed in 1977 by guitarist Jimmy Vaughan and harmonica player Kim Wilson, Vaughan was often eclipsed by his more celebrated brother, Stevie Ray, but Jimmy had a supreme gift for playing within himself, infusing studio recordings such as *T-Bird Rhythm* (1982) and *Tuff Enough* (1986) with a spontaneity comparable to that of their live concerts. When he quit the group in 1991, his replacement was Duke Robillard. When Robillard left for a solo career, the group was mothballed for a spell. Wilson had spent the intervening years working as a soloist cutting albums such as *Tigerman* (1993) for the Austin-based Antone's label, but in 1997 he was hatching plans to get the Thunderbirds back together again.

STEVIE RAY VAUGHAN

As for Stevie Ray Vaughan, he learned the guitar from Jimmy and by listening to records by artists such as Albert King, Lonnie Mack, and T-Bone Walker. After moving to Austin, he joined first the Nightcrawlers and then Paul Ray and the Cobras until forming Triple Threat Revue with vocalist Lou Ann Barton in 1977. By 1979 he had formed Double Trouble with Barton and a rhythm section of Chris Layton and Tommy Shannon; the band's name was taken from the Otis Rush classic. Vaughan's big break came in 1982 when producer Jerry Wexler added him to the line-up for the Montreux Jazz Festival, where he was spotted and hired by David Bowie for the forthcoming *Let's Dance* (1983) sessions. This was followed by Vaughan's debut album, *Texas Flood* (1983), with producer John Hammond. Combining elements of rock and the blues, 'Rude Mood' was a bouncy, abrasive instrumental which won a Grammy. Curiously, later albums such as *Couldn't Stand the Weather* (1984) betrayed less confidence in his own style and a somewhat greater reliance on inspirations such as Jimi Hendrix. Personal problems and a plethora of sessions sidelined him until *In Step* (1989) and *Family Style* (1990), the latter with his brother Jimmy. Back on track, he was killed in a helicopter crash in 1990, just as his career was set to go through the roof. Since his death, he has entered the gallery of guitar greats, providing inspiration for dozens of new young bands. Indeed, one of the brightest hopes is Storyville, which features Double Trouble's former rhythm section of Layton and Shannon along with guitarists David Grissom and David Holt and vocalist Malford Milligan. Furthermore, a sense of the blues and R&B being a part of the contemporary vernacular is evidenced by the number of young black musicians such as acoustic bluesmen Keb' Mo' and Eric Bibb, and electric guitarist Robert Cray.

ROBERT CRAY

Cray was born on 1 August 1953 in Columbus, Georgia, and formed his first band, One Way Street, while still at school. In 1973 he joined Albert 'Iceman' Collins's touring band as a guitarist after meeting Richard Cousins, Collins's bass player. In 1975 Cray and Cousins left to form their own group, the Robert Cray Band, bringing in Peter Boe on keyboards and David Olson on drums. They recorded their debut, *Who's Been Talkin'?* (1978), in between tours although it wasn't released for two years. In 1983, after almost a decade of touring, they recorded *Bad Influence*, which showed Collins's influence in Cray's use of the D-minor tuning. *False Accusations* (1985) won the Best Blues Album Award from the National Association of Independent Record Distributors; it nodded at the great soul albums of the 1960s and featured the long, lean, lyrical lines that had been used to such good effect by Steve Cropper. As if to emphasize his commitment to the blues, Cray collaborated with Collins and Johnny Copeland on *Showdown* (1985) for the Alligator label, winning a Grammy in the process. *Strong Persuader* (1987) was full of rustic charm; eschewing the desire to replicate the urban blues style of the late 1940s, it drew freely from recent memory and 'Right Next Door' echoed Eric Clapton's playing on Aretha Franklin's *Soul '69*. The circle was completed by *Midnight Stroll* (1990), on which the pugnacious Memphis Horns traded chops with Cray in a way that only Cropper had previously managed on early Otis Redding songs; that it worked was due largely to the way that perceptions of the blues had altered. Cray has steadfastly resisted the temptation to become hidebound by a putative role as B. B. King's or Muddy Waters' successor but his playing continues to combine elements of the greatest traditions of black American music, which is constantly redefining itself.

VAN MORRISON

Although Cray, Robillard, the Vaughan Brothers, and Roomful of Blues have contributed to the revival of interest in R&B in a highly selective and specific fashion, performers such as Bonnie Raitt and Van Morrison have contributed non-specifically. Both Raitt and Morrison are so thoroughly in tune with their own perception of what they are endeavouring to achieve at any given time that they tend to transcend notional terms of fashion and, in Morrison's case especially, genre or style. Morrison has for long been one of the first to put up his hand whenever a legend such as John Lee Hooker shows a willingness to have a rock 'n' roller hanging around the studios when he's recording – to the extent that Hooker's 1997 offering, *Don't Look Back*, featured Morrison as producer as well as a contributor of four songs. The point is that Morrison has never adopted the blues, jazz or, indeed, R&B the way others have; instead he has used the styles as ciphers for his own highly specific and eclectic output. And this hasn't been a recent development. Ever since leaving Them back in the mid-1960s, Morrison has charted his own course, chronicling the highs and lows as he went, and more or less forbearing utterances on influences other than to say that he liked Hooker and Ray Charles. In recent years, though, since the arrival of Georgie Fame as his band leader and the inclusion of Andy Fairweather Low as guitarist, the arrangements have become progressively bluesier and funkier.

BONNIE RAITT

Bonnie Raitt is not altogether dissimilar for although she lacks Morrison's reputation for irascibility, she has bucked the odds by being a female blues guitarist. While there are many precedents, Raitt's early career was marred by that blind prejudice which only jealousy and crass stupidity can achieve. With little or no promotion – and less encouragement – for the first ten years of her career, Raitt has developed into one of the finest slide guitarists of her generation. She was born Bonnie Lynn Raitt on 8 November 1949 in Burbank, California, and learned to play the guitar when she was eight. Initially she played folk songs and was influenced by Sippie Wallace and Odetta; after moving to Boston, Massachusetts, she majored in African Studies at Radcliffe College. In 1969 she began playing on the club and coffee-bar circuit, alongside guitarists such as Chris Smither, where she got to know bluesmen such as Mississippi Fred McDowell, Son House, Muddy Waters, and Otis Rush. Playing a mixture of blues and traditional folk, she gained a contract with Warner Brothers, cutting *Bonnie Raitt* (1971). Over the next 15 years she made nine albums. While her guitar work – particularly on the slide – improved steadily and her repertoire broadened, she gradually took on the mantle of the musicians' musician with artists such as Lowell George, Linda Ronstadt, J. D. Souther, Jackson Browne, and Tom Waits guesting on her albums, but the public at large steadfastly resisted the temptation of buying her records.

In 1989, after moving to Capitol, *Nick of Time*, with producer Don Was, finally compensated for all the lean years, winning her a shelf of Grammys and platinum discs. The same year she cut 'I'm in the Mood', a duet with John Lee Hooker, which emphasized the regard in which she was held by those who mattered. Subsequent albums such as *Luck of the Draw* (1991) – featuring a magnificent duet with Delbert McClinton on 'Good Man, Good Woman' – suggest that all the years spent in the commercial wilderness and on the road have only sharpened her resolve and given her slide guitar work that extra edge. Ironically, her touring band has included at various points accomplished musicians such as keyboardist Glen Clark and guitarist/producer Stephen Bruton.

In the 1990s, independent labels are a way of life in the US. The festival circuit is so expansive that there is a full complement of programmes covering every genre or style of music. Even the normally conservative radio stations have introduced a Triple A format that covers most non-chart-related areas of contemporary American music. This has meant that R&B musicians such as Buddy Guy, Luther Allison, Snooks Eaglin, and many others have more invitations to work than they could reasonably handle or, indeed, are inclined to handle. Guitarist Robert Ward, formerly of the Falcons, languished in obscurity, doing his day job for over twenty-five years, until in the late 1980s he decided to take up his guitar once again and have another go. This time around, he has begun to net some appreciation as his excellent Black Top albums attest.

# PUB ROCK

In the UK, revivals of interest in R&B have been more sporadic than in the US. The UK club circuit seems scarcely able to sustain more than one or two enthusiasms simultaneously. However, one of the pluses of the 1970s was that while many so-called progressive bands – there is absolutely no need to mention any names, they know exactly who they are – vied with one another to pack the largest arenas in both the UK and US, they spurred a reaction. This reaction came to be known as 'pub rock', and that sowed the seeds of punk. The ethos of pub rock was the return to the simplicity of the 1960s blues boom. In other words, bands turned up at the local pub, plugged in and started to play. Pub rock was initially fuelled by musicians who had no recording contracts or had even jettisoned the music industry in favour of regular income from some other occupation. In many instances, though, groups such as Chicken Shack, who still had a following in Europe, were considered by record companies to be deeply unfashionable and the major labels held total sway during the mid-1970s.

That was soon to change with the emergence of labels such as Stiff and Chiswick. If these labels had a mandate, it was to sign up some of the young bands that had started to gain reputations on the pub circuit. From these unpromising circumstances, Nick Lowe emerged from the underrated country-rock Brinsley Schwarz to team up with guitarist Dave Edmunds in Rockpile, Graham Parker and the Rumour started to ruffle feathers, from Canvey Island on the Thames estuary Dr Feelgood started to put the zip back into rock 'n' roll with their energetic showmanship, and the Blues Band, featuring broadcaster and former lead vocalist of Manfred Mann, Paul Jones, confirmed that R&B still had a place when approached with the requisite zest.

Cardiff-born Dave Edmunds is one of rock 'n' roll's great enthusiasts and has always been unimpressed by the machinations of an industry where appearance is all. While a member of Love Sculpture in the late 1960s, he was ripping out as many notes as fast as possible on Khachaturian's 'Sabre Dance' while his contemporaries were noodling away, trying to be meaningful. His flirtation with popular classics was brief and he set about applying his chunky chords to updated reworkings of Smiley Lewis's 'I Hear You Knocking' (1970), the Ronettes' 'Baby I Love You' (1973) and the Chordettes' 'Born to Be With You' (1973). High on production technique but short on guitar solos, *Get It* (1977) was an encyclopaedia of the rock era's variegated styles and opened the door for Rockpile. Although it was an occasional band, it included bassist Nick Lowe, guitarist Billy Bremner, and drummer Terry Williams. Edmunds lovingly recreated moments from rock's golden era with covers of songs such as the Everly Brothers' 'When Will I Be Loved?' (1980), but energy and his ability to blend styles made him a sought-after producer and he worked with Graham Parker, Jeff Beck, and Carl Perkins, to name but a few.

The spritely figure of guitarist Wilko Johnson aping a robotic Chuck Berry duckwalk was the counterpoint to the charismatic vocalist and harmonica-player Lee Brilleaux in Dr Feelgood. The Feelgoods were the crux of the R&B revival in the UK, offering frantic live shows that appealed to diehard enthusiasts as well as a new generation who would shortly reject all that the corporate ethic of the supergroups embodied with the emergence of punk. The Feelgoods, in fact, were the bridge between the two eras. While much of their material was original, their covers included Bobby Charles's 'See You Later Alligator' and Jerry Byrne's 'Lights Out'.

Despite the consistency and success of albums such as *Sneakin' Suspicion* (1977), the group remained accessible to the public that supported them; as they grew more successful, their live act became more refined, but no less raw for all that. During the late 1970s there was a string of personnel changes that included the departure of Wilko for a solo career with his own band, the Solid Senders. By 1981 Brilleaux was the only original member remaining but the group soldiered on. In the late 1980s Brilleaux put together their own record label, Grand, to co-ordinate a reissue programme of earlier material, as well as future releases. Sadly Brilleaux died on 15 April 1994, but he and the Feelgoods will always be known as the band that managed to take on supergroups and punk without suffering any loss of face at all.

In 1979, according to writer Roy Bainton in *Talk to Me Baby: The Story of the Blues Band*, the former bassist of Manfred Mann, Tom McGuinness, phoned Paul Jones and asked him if he fancied getting a band together to play the blues – but just for fun. Eighteen years later, that band – the Blues Band – is still going strong, although they did split for three years in 1982. Nowadays their reputation has meant that what started as an occasional gig for beer money has turned into something rather more demanding. Comprising Jones on harmonica and vocals, McGuinness and Dave Kelly on guitars, Gary Fletcher on bass and Hughie Flint on drums, who moved aside in 1981 to allow in Rob Townsend from Family, the Blues Band's repertoire has revolved around classics by Muddy Waters, Willie Dixon, John Lee Hooker, and Lightnin' Hopkins, combined with a liberal dosing of self-composed items. However, what they continue to do, through their mere continuance, is to espouse a genuine affection for R&B, and that is very apparent at any one of the many gigs they do throughout the year. While albums such as *The Official Bootleg Album* (1979), *Ready* (1980), *These Kind of Blues* (1986), and *Homage* (1993) illustrate the bard's zeal, their success speaks volumes for the form that many endeavour to consign to posterity.

THAT'S ENTERTAINMENT

In the late 1980s, a show called *Five Guys Named Moe* opened in London. Based very loosely on the music and the era of Louis Jordan, it was immediately a runaway success. A close analysis of the reasons for this would reveal that it wasn't just the music that appealed; it was also the spirit of the execution of that music in its staging that won over diehard fans of R&B as well as casual visitors only interested in seeing a good, lively show. Now with the millennium almost upon us, the appeal of R&B lies not just in the quality of the music but also in the showmanship that it takes to do it right. So, while R&B has thrived as a genre, the spirit, the *joie de vivre,* and the sheer 'Let's party' attitude of it all has only recently been taken on board. Certainly the on-stage theatrics between Bruce Springsteen and horn man Clarence Clemons, when Bruce would shout his exhortation, 'Blow! Big Man!' was dutifully acknowledged, but it was applauded because it demonstrated Bruce's stagecraft. Everyone knew that Bruce grew up listening to R&B, but the nature of his songs tended to militate against proper appreciation of his showmanship within the pantheon of great entertainers. An abiding wisdom – or, more accurately, folly – has arisen that if it's perceived as entertainment, it has no inherent value. Thankfully, these fallacies are now being abandoned as bands such Jools Holland and the Rhythm & Blues Orchestra, the Big Town Playboys, King Pleasure and the Biscuit Boys, the Detonators, Paul Lamb and the Kingsnakes, and Ray Gelato's Group, to name but a few, have made a point of developing their live acts before cutting records. Thankfully, too, most people recognize that the major record labels spending most of their time worrying about profitability and keeping their top performers well stocked with Louis Crystalle champagne and the best beluga caviar has very little to do with a thriving and creative musical environment. To that end, independent labels have a good prospect for survival: bands no longer need the backing of majors to keep going. Furthermore, although the UK club scene is not absolutely moribund, there is a lack of medium-sized venues but fortunately France, Germany, Holland, Sweden, and Italy provide the vital financial sustenance for groups that would have gone under long ago if they depended for their survival on touring the UK or getting albums released in the US.

The Big Town Playboys, managed by Jeff Beck's manager, Ralph Baker, have been together since 1984 and they still cut their own albums and do distribution deals later. Remember, too, that it was the Big Town Playboys who accompanied Beck on his much-maligned tribute to Cliff Gallup, Gene Vincent's guitarist in the Blue Caps. For keyboards man and co-founder, Mike Sanchez, the buzz is and always has been playing live:

> 'I remember one occasion when my biggest hero, Little Willie Littlefield, played with us . . . and as he was playing piano, I could get down into the audience to take photographs. It was just such a great feeling to think that he was playing with my band.'

These days, as if to take a step closer to their link with the great small groups of the 1940s, horn man Frank Dean is often in evidence. And Dean can and does milk the audience with every ounce of stagecraft that he can muster.

Similarly, King Pleasure and the Biscuit Boys have managed since their formation in 1987 to accompany such legends as Charles Brown and trombonist Gene 'Mighty Flea' Connors. King Pleasure, P. Popps Martin, and Bullmoose K. Shirley went to school together in Walsall in the West Midlands. After busking for a while, they won a competition in Birmingham and formed a group called the Satellites, where they were spotted by Jim Simpson of the Big Bear Booking Agency. While King Pleasure re-create the high-steppin', good-time atmosphere of the great R&B combos, it doesn't stop with the music. King Pleasure reflects:

> 'I really liked those snazzy suits they used to wear during the 1940s. And I felt that if you dress the part, you're gonna be able to play the part that much better, but also I like to run the band along quite strict lines. I fine guys who are late for rehearsals or if they don't turn up looking well turned out for a gig. It's a part of the show. And I think the rest of the guys feel the same way about it. They wouldn't stay if it were a problem'.

For all that, albums such as *Rhythm & Blues Revue* (1995) are not derivative attempts at rekindling the past, they possess a style, wit, and pzazz that are difficult to find these days.

When pianist Jools Holland left Squeeze in 1990 to concentrate on his own band, he had already built a substantial career as a television presenter. When asked by the BBC to present his own TV show entitled *Later With Jools Holland*, it did not require great perspicacity to recognize that the best studio band should be led by Jools himself. That band is now known as the Rhythm & Blues Orchestra. Featuring such respected names as trombonist Rico and former Squeeze drummer Gilson Lavis, the Rhythm & Blues Orchestra has managed the unthinkable by playing at established concert halls for affluent middle-class audiences while also plying its trade on the international festival circuit, where audiences tend to be younger. However, this is not to say there has been any compromise, for Holland has become the consummate all-round entertainer.

And that is what it is all about. Entertainment. Fuck art, let's dance. Or something along those lines. As if to vindicate those sentiments, the musical based on Leiber and Stoller's hit for the Robins (later the Coasters), *Smokey Joe's Café,* looks set to run into the next decade. Revival? What revival? R&B never went away, many audiences just stopped listening. And they probably will again. But one thing is for certain: people won't stop playing it. Of that, dear reader, you can be sure.

BIBLIOGRAPHY

The number of books that have influenced me are too numerous to mention.
Those listed here represent a cross-section.

Betrock, Alan, *Girl Groups: The Story of a Sound* Delilah, New York,
   1982
Booth, Stanley, *Rythm Oil* Pantheon, London, 1991
Brunning, Bob, *Blues in Britain* Blandford, London, 1995
Charles, Ray, with Ritz, David, *Brother Ray* Dial Press, New York, 1978
Cohn, Nik, *WopBopaLooBopLopBamBoom* Paladin, London, 1972
Cummings, Tony, *The Sound of Philadelphia* Methuen, London, 1975
Davis, Francis, *The History of the Blues* Secker & Warburg, London, 1995
Dixon, Willie, with Don Snowden, *I Am the Blues: The Willie Dixon
   Story* Da Capo, New York, 1989
Feather, Leonard, *The Encyclopaedia of Jazz* Da Capo, New York, 1960
Freeman, Scott, *Midnight Riders: The Story of the Allman Brothers Band*
   Little, Brown & Co., London, 1995
Gaar, Gillian, *She's a Rebel*, Blandford, London, 1993
Gambaccini, Paul; Rice, Tim; and Rice, Jo, *British Hit Singles* GRR
   Publications, London, 1992
– *British Hit Albums* GRR Publications, London, 1988
George, Nelson, *Where Did Our Love Go? The Rise and Fall of the
   Motown Sound*, Omnibus, London, 1985
– *The Death of Rhythm & Blues* Omnibus, London, 1988
Gillett, Charlie, *The Sound of the City* Souvenir, London, 1970
– *Making Tracks: Atlantic Records and the Growth of a Multi-Billion
   Dollar Industry* Souvenir, London, 1974

Greig, Charlotte, *Will You Still Love Me Tomorrow?* Virago, London, 1989

Gregory, Hugh, *Soul Music A–Z* Da Capo, New York, 1995

– *Who's Who in Country Music*, Weidenfeld & Nicolson, London, 1993

– *1000 Great Guitarists* Miller Freeman, San Francisco, 1994

Guralnick, Peter, *Sweet Soul Music* Virgin, London, 1986

– *Feel Like Going Home* Omnibus, London, 1981

Hardy, Phil, and Laing, Dave, *The Faber Companion to 20th Century Popular Music* Faber, London, 1990

Hirshey, Gerri, *Nowhere to Run* Macmillan, London, 1984

Hoare, Ian; Anderson, Clive; Cummings, Tony; and Frith, Simon, *The Soul Book* Methuen, London, 1975

Hoskyns, Barney, *Say It One Time For the Broken Hearted: The Country Side of Southern Soul* Fontana, London, 1987

Jackson, John, *Big Beat Heat* Schirmer, Munich, 1991

Jonex, Leroi, *Black Music*, William Morrow & Co., New York, 1968

Larkin, Colin (ed.), *The Guinness Encyclopaedia of Popular Music* Guinness Publishing, London, 1993

Marcus, Greil, *Mystery Train* Omnibus, London, 1979

Marsh, Dave, *The Heart of Rock and Soul* Penguin, London, 1989

Mezzrow, Mezz, *Really the Blues* Flamingo, London, 1993

Millar, Bill, *The Coasters* Star Books, London, 1974

– *The Drifters* Studio Vista, London, 1971

Nicholson, Stuart, *Ella Fitzgerald* Gollancz, London, 1993

Propes, Steven, *Those Oldies But Goodies* Collier, 1973

Ritz, David, *Divided Soul: The Life of Marvin Gaye* Grafton, London, 1986

Sawyer, Charles, *B. B. King: The Authorised Biography* Blandford, London, 1981

Shaar Murray, Charles, *Crosstown Traffic* Faber, London, 1989

Shaw, Arnold, *Honkers and Shouters* Collier, 1978

Tosches, Nick, *The Unsung Heroes of Rock 'n' Roll* Secker & Warburg, London, 1991

– *Country* Secker & Warburg, London, 1985

Wade, Dorothy, and Picardie, Justine, *Music Man* W. W. Norton, New York, 1990

Warner, Alan, *Who Sang What in Rock 'n' Roll* Blandford, London, 1990

Wexler, Jerry, with Ritz, David, *Rhythm and the Blues* Random, New York, 1993

Whitburn, Joel, *The Billboard Book of US Top 40 Hits* Billboard Publications, London, 1992

– *The Billboard Book of US Top 40 Albums* Billboard Publications, 1987

Williams, Richard, *The Sound of Phil Spector: Out of His Head* Abacus, London, 1974

DISCOGRAPHY

This is not a comprehensive list, but offers a starting point for those seeking more information.

Johnny Ace, *Memorial Album*, (MCA)

Johnny Adams, *Sings Doc Pomus* (Rounder)
– *Goodmorning Heartache* (Rounder)
– *I Won't Cry: The Original Ronn Recordings* (Rounder)

The Allman Brothers Band, *Live at Fillmore East* (Polydor)

LaVern Baker, *Real Gone Gal* (Charly)

Hank Ballard, *Let 'Em Roll* (Charly)

Lou Ann Barton, *Old Enough* (Antone's)

Jesse Belvin, *Goodnight My Love* (Ace)

Chuck Berry, *The Chess Box* (Chess)
– *His Best, Volume 1* (MCA/Chess)

Big Maybelle, *Sings the Blues* (Charly)

Big Town Playboys, *Hip Joint* (Ace)

Elvin Bishop, *Big Fun* (Alligator)
– *Ace in the Hole* (Alligator)

Bobby Bland, *Ask Me Nothing 'Bout the Blues* (MCA/Half Moon)
– *Two Steps From the Blues* (MCA/Duke)
– *The Dreamer* (MCA)

Mike Bloomfield, *Essential Blues 1964–69* (Columbia/Legacy)

James Booker, *The New Orleans Piano Wizard: Live!* (Rounder)
– *Spiders on the Keys* (Rounder)

Earl Bostic, *Flamingo* (Charly)

Tiny Bradshaw, *The Great Composer* (King)

Hadda Brooks, *Time Was When* (Virgin/Pointblank)

Lonnie Brooks, *Let's Talk It Over* (Delmark)
– *Deluxe Edition* (Alligator)

Big Bill Broonzy, *Good Time Tonight* (Columbia)
– *Sings Folk Songs* (Smithsonian/Folkways)

Charles Brown, *Driftin' Blues: The Best of . . .* (EMI)
– *One More For the Road* (Alligator)
– *All My Life* (Rounder)

Clarence 'Gatemouth' Brown, *The Original Peacock Recordings* (Rounder)
– *Pressue Cooker* (Alligator)
– *The Best of . . .* (Verve)
– *The Man* (Verve)

James Brown, *20 All Time Greatest Hits* (Polydor)
– *Live at the Apollo* (Polydor)
– *Star Time* (Polydor)

Roy Brown, *The Complete Imperial Recordings* (Capitol)

Ruth Brown, *Rockin' With Ruth* (Atlantic)
– *R+B Ruth Brown* (Bullseye Blues)

The Paul Butterfield Blues Band (Elektra)
– *East West* (Elektra)
– *The Resurrection of Pigboy Crabshaw* (Elektra)

Cab Calloway, *Cab Calloway and the Missourians* (JSP)
– *The Cab Calloway Collection* (Columbia)

Canned Heat, *The Best of . . .* (EMI America)

Ray Charles, *The Birth of Soul: The Complete Atlantic Rhythm & Blues Recordings 1952–1959* (Atlantic)
– *Greatest Country & Western Hits* (Castle)

Clifton Chenier, *Zydeco Dynamite: The Clifton Chenier Anthology* (Rhino)
– *Zydeco Sont Pas Sale* (Arhoolie)

Eric Clapton, *Crossroads* (Polydor)
– *From the Cradle* (Reprise)

Clovers, *Down in the Alley: The Best of the Clovers* (Atlantic)

Coasters, *The Ultimate Coasters* (Atlantic)

Albert Collins, *The Complete Imperial Recordings* (EMI)
– *Deluxe Edition* (Alligator)
– *The Best of . . .* (Virgin/Pointblank)

Albert Collins/Robert Cray/Johnny Copeland, *Showdown!* (Alligator)

Ry Cooder, *Borderline* (Reprise)
– *Bop 'Til You Drop* (Reprise)
– *Get Rhythm* (Reprise)

Robert Cray, *Bad Influence* (Hightone)
– *False Accusations* (Hightone)
– *Strong Persuader* (Mercury)
– *Don't Be Afraid of the Dark* (Mercury)
– *Midnight Stroll* (Mercury)
– *Sweet Potato Pie* (Mercury)

Pee Wee Crayton, *Things I Used to Do* (Vanguard)
– *The Modern Legacy, Volume I* (Ace)
– *The Complete Aladdin/Imperial Recordings* (Capitol)

Creedence Clearwater Revival, *Chronicle, Volumes 1/2* (Fantasy)

Cream, *Those Were the Days* (Polydor)

Arthur 'Big Boy' Crudup, *That's All Right Mama* (RCA Bluebird)

Dells, *On Their Corner* (Chess/MCA)

Bo Diddley, *His Best* (Chess/MCA)

Willie Dixon, *The Chess Box* (Chess/MCA)

Bill Doggett, *Leaps and Bounds* (Charly)

Don & Dewey, *Jungle Hop* (Ace)

Lee Dorsey, *Working in a Coalmine* (Charly)

Thomas A. Dorsey, *Precious Lord* (Columbia/Legacy)

Drifters, *Let the Boogie-Woogie Roll* (Atlantic)
– *All-Time Greatest Hits, 1959–1965* (Atlantic)

Snooks Eaglin, *Country Boy In New Orleans* (Arhoolie)
– *Out of Nowhere* (Black Top)
– *Soul's Edge* (Black Top)

Fabulous Thunderbirds, *Walk That Walk, Talk That Talk* (Epic)

Five Guys Named Moe, The Original Decca Recordings, Volume 2 (MCA)

Five Royales (King)
– *Dedicated To You* (King)

Flamingoes, *The Complete Chess Masters* (Chess/MCA)

Aretha Franklin, *The Great Aretha Franklin: The First 12 Sides* (Columbia)
– *I Never Loved a Man* (Atlantic)
– *Live at Fillmore West* (Atlantic)
– *Her Greatest Recordings* (Atlantic)

Lowell Fulson, *Hung Down Head* (Chess/MCA)
– *Tramp/Soul* (Flair)
– *It's a Good Day* (Rounder)
– *Them Update Blues* (Bullseye Blues)

Ray Gelato's Giants of Jive (Blue Horizon)

Al Green, *Let's Stay Together* (Hi)
– *Greatest Hits* (Hi)

Guitar Slim, *Sufferin' Mind* (Specialty)

Buddy Guy, *Complete Chess Studio Sessions* (Chess/MCA)
– *A Man and the Blues* (Vanguard)
– *Stone Crazy* (Alligator)
– *Damn Right, I've Got the Blues* (Silvertone)
– *Feels Like Rain* (Silvertone)
– *The Real Deal* (Silvertone)

Lionel Hampton, *Flying Home* (Decca)

Slim Harpo, *Tip on In* (Ace)

Wynonie Harris, *Good Rockin' Tonight* (Charly)

Erskine Hawkins, *The Original Tuxedo Junction* (RCA Bluebird)

Screamin' Jay Hawkins, *Frenzy* (Demon)
– *Portrait of a Man* (Demon)

Jimi Hendrix, *Electric Ladyland* (Polydor)

Earl Hooker, *Two Bugs and a Roach* (Arhoolie)

John Lee Hooker, *The Best of . . .* (MCA)
– *The Real Folk Blues* (Chess/ MCA)
– *The Country Blues of . . .* (Original Blues Classics)
– *Detroit Special* (Atlantic)
– *Mr Lucky* (Silvertone)
– *Don't Look Back* (Virgin/Pointblank)
– *Alternative Boogie* (Capitol)

Lightnin' Hopkins, *The Complete Aladdin Recordings* (EMI)
– *Texas Bluesman* (Arhoolie)

Howlin' Wolf, *Rides Again* (Flair)
– *Moanin' in the Moonlight* (Chess/MCA)
– *The Real Folk Blues* (Chess/MCA)
– *More Real Folk Blues* (Chess/MCA)

Ivory Joe Hunter, *16 of His Greatest Hits* (King)
– *His Greatest Hits* (Atlantic)

Impressions, *The Best of . . .*, featuring Curtis Mayfield (MCA/Half Moon)

Ink Spots, *The Best of . . .* (MCA/Half Moon)

Bullmoose Jackson, *Badman Jackson, That's Me* (Charly)

Illinois Jacquet, *Big Horn* (Charly)

Elmore James, *King of the Slide Guitar* (Charly)

Etta James, *These Foolish Things* (Chess/MCA)
– *Her Best* (Chess/MCA)
– *Deep in the Night* (Rounder)
– *The Genuine Article* (MCA)
– *Mystery Lady: The Songs of Billie Holiday* (Private)

Blind Lemon Jefferson (Milestone)

Little Willie John, *Fever* (King)

Blind Willie Johnson, *The Complete Recordings* (Columbia/Legacy)

Lonnie Johnson, *The Complete Folkways Recordings* (Smithsonian/Folkways)

Robert Johnson, *The Complete Recordings* (Columbia)

Louis Jordan, *The Best of . . .* (MCA)

Albert King, *Born Under a Bad Sign* (Atlantic)
– *King of the Blues Guitar* (Atlantic)
– *The Best of . . .* (Stax)

B. B. King, *Singin' the Blues/The Blues* (Ace)
– *My Sweet Little Angel* (Ace)
– *Live at the Regal* (MCA)
– *The King of the Blues* (MCA)
– *Blues Summit* (MCA)

King Curtis, *The Complete Enjoy Sessions* (Charly)
– *Live at Fillmore West* (Atlantic)

King Pleasure and The Biscuit Boys, *Blues & Rhythm Revue, Volume 1* (Essential)

Paul Lam, *Fine Condition* (Indigo)
– *She's a Killer* (Indigo)

Smiley Lewis, *I Hear You Knockin': The Best of . . .* (EMI)

Jimmy Liggins and His Drops of Joy (Ace)

Joe Liggins and the Honerdrippers (Ace)

Little Esther, *I Paid My Dues* (King)

Little Milton, *If Walls Could Talk* (Chess/ MCA)

Little Richard, *22 Classic Cuts* (Ace)
– *The Specialty Sessions* (Ace)

Frankie Lymon and the Teenagers, *Greatest Hits* (Roulette)

Jay McShan, *Blues From Kansas City* (Decca)

John Mayall and Eric Clapton, *Bluesbreakers* (Decca)

John Mayall's Bluesbreakers, *A Hard Road* (Decca)
– *Crusade* (Decca)

Percy Mayfield, *Poet of the Blues* (Ace)

Meters, *Crescent City Groove Merchants* (Charly)

Amos Milburn, *The Complete Aladdin Recordings* (Capitol)

Mills Brothers, *Greatest Hits* (MCA)

Roy Milton, *Groovy Blues* (Ace)

Roy Milton and His Solid Senders (Ace)

Mississippi Sheiks, *Stop and Listen* (Yazoo)

Moonglows, *Their Greatest Hits* (Chess/MCA)

Van Morrison, *It's Too Late to Stop Now* (Polydor)
– *Enlightenment* (Polydor)
– *Days Like This* (Polydor

Art Neville, *His Specialty Recordings* (Ace)

Neville Brothers, *Fiyo on the Bayou* (A&M)
– *Nevillization* (A&M)
– *Treacherous: A History* (Rhino)

NRBQ (Columbia)

Johnny Otis, *Creepin' With the Cats: The Legendary Dig Masters* (Ace)
– *Live at Monterey* (Epic)

Penguins, *Earth Angel* (Ace)

Esther Phillips, *The Complete Savoy Recordings* (Savoy)
– *Confessin' the Blues* (Atlantic)
– *From a Whisper to a Scream* (Kudu)
– *Alone Again Naturally* (Kudu)
– *What a Difference a Day Makes* (Kudu)

Elvis Presley, *The Complete '50s Masters* (RCA)

Lloyd Price, *Lawdy!* (Ace)

Professor Longhair, *New Orleans Piano: Blues Originals, Volume 2* (Atlantic)
– *Crawfish Fiesta* (Alligator)

Bonnie Raitt, *Collection* (Warner Bros)
– *Give It Up* (Warner Bros)
– *Nick of Time* (Capitol)
– *Luck of the Draw* (Capitol)

Otis Redding, *The Otis Redding Story* (Atlantic)

Jimmy Reed, *The Best of . . .* (GNP Crescendo)

Rising Sons, featuring Taj Mahal and Ry Cooder (Columbia)

Duke Robillard, *You Got Me* (Munich)
– *After Hours Swing Session* (Munich)
– *Duke's Blues* (Virgin/Pointblank)

Duke Robillard and The Pleasure Kings, *Rockin' Blues* (Rounder)

Jimmy Rogers, *The Complete Chess Recordings* (Chess/MCA)

Roy Rogers, *Slide of Hand* (Liberty)

Roomful of Blues (Varrick)
– *Hot Little Mama* (Varrick)
– *Dance All Night* (Bullseye Blues)
– *Turn It On, Turn It Up* (Bullseye Blues)
– *Under One Roof* (Bullseye Blues)

Otis Rush, *Mourning in the Morning* (Atlantic)
– *Lost in the Blues* (Alligator)

Jimmy Rushing, *The Essential* (Vanguard)

Boz Scaggs (Atlantic)
– *Come on Home* (Virgin America)

Shirelles, *The Best of . . .* (Ace)

Bessie Smith, *Collection* (Columbia Jazz)

Soul Stirrers, *Jesus Gave Me Water* (Ace)

Spaniels, *Dearest* (Charly)

Storyville, *A Piece of Your Soul* (Code Blue)

Hubert Sumlin, *Blues Party* (Black Top)

Swallows, *Dearest* (Charly)

Taj Mahal, *The Natchr'l Blues* (Columbia)
– *Giant Step/De Ole Folks at Home* (Columbia)
– *Dancing the Blues* (Private)

Hound Dog Taylor and The Houserockers (Alligator)

Koko Taylor, *The Chess Years* (Chess/MCA)
– *Force of Nature* (Alligator)

Big Mama Thornton, *The Original Hound Dog* (Ace)

Allen Toussaint, *The Minit Records Story* (EMI)
– *Collection* (Warner Bros)
– *Southern Nights* (Warner Bros)

Ike Turner's Kings of Rhythm (Charly)

The Ike & Tina Turner Revue: Live! (Kent)

Ike and Tina Turner, *Fingerpoppin': The Best of the Warner Bros Years* (Edsel)

Big Joe Turner, *Jumpin' With Joe: The Complete Aladdin Recordings* (EMI)
– *Greatest Hits* (Atlantic)
– *Tell Me Pretty Baby* (Arhoolie)
– *The Boss of the Blues* (Atlantic)

Stevie Ray Vaughan & Double Trouble, *Texas Flood* (Epic)
– *Soul to Soul* (Epic)
– *In Step* (Epic)

The Vaughan Brothers, *Family Style* (Epic)

Eddie 'Cleanhead' Vinson, *Kidney Stew Is Fine* (Delmark)
– *Meat's Too High* (JSP)

T-Bone Walker, *The Complete Capitol/ Black & White Recordings* (Capitol)
– *The Complete Imperial Recordings* (EMI)
– *T-Bone Blues* (Atlantic)
– *I Want A Little Girl* (Delmark)

Billy Ward and His Dominoes, with Clyde McPhatter and Jackie Wilson (King)

Billy Ward and His Dominoes, *Sixty Minute Man* (Charly)

Robert Ward, *Fear No Evil* (Black Top)
– *Rhythm of the People* (Black Top)

Dinah Washington, *The Queen of the Blues* (Charly)

Walter 'Wolfman' Washington, *Wolf at the Door* (Rounder)
– *Out of the Dark* (Rounder)

Muddy Waters, *The Complete Muddy Waters*: 1947–1967 (Chess)
– *Hard Again* (Blue Sky)
– *I'm Ready* (Blue Sky)

Johnny 'Guitar' Watson, *Three Hours Past Midnight* (Ace)

Larry Williams, *The Best of …* (Ace)

Sonny Boy Williamson (Rice Miller), *Real Folk Blues* (Chess/MCA)

Jackie Wilson, *The Very Best of …* (Ace)

Johnny Winter, *Second Winter* (Epic)
– *Guitar Slinger* (Alligator)

Jimmy Witherspoon, *Blowin' in From Kansas City* (Ace)
– *Spoon So Easy* (Chess/MCA)
– *The Spoon Concerts* (Fantasy)

ANTHOLOGIES

The Alligator Records 20th Anniversary Collection (Alligator)

The Alligator Records 25th Anniversary Collection (Alligator)

Antone's Tenth Anniversary Anthology (Antone's)

Atlantic Rhythm & Blues: 1947–1974 (Atlantic)

Authentic Excello R&B (Ace)

Best of Chess Rock 'n' Roll (Chess/MCA)

Better Boot That Thing: Great Women Blues Singers of the 1920's (Columbia)

The Blind Pig 20th Anniversary Collection (Blind Pig)

Chess Blues (Chess/MCA)

The Cobra Records Story: 1956–58 (Capricorn)

The Cocktail Combos (Capitol)

The Complete Stax-Volt Singles, 1959–1968 (Atlantic)

Cool Cats & Hip Chicks: Jumpin' Like Mad (Capitol)

Crescent City Soul: The Sound of New Orleans, 1947–1974 (EMI)

The Hoy Hoy Collection: Rock Before Elvis (Stash)

Kansas City Blues (Capitol)

The King R&B Box Set (King)

The Living Chicago Blues, Vols 1–4 (Alligator)

Louisiana Swamp Blues (Capitol)

Old Town Doo Wop, Vols 1–3 (Ace)

Saxomania: Honkers and Screamers (Charly)

Very Best of Cajun (Dino)

INDEX

ACKNOWLEDGEMENTS

Books of this nature don't happen without extensive guidance and assistance from all sorts of different people. In the first instance this book would not have come about had it not been for Senior Commissioning Editor, Stuart Booth of Cassell. It was a subject we had kicked around for many years one way or another, and when it finally came about I was at once interested, but not without apprehension. There were times when, as one deadline receded into the middle distance, that Stuart, too, may have experienced similar misgivings. Be that as it may.

Along the way, numerous people have taken time out to talk and numerous record companies have been equally wholehearted in their support with photos and the like. Here is a rough list – and I crave the indulgence of those who I haven't mentioned: Ralph Baker, Catrina Barnes, Clarence 'Gatemouth' Brown, Stephen Bruton, Tony Eagle (Topic), Miles Evans, Christopher Fagg, John Hammond, Alan Hodgson (Universal), Julia Honeywell (Ace Records), Claire Horton (Manor House), Bruce Iglauer (Alligator), Howard Jones (Sheridans), King Pleasure, Delbert McClinton, Irving Mildener (Clayman & Co.), Lorne Murdoch (MCPS), National Sound Archive, Richard Porter (Direct Distribution), Duke Robillard, Mike Sanchez, Harriet Simms (Topic), Jim Simpson (Big Bear), Phil Straight (Warner Bros), Del Taylor (Indigo), Judith Weaterton (Polydor) and Richard Wootton (Manor House).

Editor Eric Smith has done a stupendous a job in rectifying anomalies and oversights; while Antonia Maxwell and Jane Birch have ensured that, despite my indolence, proofs were checked and that everything kept on moving.

Finally, Sara-Jane, Caitlin and Luke have given me the space to do it. That's all folks!

Hugh Gregory